INFORMAL POLITIC

M000196813

SUZI MIRGANI

(*Editor*)

Informal Politics in the Middle East

جـامـعـة جـورجـتـاون قـطـر
GEORGETOWN UNIVERSITY QATAR

Center *for* International *and* Regional Studies

OXFORD
UNIVERSITY PRESS

OXFORD
UNIVERSITY PRESS

Oxford University Press is a department of the
University of Oxford. It furthers the University's objective
of excellence in research, scholarship, and education
by publishing worldwide.

Oxford   New York

Auckland   Cape Town   Dar es Salaam   Hong Kong   Karachi
Kuala Lumpur   Madrid   Melbourne   Mexico City   Nairobi
New Delhi   Shanghai   Taipei   Toronto

With offices in

Argentina   Austria   Brazil   Chile   Czech Republic   France   Greece
Guatemala   Hungary   Italy   Japan   Poland   Portugal   Singapore
South Korea   Switzerland   Thailand   Turkey   Ukraine   Vietnam

Oxford is a registered trade mark of Oxford University Press
in the UK and certain other countries.

Published in the United States of America by
Oxford University Press
198 Madison Avenue, New York, NY 10016

Copyright © Suzi Mirgani 2021

All rights reserved. No part of this publication may be reproduced,
stored in a retrieval system, or transmitted, in any form or by any means,
without the prior permission in writing of Oxford University Press,
or as expressly permitted by law, by license, or under terms agreed with
the appropriate reproduction rights organization. Inquiries concerning
reproduction outside the scope of the above should be sent to the
Rights Department, Oxford University Press, at the address above.

You must not circulate this work in any other form
and you must impose this same condition on any acquirer.

Library of Congress Cataloging-in-Publication Data is available
Suzi Mirgani.
Informal Politics in the Middle East.
ISBN: 9780197604342

Printed in India on acid-free paper

CONTENTS

CONTENTS

LIST OF TABLES AND FIGURES

ABOUT THE CONTRIBUTORS

Nejm Benessaiah is a teaching assistant professor in the anthropology department at Georgetown University. His research interests include the everyday politics of water, infrastructures, environmental justice, social movements, AI, oases, the Sahara, the Middle East and North Africa, and Algeria. He is currently investigating the potential for upscaling ways to commonly govern important goods for humankind, such as water, the atmosphere, and digital data security. His most recent work investigates the role of voluntary associations in contemporary water management in North Africa, conceptualizing them as "micro-movements" in order to contrast how they may be key to managing (new) change, as opposed to customary governance regimes, which are configured to maintain the status quo. He has published in *Ethnobiology Letters* and *Quaternary International* and has book chapters in *Law and Property in Algeria: Anthropological Perspectives* (Brill) and *African Anthropologies in the Post-colony* (HSRC Press). He has also written for Truthout and the Daily Maverick.

Clemens Chay holds a PhD from Durham University and is currently a research fellow at the National University of Singapore's Middle East Institute. His research focuses on the history and politics of the Gulf states, with a particular emphasis on Kuwait and Saudi Arabia. His most recent publications include a chapter that examines Kuwait's parliamentary politics in *The Routledge Handbook of Persian Gulf Politics* (2020), and another article appearing in the *Journal of Arabian Studies*, titled "The Dīwāniyya Tradition in Modern Kuwait: An Interlinked Space and Practice."

Paulino Robles-Gil Cozzi is a PhD candidate at the Gulf Studies Program of Qatar University. He is also a diplomat working as the Cultural and Press

Attaché at the Embassy of Mexico in Qatar. He graduated with a degree in political science from the National University of Mexico and completed an MA in Contemporary Muslim Societies at Hamad Bin Khalifa University in Qatar. Cozzi's research interests include theoretical and ethnographic work related to Middle Eastern studies, sectarianism, Islam in the Persian Gulf, minorities in the Muslim world, and new anthropological approaches of the Arabian Peninsula.

Michelangelo Guida is Professor and Head of the Department of Political Science and International Relations at Istanbul 29 Mayıs University. Previously, he worked at the Department of Political Science and Public Administration at Fatih University. Guida teaches courses on Turkish politics and society, civil society, democracy, and political sociology. His main research interest is in conservative thought in Turkey. He is coauthor of *Türkiye'de Seçim Kampanyaları* [Electoral Campaigns in Turkey] (Orion 2011). Other recent publications in English include: "Negotiating Values in the Islamist Press after 2013" in *Middle East Critique* (2018); "Turkish Islamists' Enthusiasm for Versace: Islamism between Rejection and Adoption of the West" in *Muslims and Capitalism: An Uneasy Relationship?* (Ergon, 2018); and "Nurettin Topçu and Necip Fazıl Kısakürek: Stories of 'Conversion' and Activism in Republican Turkey" in the *Journal for Islamic Studies* (2014). Guida has published numerous academic articles in English, Turkish, and Italian.

Shahla Haeri is an associate professor in anthropology at Boston University, where she served as Director of the Women's Studies Program from 2001–10. She has conducted research in Iran, Pakistan, and India, and has written extensively on religion, law, politics, and gender dynamics in the Muslim world. Her book, *The Unforgettable Queens of Islam: Succession, Patriarchy, Gender*, is published by Cambridge University Press (2020). She has also authored *No Shame for the Sun: Lives of Professional Pakistani Women* (Syracuse University Press, 2002) and *Law of Desire: Temporary Marriage in Shi'a Iran* (Syracuse University Press, 1993; revised 2014). Her video documentary, *Mrs. President: Women and Political Leadership in Iran*, is distributed by Films for the Humanities and Sciences (2002). She has been awarded a number of grants and postdoctoral fellowships, including Visiting Fellow at CIRS, Georgetown University in Qatar (2012), Women's Studies in Religion at Harvard Divinity School (2005–06), and Fulbright (1999–2000; 2002–03), among others.

Amr Hamzawy studied political science and developmental studies in Cairo, The Hague, and Berlin. He was previously an associate professor of political science at Cairo University and a professor of public policy at the American University in Cairo. Between 2016 and 2017, he served as a senior fellow in the Middle East program and the Democracy and Rule of Law program at the Carnegie Endowment for International Peace, Washington, DC. His research and teaching interests as well as his academic publications focus on democratization processes in Egypt, tensions between freedom and repression in the Egyptian public space, political movements and civil society in Egypt, contemporary debates in Arab political thought, and human rights and governance in the Arab world. His new book *On The Habits of Neoauthoritarianism: Politics in Egypt Between 2013 and 2019* appeared in Arabic in September 2019 (Beirut: El Rayyes Publishers). Hamzawy is a former member of the People's Assembly after being elected in the first parliamentary elections in Egypt after the January 25, 2011 revolution. He is also a former member of the Egyptian National Council for Human Rights. Hamzawy contributes a weekly op-ed to the Egyptian independent newspaper *Shorouk* and a weekly op-ed to the London-based newspaper *al-Quds al-Arabi*.

Suzi Mirgani is assistant director for publications at the Center for International and Regional Studies (CIRS), Georgetown University in Qatar, and book review editor at the *Journal of Arabian Studies*. Her research focuses on the intersection of politics and popular culture. Mirgani is author of *Target Markets: International Terrorism Meets Global Capitalism in the Mall* (Transcript Press, 2017); editor of *Art and Cultural Production in the Gulf Cooperation Council* (Routledge, 2018); and coeditor of *Bullets and Bulletins: Media and Politics in the Wake of the Arab Uprisings*, with Mohamed Zayani (Oxford University Press/Hurst, 2016), and *Food Security in the Middle East*, with Zahra Babar (Oxford University Press/Hurst, 2014). She has published in the *International Feminist Journal of Politics* (2007); *Journeys Home: An Anthology of Contemporary African Diasporic Experience* (2009); and *Critical Studies in Media Communication* (2011). Mirgani is an independent filmmaker working on highlighting stories from the Arab world.

Charles Schmitz is a professor of geography at Towson University in Baltimore, where he has taught since 1999. He is a specialist on the Middle East and Yemen, and began his academic career as a Fulbright Scholar and American Institute for Yemeni Studies fellow in Yemen in the early 1990s. His issues of expertise include development, international law, and geopolitics, and his current research interests include the political economy of development in Yemen and the sociology of contemporary Yemeni society. He is coauthor of *Historical Dictionary of Yemen* (Rowman and Littlefield, 2018), and author of "Yemen's National Dialogue" (Middle East Institute Policy Paper Series, 2014); "Obama, Guantanamo, and the Devil in the Details" (Middle East Institute, 2013), and "Crisis in the Yemeni Economy: A Troubled Transition to Post-Hydrocarbon Growth" (Middle East Institute Scholarly Policy Paper, 2011), among others.

Deen Sharp is an LSE Fellow in Human Geography in the Department of Geography and Environment at the London School of Economics and Political Science and the co-director of Terreform, Center for Advanced Urban Research. He was previously a post-doctoral fellow at the Aga Khan Program for Islamic Architecture at the Massachusetts Institute of Technology (2018–19). He is the coeditor of *Beyond the Square: Urbanism and the Arab Uprisings* (Urban Research, 2016) and *Open Gaza* (American University in Cairo Press and Terreform, 2021). His most recent journal article, "Difference as Practice: Diffracting Geography and the Area Studies Turn," was published in *Progress in Human Geography* (2019). His doctoral dissertation, "Corporate Urbanization: Between the Future and Survival in Lebanon," focuses on corporations and urban development in the Eastern Mediterranean. Previously, he was a freelance journalist and consultant based in Lebanon. He has written for a number of publications, including *Jadaliyya, Portal 9*, the *Middle East Report* for the Middle East Research and Information Project, the *Arab Studies Journal*, and *The Guardian*. He has worked for several UN agencies, including the UN Development Programme and UN-Habitat, as well as for governments and international NGOs.

ACKNOWLEDGEMENTS

The chapters in this volume grew out of a two-year research initiative at the Center for International and Regional Studies (CIRS), Georgetown University in Qatar. My thanks to Mehran Kamrava for initiating this project and ensuring its smooth completion, and to the staff at CIRS—Zahra Babar, Elizabeth Wanucha, Misba Bhatti, and Maram Al-Qershi—for their impeccable organization of the project overall, and the two working group meetings held in Washington, DC, and Doha. I am indebted to Jackie Starbird for her copyediting expertise, and to CIRS student fellows Chaïmaa Benkermi and Shaza Afifi for all their help with CIRS publications over the years and for providing daily good humor.

1

AN OVERVIEW OF INFORMAL POLITICS
IN THE MIDDLE EAST

Suzi Mirgani

Introduction

The culture of politics within any system of governance is influenced by how states and societies interact with each other, and how these relationships are mediated by existing political institutions—whether formal or informal. State–society relationships in the Middle East have been largely defined by patriarchal and patrimonial principles that serve to strengthen the authority of the state and to keep society in check.[1] The characteristic of authoritarian governance has been a historical feature of most Middle Eastern countries long before the formation of nation states, and has continued unabated despite these nations' attempts at modernization and their increased integration into a global market economy.[2] The imbalanced relationships of power between states and societies in Middle Eastern countries have been key to maintaining societal subservience, and ensuring the lack of a fully functioning—and thus challenging—civil society.

Everyday sociopolitical behavior in private and public spheres has been shaped, guided, and supervised by concentric circles of control—a pyramid scheme of influence headed by the state, and its inevitable strongman, that must simultaneously dance to the vagaries of the market as it attempts to contain the effects of growing socioeconomic inequalities.[3] The state puts pressure on the country's sociopolitical substructure, the legal system, the policing apparatus, religious authorities, educational entities, the family institution, and, finally, the ordinary individual who occupies the weakest position. These institutions constitute both formal and informal regulatory networks that take turns at identifying, punishing, reforming, or excising deviant behavior—especially aberrant political behavior, which, in many cases, amounts to speaking out. In this environment, opinions, ideas, and actions that challenge the political status quo on a mass public scale are rare. But, every so often, when frustrations reach a breaking point and can no longer be contained, there is an abrupt demonstration of mass civil disobedience—most recently witnessed in the Arab uprisings beginning in 2010. In many ways, these nation-wide protests were "a response to the absence of effective institutionalized mechanisms of conflict resolution."[4]

In between these moments of mass outburst, however, there are quiet, determined, and enduring pockets of political mobilization and group action—women's associations, farmers' collectives, and labor and student unions—all working towards improving daily life, and perhaps even effecting sociopolitical transformation, in one family, neighborhood, farm, factory, and university at a time.[5] For many, it is not a choice to engage in informal political activity and civil mobilization, but a necessity in order to secure, collectively, some kind of social security through communal reciprocity and everyday activism. Ironically, because these "self-help" schemes are allowing certain social groups to get by, reducing their instinct to make demands and to seek subsistence from the state, authorities often turn a blind eye to informal activities. Not only are people discouraged from political action and dissent, they are simultaneously—and seemingly paradoxically—encouraged to seek their own betterment, often leading to the many politicized groups and associations discussed in this volume.

In many countries of the region, states and societies survive by bypassing, exceeding, or undermining formal institutions in a nondemocratic environment controlled by largely unaccountable governments. The enveloping market-centric and politically authoritarian environment has pushed people towards increasing informality. In this sense, both formal and informal economies exist side by side, and are mirror images of each other. It is within this precarious environment that we see the emergence of "a salient feature of grass-roots activism in the region: it is characterized less by demand-making movements than by direct actions, be they individual, informal, or institutional."[6] Consequently, relationships of affinity are formed among like-minded groups of people, in both rural and urban areas, who are attempting to better their daily lives and to gain advantage in countries of the Middle East that do not offer reliable safety nets—a condition of existence for many.

In the immediate post-independence period, wealth accrued from industry—whether hydrocarbon, agricultural, or manufacturing—on the one hand, and remittances on the other, kick-started Middle Eastern governments into establishing basic social welfare services as a means of gaining support from the general public in the early days of nation-building. The states took broadly varying paths "largely dominated by either nationalist-populist regimes (such as Egypt, Syria, Iraq, Libya, Sudan, Turkey) or pro-Western rentier states (Iran, Arab Gulf states)."[7] In whichever direction these nations veered, the characteristics they steadfastly shared was an authoritarianism with fixed patriarchal underpinnings, and the establishment of networks of patronage and privilege among business and political elites.[8] Having been initiated in the guise of provider—whether actual or imagined—the postcolonial Middle Eastern state has, from its inception, enacted an ideological, patrimonial, and patriarchal role that offers little room for challenge, for participation, or for diversity of thought—those elements that form the basic building blocks of civil society.

A global move toward market deregulation in the 1980s encouraged Middle Eastern governments to enact various degrees of economic restructuring in order to operate within an increasingly neoliberal environment. While these development reforms were hugely beneficial to some—business and political elites and the private sector in particular—for the public sector and for society in general, benefits were stripped and opportunities diminished, creating deteriorating social conditions and an emerging anxiety-filled class of unemployed people, or what Standing terms "the precariat,"[9] a disempowered generation beset by "the gradual closing of the commons, the disenfranchisement of workers and demise of citizen rights and due process."[10] Even those who are employed are affected by this combination of deteriorating conditions, producing a "global class of people who labor in circumstances of extreme structural insecurity."[11]

In the contemporary period, states have failed to live up to "the social responsibilities that characterized their early populist development. Many social provisions have been withdrawn, and the low-income groups largely have to rely on themselves to survive."[12] Subsidies, provisions, the commons, and welfare are no longer words recognized in the new neoliberal language. Instead, the average individual has had to learn—the hard way—the meaning of terms such as privatization, closures, austerity, downsizing, survival strategy, and crony capitalism.[13] Neoliberal policies are geared towards ensuring less reliance on government and more submission to the market—despite the many structural obstacles and socioeconomic challenges that fail to secure jobs in a limited labor market.

In order to wring out a living, or to have some sense of control within their own precarious positions, teetering on the edge of the formal—often corrupt or corrupting—institutions, many are doing exactly what is being asked of them in a market economy: they are no longer relying on the state, but instead exhibiting all the skills and knowhow of survival through their own efforts and other "direct actions of individuals and families to acquire the basic necessities of their lives (land for shelter, urban collective consumption, informal jobs, business opportunities) in a quiet and unassuming, illegal fashion."[14] Some individuals are indeed helping themselves: they are helping themselves to unoccupied plots of land by squatting and through unlawful construction; they are helping themselves to water and electricity by illegally tapping into mains and redirecting resources to their makeshift homes; and they are helping themselves to market share and ad hoc employment opportunities by setting up small businesses in a parallel informal and black market economy.[15]

The underlying paradox, however, is that "when states are unable to meet the needs of these classes, they resort to (and encourage the establishment of) civil associations to fulfill them,"[16] and can tacitly support community self-help schemes. On the one hand, informal social schemes relieve the state of responsibility as people make their own way—whether building their own slum housing, creating small businesses, or resorting to charity—but, on the other, these processes challenge the authority of the state by growing in directions that cannot always be controlled or monitored, taking on a life of their own. Such self-help mechanisms are both encouraged and yet are under suspicion by ruling authorities.

The studies in this collection highlight two different types of informal political engagement in the Middle East: civil action that works in tandem with the state apparatus, and civil action that poses a challenge to the state—in either case, these are informal political engagements that can and have achieved tangible results for particular groups of people, as well as for the state (albeit indirectly). These studies highlight the informal political activity that is practiced by both states and societies as they navigate through the nondemocratic environments of the Middle East. As with any edited volume, this collection of studies is not, and cannot be, comprehensive in its coverage of the politics of the Middle East. We acknowledge the impossibility of covering all topics related to the central theme and are aware that geographic omissions and subject selections are a condition of space constraints. Nevertheless, the studies presented in this collection serve as case study examples of the varying, nuanced, and evolving ways in which formal and informal political actors and institutions interact in different Middle Eastern contexts.

Converging Formal and Informal Politics

To begin, the first part of this collection highlights some of the ways in which formal and informal political processes engage in a symbiotic manner in the countries of the Middle East. While these state and society groups engage with each other on the margins of constitutional or legal lines, this type of ruling bargain is often a continuation of preexisting sociopolitical formations that predate the formation of the nation state. Even after independence, many Middle Eastern countries have retained various sociopolitical configurations that allow tribal and kinship bonds to reach beyond socioeconomic, political, and rural–urban divides.

In this collection, Charles Schmitz, Michelangelo Guida, Clemens Chay, and Paulino Cozzi examine the deeply-rooted relationships between the state and society, and the ways in which they work together to different degrees and with varying results. The politically powerful—yet politically informal— institutions discussed in this volume include communities that have direct and symbiotic relationships with the formal state, such as the tribes of Yemen and their continued fundamental importance to country-wide politics; villages and rural leaders and their power over regional vote mobilization in Turkey; the public–private power of the *dīwāniyya* in Kuwait where elite members of society engage in social politicking from within this household debate space; and, finally, the discreet yet persistent Shiʿa community in Qatar that has managed to negotiate its continued existence within the Sunni state. These communities experience similar endemic issues, but address them in different ways depending on their geographic and historical specificity.

These interactions between formal and informal institutions are mutually maintained by both political authorities and by social groups as a matter of course and in order to negotiate political and daily survival on both sides. Tribal and kinship networks of patronage have been historically cultivated and exploited by both the state and social groups—though imbalanced and with varying degrees of success—through entrenched, complex, and overlapping interactions. Regardless of how skewed the balance of power is between formal and informal political institutions in these cases, these sectors of society work directly with political authorities as a condition of daily life. In these contexts, both state and society rely on each other in a mutual two-way process of gaining benefits.

Although tribalism and political ethnicity have long and strong historical roots that extend into the contemporary period, these networks evolve and transform over time and according to the prevailing political context. As we have seen recently in situations of conflict and complete or near state collapse in Lebanon, Libya, Iraq, Syria, and Yemen, the founding principles that serve to form cohesion among ethnic and kinship groups can be fluid, flexible, and especially sensitive to times of crisis. Such groups can form new politically motivated alliances and pragmatic bonds that may or may not complement traditional kinship loyalties. In the contemporary period:

> [...] numerous countries in the Middle East are currently in the grip of intense civil conflict that is tearing apart the social and cultural fabric that has held these societies together. With increasing sectarianism spreading across much of the region, the collapsing of state structures and evaporation of national borders, and open conflict and warfare engulfing whole swathes of the region's geography, questions of the resilience of ethnicity and religious identity are becoming increasingly relevant.[17]

This is especially true in relation to the informal means through which many communities of the Middle East struggle to survive.

In his contribution, "Weighing the Tribal Factor in Yemen's Informal Politics," Charles Schmitz looks at how formal and informal politics are extensions of each other in the case of Yemen; one creates, relies on, and sustains the other. Specifically, in the political quagmire that is Yemeni politics, the central government must engage in multiple alliances with competing local and regional actors, who, in turn, benefit from these networks of patronage. In the fractured Yemeni political scene, relationships of power are ever-shifting and dependent on varying tribal structures and networks of patronage. Schmitz complicates the notion of formal politics by introducing the structural relationship of dependence between tribes and a central government that operates through a system of balances of power. He argues that "if we understand formal politics to be the institutions of government and the public political processes of modern states (political parties and elections), and informal politics to be relationships of power outside those formal institutions, then governance in Yemen is mostly informal." Similarly, tribes can also be considered as having both informal as well as formal power in that they exist both within and outside of the formal institutions of state, acting as both a part of, and a challenge to, the state's sovereignty. Tribes guard their own geographies and domains of power, and exercise a certain degree of autonomy over their particular entities by having their own alternative security apparatus, rule of law, and conflict dispute mechanisms—powers that pose a challenge to the central government, even as they are sometimes exploited by formal political institutions and authorities.

Schmitz continues by arguing that the central government deliberately pits tribes against one other in order to weaken potential alliances between them and to ensure that all institutions—military, economy, political parties, and tribes—however weak, fall under the orbit of the president as a means of preserving state power and control. Largely because there is no consensus or strong alliance between different tribes, tribal leaders have looked elsewhere for support, forming relationships of convenience—rather than conviction— with outside forces, whether the Muslim Brotherhood, the Ba'th Party, pro-Houthi, pro-Salafi, pro-Saudi, or pro-Iraq groups. These relationships, however, are fragile, noncommittal, and easily manipulated, and in the current contentious political quagmire, tribes do not necessarily take a steadfast political position but change depending on what can be gained from any one alliance. However, even though some tribes might engage in questionable transnational relationships, the influence of tribes scarcely goes beyond their territories of influence: while "local tribes may challenge the state's local authority," Schmitz argues, "they do not threaten the formal institutions of the state at the national level because they are politically fractured and because they benefit from national political institutions." As Yemen continues to be the battleground for foreign forces, the country's tribal divisions and informal political makeup mean that factions will continue to remain disconnected from each other, and thus easier to manipulate by regional powers in an attempt to impose their foreign policy agendas vicariously through Yemen.

Similarly, Guida's study, "Çay Politics: Informal Politics in Turkey and Vote Mobilization in Istanbul and Şanlıurfa," highlights how the state and politically lucrative communities reach out to each other across the urban-rural divide through "çay politics," or tea politics, in Turkey. This is a hybrid formal–informal political strategy in which politicians make pilgrimages to various villages ahead of elections in order to solicit their votes over a friendly conversation and a glass of tea. As elsewhere in the world, the centers of power are located in the capital city and other major urban areas, and so in order to reach out to political constituencies in the vast rural areas, politicians must appeal to small towns and villages by assuming a more informal character and through mirroring traditional values by forming personal relationships with residents. In many of these rural areas, villages engage in communal voting (*birleşik oy*, or "united vote"), which is a collective vote often decided on and dictated by village leaders. City politicians thus find it crucial to engage in social visits with village leaders in order to gain or sway their vote—and, with it, the vote of the entire village and sometimes surrounding villages as well. Guida argues in his chapter that "aside from formal campaigning, political parties must resort to a series of *informal* tools to maintain or gain consent. Among these tools is the exploitation of 'kin-like networks'" specifically for vote mobilization.

Through his study, Guida highlights how, in the contemporary period, "despite the demographic, social, political, and economic transformations, tribal identities have not disappeared—they evolved into a functional and dynamic network of patronage." Indeed, this relationship of informality between the state and society is an inheritance from the Ottomans, who fully exploited tribal and kin networks as a means of administering state policies without instruments of the state having to be physically present in rural areas at all times. These absentee political methods have been inherited into modern Turkey and carried into its democratic electoral system, in which political parties are able to reduce the costs of political campaigning, trading expensive media campaigns for a cup of tea with a village leader. In this sense, formal political leaders not only exploit but also encourage the maintenance and strengthening of informal kinship networks because, Guida argues, "influencing groups that are bound by different forms of identity is cheaper and easier than campaigning for the consent of individuals throughout the country."

Clemens Chay focuses on another type of enduring formal–informal political bond through his study of the *dīwāniyya*, a small reception room attached to private homes in Kuwait. In his study, "Dissecting the Spatial Relevance of the *Dīwāniyya* in Kuwait: An Inquiry into its 'Publicness,'" he highlights how the space "offers a profile of power relations." The *dīwāniyya* provides a meeting space that is neither entirely private, nor entirely public—

an interstitial space in which power relations are regularly negotiated. The *dīwāniyya* plays different roles that are intimately related to local custom and serve "to connect the private realm of the family to the public domain" through intimate physical encounters between friends, relations, and strangers in the same space.

The rapid urbanization of Gulf cities may have dramatically altered lifestyles, but it did not necessarily change the fundamental relationships between tribal leaders and their communities in the early years of nation-building, and between the ruling families—the state—and society in later years. Enduring clientelist relationships and kinship bonds between the ruling regimes, business networks, and social groups are the underlying condition of all the Gulf monarchies, which is writ large in the case of Saudi Arabia, the most populous nation in the Arabian Peninsula and the traditional regional hegemon. However, along with the growth of state institutions, informal networks have been adept at navigating and reconstituting their evolving relationships with formal state structures, sometimes in cooperation and sometimes in competition. Thus, Chay argues, when studying governance in the Gulf states, "the relationship between the ruling family and the ruled is often the focal point of sociopolitical discussion." Chay gives several historical examples of how public spaces in Gulf towns, including squares, streets, and souks, gave concrete embodiment to the formal and informal public performances—from pearling protests against British rulers to grievances aired to tribal leaders—between ruler and ruled.

Whereas highly urbanized environments are often characterized by a concomitant shift from an integrative community to urban anonymity, this has not necessarily been the experience of the Gulf states—largely a result of enduring kinship networks and a condition of socioeconomic dependence and binding rentier arrangements in the contemporary period. However, because Gulf states have unreservedly submitted to the forces of neoliberal exploitation of public spaces in their rapidly rising metropolises, many are being privatized such that noncommercial communal spaces are few and far between. Bahrain's Pearl roundabout serves as an example of a contested and constrained public space that was rendered the center of an unprecedented uprising,[18] attracting a critical mass of dissenters, as much for its physical capabilities as for its highly symbolic nature. Unsurprisingly, state authorities promptly demolished the roundabout in the hope of also demolishing the air of protest, and dispersing the protestors.[19] Public debates in the Gulf Cooperation Council states are not always so overt, loud, or spectacular, however, and the *dīwāniyya* is one example of how political issues are negotiated. Even though the *dīwāniyya* is mostly reserved for a narrow group of people—citizens of the state—the space has seen a relaxing of its boundaries to include some foreigners, but especially foreign diplomats and those engaged with politics at the state level.

Through his examination of the *dīwāniyya*, Chay expands our understanding of what public space means, and adds further nuance to the literature on how public space has been traditionally defined in particular contexts of the Middle East. The *dīwāniyya* is both physical and conceptual in that it is both a place and an indigenous culture—it is the dual nature of the *dīwāniyya* that has enabled it to survive through the centuries as a customary practice. Commenting on the durability of its purpose and form, Chay notes: "from Kuwait's pre-oil landscape catering to a bustling port town, to today's suburbanized residential areas, the *dīwāniyya* continues to find its place in the urban landscape despite the demise of other built environments." The *dīwāniyya* has been adapted over time to fit into modern urban environments as well as into Kuwait's evolving governance structures and political system.

Cozzi's contribution to this volume, "Shi'a-State Relations in Qatar: The Negotiation of Coexistence," traces the ways in which the Shi'a have been integrated into Sunni-dominated Qatari society, and how they live largely below the radar in a space that is both allowed and controlled by the Qatari state. Cozzi argues that Shi'i communities have existed as minorities in Qatar for some time, but their daily lives and the ways in which they navigate public space have been the products of years of negotiation with the Sunni establishment. Since the State of Qatar was established as a largely homogenous nation at the time of independence from British protectionism, minorities, and especially religious minorities, have had little room to assert themselves and so have had to adapt to the overall Wahhabi state by collaborating, negotiating, and tacitly accepting certain constraints while enjoying some freedoms. The state, for its part, has similarly had to negotiate a particular set of institutional mechanisms to find some kind of balance in accommodating this internal Islamic other.

Cozzi highlights the many complex layers of the arrangements that have enabled the peaceful coexistence of both religious orientations within the state, all of which have been carried out and instituted through informal channels. Differing significantly from the surrounding region, "the Shi'a in Qatar have a very high degree of independence compared with communities in neighboring countries, which are actively engaged in transnational networks." Because of their long-term residence in Qatar, and their strong economic bonds and business ties to the state, these Shiʿa communities tend to maintain few transnational networks, Cozzi argues, preferring to largely coexist as part of Qatari society.

As a means of maintaining social stability in a region fueled by sectarian tensions, Cozzi argues that the Qatari state attempts to downplay the relevance of religious denomination through its omission of public statistics about religious identities, which is a policy that markedly "differs from that of neighboring countries like Saudi Arabia and Bahrain, which repeatedly mobilize sectarian identities for political reasons." Cozzi relies on published secondary data as well as primary ethnographic research to get a sense of the number of Shiʿa in Qatar, suggesting that 10 percent of the inhabitants (including migrants) are Shiʿa. It is precisely because of their minority status in Qatar that Shiʿa groups have been accommodated within the government's broader nation strategy, which differs greatly from policies instituted in other Gulf states like Saudi Arabia and Bahrain. These countries have dealt with their sizeable, and contentious, Shiʿa populations through a deliberate and repressive authoritarian apparatus in an attempt to dismantle, disempower, and dominate Shiʿa networks, especially since these domestic religious groups are feared to have a more transnational character and allegiance that threaten the enforced cohesion of national identity.

Diverging Formal and Informal Politics

The second half of this collection focuses on organized or ad hoc collectives that are far from integrated into the state structures of the Middle East. While these groups largely remain on the margins, their collective action often brings their issues to the—not always positive—attention of the state. In other cases, such informal pressure groups succeed in coercing the state to concede to their demands, whether temporarily or over the long term, and whether meaningfully or cosmetically. In this volume, studies of the ways in which activists push back against the state focus on the strategies of slum dwellers in informal settlements of Egypt and elsewhere in the Middle East; organized voluntary agricultural associations in rural Algeria; outspoken women in Iran demanding political rights; and political activists determined to keep alive the spirit of recent uprisings and to continue to hold Arab governments to account.

While effective mechanisms for public participation have been excluded from the sphere of official politics by design in many countries of the Middle

East, the more underprivileged groups of people—unemployed, youth, women, or the poor—are denied access to formal institutions, the more they find solace in creating their own informal organizations, by joining others, or by carving out their own working arrangements and creating their own living spaces.

The *'ashwa'iyyat* phenomenon of Egypt—informal settlements and their inhabitants—is largely the result of corporate, clientelist, and often corrupt urban development schemes, and is the subject of Deen Sharp's contribution to this volume. In his chapter, "Threatening Urban Informality in the Middle East," Sharp introduces the topic by noting that "urbanization is always embedded within struggles over social power. Who gets to build what, where, and how are political, social, and economic questions that can have far-reaching spatial and temporal consequences." He traces the historical development of these living conditions, noting that urban policies instituted in the 1950s by the post-revolutionary Nasserist state reduced government funding for housing in order to make way for increased investments in the construction of factories in an industrializing Egypt.

Informal settlements in Egypt increased as a direct result of an *infitah*, or "open door," deregulation policy, which attracted a sharp rise in foreign investment; paved the way for Egyptian migrants to travel to the oil-rich Gulf countries and send back remittances; and instituted a boom in urban development projects, both formal and informal. Ironically, Sharp demonstrates that as formal urbanization increased so did informal settlements—many of whose inhabitants were factory workers who were given no accommodation in the surrounding areas. Especially in the increasingly congested metropolises of the Middle East, a "large number of public-sector workers and rural laborers, as well as educated, once well-to-do members of the middle class (government employees and college students), have been pushed into the ranks of the urban poor in labor and housing markets."[20] Unsurprisingly, Sharp argues, this led to a housing crisis, especially in the urbanizing agricultural areas around these factories, forcing workers to create their own settlement solutions by congregating in *'ashwa'iyyat*, haphazard or random, informal settlements.

This housing crisis in Egypt did not abate, and, in the contemporary period, people are being increasingly pushed out—and priced out—of their previous habitats, forced to seek ad hoc shelter elsewhere in slums and informal settlements, often with no basic sanitation or services. Through microloans and with help from others in these ramshackle communities, many live a precarious subsistence on the margins of expanding cities and urban fringes by constructing their own informal accommodation and by illegally tapping into water and electricity facilities.

But it is not only the chaotic impoverishment and national embarrassment of these places that has become a concern for the Egyptian state. Informal settlements have also become the domain of political opposition entities and Islamic groups—often charitable, sometimes evangelical—and thus also considered a threat to the larger state and the target of the government's securitization policies, or what Sharp terms the "weaponization" of urban informality. It was precisely because the 2011 uprisings empowered marginalized groups associated with the *ashwa'iyyat* that the Sisi government has made informal urban settlements an especially direct target. Sharp argues that the government's attempt to impose order by instituting a backlash against informal settlements is disingenuous; the government often targets some of the most vulnerable in order to demonstrate power and to exhibit a semblance of order. He argues that the Egyptian government is not really concerned about people's lives, livelihoods, or chaotic living conditions, but is more concerned that informal settlements reveal an alternative form of potential collective power beyond the reach of the state.

Despite the many barriers to activism in the Middle East, groups of people gather to form networks of allegiance, most often about specific issues or within particular geographical locations. Asef Bayat reminds us that informal political communities are often temporary, ad hoc, and cause-based, and are rarely sustained over time to form strong political entities that can act as a true opposition to the formal state. Bayat argues that the formation of pressure groups:

> [...] tend to happen in extraordinary social and political circumstances—in revolutionary conditions or in times of crisis and war, when the state is undermined or totally absent, as in Palestine. Thus, few such activities become a pattern for sustained social mobilization and institutionalization in normal situations. Once the exceptional conditions come to an end, the experiments begin to wither away or get distorted.[21]

While this is generally the case in the Middle East, the chapters in the second half of this collection point to the many sustained below-the-radar movements and voluntary associations.

Collective activism, whether demonstrative or inconspicuous, is making life bearable for some of those who must contend with harsh living and working conditions. As has occurred elsewhere in the world, rural and agricultural communities in the Middle East have been especially marginalized and consigned to the peripheries of formal politics. Many have been largely abandoned by central, urban-based governments that direct their efforts towards large-scale, market-centric modernization projects in an attempt to compete in the international sphere. In many cases, rural communities are finding themselves having to form a variety of collectives as a survival strategy in an attempt to secure basic services.

Because of the reactionary nature of authoritarian governments in the Middle East, brash forms of activism are often immediately identified and quashed by security forces. Exasperated farmers' collectives, enraged labor unions, vociferous women's movements, and raucous youth groups, while gaining needed public attention to their cause, also attract the ire of authorities. Within each one of these spheres, however, activist groups have spent years "foster[ing] quiet encroachment as a viable strategy that gives the urban [and rural] grass-roots some power over their own lives and influence over state policy."[22] It is this type of quiet encroachment that is the subject of Nejm Benessaiah's contribution, or what he terms "micromovements" in his chapter, "Voluntary Associations as Social Micromovements: The Case for Gradual Sociopolitical Change in Algeria." Benessaiah undertook twelve months of ethnographic fieldwork studying a Tazdait (date palm in Tamazight) association that was formed to safeguard the livelihoods and traditional knowledge of date palm farmers and climbers.

Rather than challenging the overwhelming mechanics of a largely unaccountable "deep state," Benessaiah argues that social change in some parts of Algeria is gradual, and perhaps even sometimes imperceptible, although effective over the long term. His study informs the literature on informal politics by examining the politics of natural resources in general, and environmental social movements in particular. Through a case study of the M'zab valley oasis, Benessaiah highlights agricultural civic organizations and their right to take part in the governance of natural resources in the changing political culture of Algerian oases—historically strategic economic nodes that served to link trade routes across the desert. While oases play a less central role in the country's overall political economy, Benessaiah argues that they maintain their importance in the Western imaginary as hideouts for illegal migrants, religious extremists, and illicit trade. Such areas are thus subject to decreased social services and increased securitization, both by the state as well as its foreign partners, leaving the rural communities who reside there disempowered and the subject of both suspicion and targeting.

While many of these rural collectives see value in continuing the custom of tribal politics—governed by clan and kinship ties, political allegiances, and religious authorities—new forms of "voluntary associations" are emerging and merging with traditional community structures, forming new hybrid groups that are decidedly less hierarchical and patriarchal; they are more consensual, with leadership positions elected through member voting. Such voluntary groups show how traditional communities can adapt to contemporary challenges. Benessaiah argues that "Mozabite voluntary associations can challenge the hierarchy of the local elites, not by violence or even direct conflict, but by simply doing things differently." This is an example of below-the-radar community action that is "characterized by quiet, largely atomized, and prolonged mobilization with episodic collective action—open and fleeting struggles without clear leadership, ideology, or structured organization."[23] As a demonstration of how small, rural voluntary associations are inherently political, Benessaiah's study zones in on a community collective whose aims are not revolution, disruption, or direct challenge of the state, but one that is directed towards gradual, quiet, and effective change of the ways in which natural resources are governed—and, thus, the ways in which rural communities live their daily lives.

Similarly, despite the myriad restrictions placed on women in Middle Eastern societies, many have been working tirelessly and relentlessly on issues of social justice, and are presenting real—and legal—challenges to the state. In her study, "Perilous Adventures: Women and Civil Society Participation in Iran," Shahla Haeri notes that "from the early days of the establishment of the Islamic Republic, educated urban Iranian women have actively engaged with the state and civil society in all spheres and domains, despite the many legal and political hurdles thrown in their paths by the state's 'medieval' gender policies." Iranian women are exposing the hypocrisy of the state, especially its claim of upholding the elevated status of women in Islam. Haeri argues that while an Iranian woman is often encouraged by the state to pursue education, "her legal rights are institutionally restricted, inferior, and conditional, which limit her social capital, restrict her professional options, and control her sociopolitical mobility." She points to the brewing social injustice of the state's encouragement of women's education, only to limit their skills, abilities, and applications in the labor market and through enveloping sociopolitical restrictions.

These women have not remained quiet, however, and Haeri examines how many activists are demanding a seat at the political table by challenging the language of the constitution and legal doctrines—the very foundations of the Islamic Republic. She engages with the absurdity of government policy, arguing that within the same generation, women were first forced to unveil under Reza Shah Pahlavi's Unveiling Act of 1936, and later forced to veil under the rules of the conservative Islamic Republic. "In both cases," she argues, "a woman's body became the symbolic site of forced modernization or Islamization of Iranian society," and thus used as an experimental litmus test for government policy.

Haeri shines a light on the many individual and collective female activists who are striving to amplify the voices of Iranian women, and for their demands to be heard. Female-led political campaigns for social equality include the solo protests of Girls of Revolution Avenue against forced veiling; the call to change the masculine face of parliament; challenging the constitutionality of preventing women from running for president; and the One Million Signatures campaign against discriminatory laws. Importantly, legal challenges, politics, and skewed gender relationships of power are being addressed through artistic practice, through women's literary productions, as well as through cinema, which has become an internationally respected and celebrated cultural-political form,[24] and thus is also attracting worldwide attention to the predicament of women in the Islamic Republic.

Concluding this volume is Amr Hamzawy's study, "Post-2013 Egypt: Declining Formal Politics and Resilient Social Activism," which maintains that although acts of civil disobedience have long been an undercurrent of Egyptian daily life, activists, students, and human rights groups have tasted what is possible through successful protest. Moreover, some groups have remained emboldened in post-2013 Egypt, even if they often lack organizational capabilities and whether they remain committed to a single cause related to human rights abuses, such as extrajudicial killings, forced disappearances, or torture in places of custody. Additionally, conditions for some have worsened, and in the post-2013 environment, the ways in which Egypt's crony capitalism has become even more embedded into the state system has further entrenched corruption,[25] leading many to believe that life has worsened for the average individual. The deep entanglement of the military and the state is another cause for concern, and has become even stronger in the post-uprisings era. To this effect, Shama argues that "civil-military relations in the Arab world are marred by excessive military intervention in political affairs, heavy permeation of the state bureaucracy, and indulgence in commercial activities that includes the establishment of autonomous economic fiefdoms."[26]

In aiming to raise citizens' awareness and mobilize them to demand an end to human rights abuses, Hamzawy argues that these initiatives have to navigate the current social and political environment of malaise, in which large segments of the population are either resigned to the current status quo, and thus less interested in standing up for the victims of abuses, or are fearful of being targeted themselves by an increasingly repressive regime. Despite these setbacks, Hamzawy's analysis concludes this volume on a high note, and with renewed hope for social empowerment, arguing that political activism has been injected with new vigor on the Egyptian political scene, with direct implications for the rest of the Middle East.

Conclusion

The relationships between states and societies in the Middle East have been largely characterized by authoritarian rule and submissive subjects bound by a series of political oppressions, economic depressions, societal repressions, and religious persecutions. Whether urban or rural, politically minded communities are sometimes voicing concern and at other times taking matters into their own hands through direct action. In the contemporary environment, communal networks and demonstrations of discontent employ all the tools available to them in the contemporary era, including "traditional strategies of communication within the community, as well as modern tactics such as engaging the media, lobbying politicians, and resorting to the court system as a means of registering opposition."[27] What is seemingly a rural or peripheral issue becomes a country-wide cause, gaining momentum, millions of members, and global media attention.

In many countries where opposition parties are either banned or of dubious nature, people organize in various informal groupings that serve as pressure valves, giving space for limited forms of expression. In the wake of the Arab uprisings, and "given these challenges, many youth activists see changing the political culture, including normalizing the right to protest, as a prerequisite to achieving fundamental political change. They are pushing against red lines and introducing innovative ways to organize and express dissent."[28] They are fighting an uphill battle in many cases, and the response from many of the region's governments is often "retaliating with new restrictions on assembly and political expression."[29] Sentiments of pessimism and precarity are repeated across the Middle East, especially for those trying to survive in countries facing near or total state collapse: traumatized populations in war-torn Yemen and Iraq or those trying to navigate Lebanon's many trials and tribulations, from a nation-wide economic collapse to the effects of the 2020 Beirut port blast on the urban and social fabric of an already scarred city.[30] These feelings of hopelessness and helplessness are not confined to nations in states of crisis: at the time of writing in the fall of 2020, the novel coronavirus pandemic has only served to magnify these collective fears by halting lives, stunting livelihoods, surveilling bodies, crippling economies, and shaking the foundations of even the wealthiest of Gulf nations. In light of the pandemic and the many disruptions to daily life it has induced (and will continue to induce for the foreseeable future), the informality of politics in the Middle East will only be further normalized, but so will political activism..

For the people of the Middle East, spaces for expression are opening and closing on a regular basis. While in some cases this encourages informal activities as a means of communal survival, the central state also sees these as a threat: "most governments in the region are still apprehensive of and tend to restrict independent collective mobilization for fear of losing political space."[31] Middle Eastern governments make every attempt to weaken or even destroy civil and political groups whenever necessary and wherever they become a popular and powerful force. The collection of studies in this volume examine these diverse forms of informal political engagements, highlighting specific incidences in which groups of people who, if not powerful, have a certain type of influence and ability to address particular problems or achieve certain goals—to get things done for themselves or for others within their immediate circles—and thus become potentially powerful and a force to be reckoned with.

PART I

CONVERGING FORMAL
AND INFORMAL POLITICS

2

WEIGHING THE TRIBAL FACTOR IN YEMEN'S INFORMAL POLITICS

Charles Schmitz

Introduction

The Yemeni state is weak. To govern, the central government contends with a myriad of competing local and regional powers in a style of government that has been called the "politics of patronage,"[1] the "politics of chaos,"[2] the "politics of permanent crisis,"[3] and "dancing on the head of snakes."[4] In Sanaa, one gets the impression the government runs on rumors. Abrahamian's description of Qajar rule in the nineteenth century fits contemporary Yemen well: "less through bureaucratic institutions, coercion, or grand appeals to divinity and history ... than through the systematic manipulation of social divisions, especially clan, tribal, ethnic, regional, and sectarian differences."[5] If we understand formal politics to be the institutions of government and the public political processes of modern states (political parties and elections), and informal politics to be relationships of power outside those formal institutions,[6] then governance in Yemen is mostly informal.[7] To the consternation of development agencies and modernist state builders, the Yemeni regimes govern Yemen through what might be called an informal policy of managed chaos by playing factions against one another,[8] just as the Qajar regime did in the nineteenth century. A centralized but diffuse patronage network pulls all factions towards the personal rule of the president—the state, the economy, political parties, militant groups, influential personalities, and tribes are all elements of the patronage system.[9]

However, the formal institutions of state are still central to Yemeni politics; the patronage politics of the regime do not abolish state institutions but live through them. Formal politics legitimize the national political leadership and tie together the disparate local and regional centers of power in Yemen. The tribes of the far north have an ironic role in these formal institutions of state government: they challenge state sovereignty yet are empowered by the formal institutions of state at the same time.[10] On the one hand, tribes in the north are sovereign and are in themselves small states. Their tribal order operates on a principle of collective responsibility and a relative moral balance that conflicts with the notion of the individual's responsibility before the universal law of the state. The shaykh representing the collective stands between the state and the individual members of a tribe,[11] and conflict is resolved by negotiation, not by the application of state law. In this way, tribes challenge state sovereignty.

At the same time, the formation of the Yemeni Arab Republic in the 1960s brought northern tribal shaykhs into the highest positions of power in the new state institutions. In this "republic of shaykhs," tribal shaykhs of the north used their positions in state institutions to ensure that the tribal system remained autonomous in the north; that the national military was never independently powerful enough to subdue the region; and that the very shaykhs in state power remained the intermediaries between the central state and local tribal society. The tribes of the north both challenged the formal state by constituting an alternative formal power in local areas and joined and benefitted from formal power by participating in parliament, the military, and the state bureaucracy.

The predominance of tribal shaykhs in Yemen's central state institutions would seem to imply that tribes run Yemen and that tribal shaykhs command Yemeni politics. In yet another irony of Yemeni politics, tribes are often divided and cannot agree on anything except the continuance of the tribal system. Tribes very much agree to disagree, by design, and as such cannot represent a single political bloc.[12] Instead, tribes tend to reflect the conflicts of wider Yemeni society. All the national political parties are found strewn about

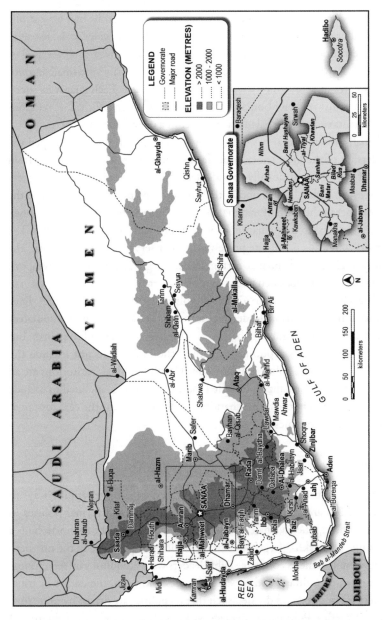

Fig. 2.1: Map of Yemen's administrative divisions and major roads and cities.

the tribal north, with none dominant. Competition between wider conflicting religious currents also takes place within tribal society, most significantly the Salafi-Zaydi conflict. While individual members of a tribe may have strong political or religious convictions of one sort or another, wider social forces in tribal territories (such as political parties or religious movements) are used by tribal society to balance power between local tribes. Tribes are small autonomous states surrounded by a sea of similar small states. Each guards its sovereignty against its neighbor, and the support of wider political or religious movements can counterbalance the power of a neighboring tribe.

Finally, the informal patronage politics of the central regime shaped the leadership of the local tribe. Tribal leadership is customary. Often a certain clan of the tribe traditionally provides leadership, but leadership is ultimately consensual. Tribal leaders obtain their position by providing benefits to the tribe either in the form of material benefits (for example, cash and weapons), or wise leadership in mediation or in relations with neighboring tribes. The person who leads is the one perceived to best serve the tribe's interest. The central regime could enhance certain leaders by giving them cash or weapons or by employing tribesmen in the state bureaucracy.

The Houthi are masters of tribal politics in the north, yet they have reduced the role of tribal leadership in their state. The Houthi manipulated, coerced, and reconfigured tribal politics in their conquest of the north, but unlike the previous republican regimes, the Houthi do not include the shaykhs in national politics. Admittedly, Houthi national institutions are ad hoc and not yet formalized, but the Houthi do not seem inclined to include tribal leadership in the formal national leadership, as was the case for previous republican regimes.

Weighing Up the Tribal Factor

Weighing up the role of tribes is complicated by the overlapping ways in which tribes and tribalism interact with informal and formal politics in Yemen. During the past half century, tribal leaders from the far north built a "republic of shaykhs," largely due to the military importance of the northern tribesmen in Yemen's conflicts. Tribal leaders were ubiquitous in Yemen's legislature, in its military, and its state agencies. However, the nature of tribal society is fractured and divided such that its politics are driven by non-tribal outside parties. Political tendencies within tribal society reflect the rest of Yemen rather than lead the country. There is no tribal position:[13] tribal leaders can agree only to maintain tribal society to assure their own leadership position. All Yemen's different political forces are scattered amongst the tribes precisely for tribal reasons.[14] The Muslim Brotherhood, the Ba'th Party, pro-Houthi, pro-Salafi, pro-Saudi, and pro-Iraq—all outside forces—can find tribal backers because the tribal calculus is the survival of the small local tribal unit. As such, tribal society is ideally suited for incorporation in a patronage system. Longtime ruler Ali Abdallah Saleh was a master at using tribal relations to his benefit, and he preserved tribal social order precisely because it is so divided. The Houthi are a little different; they too are adept at the nuances of tribal society, but the Houthi are not inclined to allow tribal shaykhs a role in formal government.

Tribes might be considered an alternative formal power—a source of power outside the formal institutions of state, a challenge to the state's sovereignty. At the local level, tribes jealously guard their political dominion, the tribe's territory. Tribal leaders represent the tribe to outsiders and attempt to prevent the state from encroaching on their domain. Tribal social order provides security and a means of settling disputes, an alternative legal order. In this sense, tribes challenge the state; they are small sovereignties,[15] an alternative formal power in tribal regions. However, tribes do not constitute a single political bloc, and tribal social order is inherently fractured. It is a mistake to speak of "the tribes" as an entity because tribes are politically disunited by design. Each tribe guards its autonomy against its neighbors in a sea of equally autonomous tribes. Advantage to one tribe will be countered by neighboring tribes, preventing them from acting as a single bloc of power. According to Dresch:

> Within a tribe the relation between sections is usually that purely of opposition, each section guarding its own against others. The whole tribe in turn is opposed to other tribes, but in times of conflict part of the tribe may stand aside, and in times of calm little stress can be put on the sections' common identity: it becomes scarcely relevant.[16]

The local tribes challenge the state's authority, but they do not threaten the formal institutions of the state at the national level because they are politically fractured and because they benefit from national political institutions. Tribes are too easily manipulated by outside powers; rather than constituting a tribal political bloc, tribal territory is often the scene of outsiders' political conflicts.[17] Political parties and movements seek tribal supporters, but tribal society balances the support of one faction with support for another and tends to contain rather than exacerbate conflict. Tribal leaders are found in all political parties—from the conservative Islamic Islah Party to the Ba'th

Party and even the Movement of Arab Nationalists. During the civil war of the 1960s, some tribes were allied to the royalist forces and others to the republic forces; in the war of 1994, some tribes supported Sanaa, while other tribes supported Aden.

In the republican era after 1962, tribal leaders from the far north became national leaders, entering the formal institutions of government. Tribal shaykhs occupied Yemen's parliament, its administration, and its military. Their military importance to the republican regime enabled tribal leaders to ensure that northern tribes and their shaykhs governed tribal territory, and that tribal militias and tribesmen in regular military units could keep a check on the power of the central state. Here, tribal leaders are shaping the formal institutions of government to maintain the tribal order in the north and to preserve their own roles as tribal leaders.

The military importance of tribes lies in the abilities of tribesmen, not the tribes themselves. States have historically used the far north as a reservoir of fighting men for states' formal military units and for informal fighting units called alternatively tribal militias,[18] irregulars,[19] irregular militias,[20] tribal levies,[21] or mercenaries.[22] These are not tribes, but agents of states or political movements. They are not acting on tribal motives; they are hired guns. Tribal wars—battles between tribesmen over tribal affairs—are limited skirmishes enacted to make a point, not to conquer territory or destroy an enemy. Tribal means of conflict include closing roads to outsiders and taking hostages. The royalists and republicans battling in the 1960s made use of tribal fighters, but the war was not so much between tribes as it was between a republican government and a royalist government. Within tribes, conflict is contained by tribal customs.[23]

Local tribal leaders are intimately involved in local affairs, and the reputations of tribal leaders are made by their ability to resolve disputes and secure economic or social benefits for the tribe. Ironically, however, the success of tribal leaders in shaping the national government also pulls shaykhs into the central regime's patronage networks, and potentially diminishes their role in tribal territories. Shaykhs are no longer just shaykhs: they are businessmen, military leaders, members of parliament, and state functionaries. Their interests change; they become part of Yemen's national political system rather than just a representative of a local tribe. When tribal leaders become involved in national politics, they can lose their connection to tribal areas and become "city shaykhs."

Over the years, the Yemeni regimes promoted tribalism, rather than opposed it, with the notable exception of the socialist People's Republic of

South Yemen and People's Democratic Republic of Yemen (PDRY) in the south between 1967 and 1990.[24] The Yemeni state acted as the largest tribe among tribes. The regime would call for shaykhs to mediate disputes between a tribe and the state according to tribal custom. Saleh encouraged the retribalization of southern Yemen after the civil war of 1994 and the collapse of the Yemeni Socialist Party. Promoting tribalism facilitated the Yemeni regimes' informal politics of patronage. Tribal leaders and the central regimes together colluded in weakening the formal institutions of government.[25]

Finally, the Yemeni regimes manipulate the internal politics of tribes themselves. Positions of tribal leadership are consensual and fluid, and leadership depends upon the ability to bring material benefits to the tribe and secure the tribe's interests in a local context. Outsiders can promote leaders within tribes by steering water projects, employment, weapons, or cash to chosen leaders. Saleh had a network of supportive shaykhs all throughout the north, but these were largely overturned by the Houthi during their rise to power.[26] The central political leadership thus intervened in the domestic politics of tribes—a form of informal tribal politics.

There are some indications that tribalism is under stress. The Houthi wars between 2004 and 2010 brought a new level of violence to tribal conflicts. New forms of tribal militias, under both the Houthi and the government, fought bloody and violent battles far outside the scope of tribal custom. Tribalism seemed unable to play its traditional role in containing violence. At the same time, the material rewards of state connections seem to have changed the customary relationship between shaykhs and members of a tribe. Shaykhs have pursued their individual interests at the expense of common tribe members. Tribal areas are tellingly poor in general, despite the substantial largess the state channels towards tribal shaykhs. The gap between leaders and members of a tribe was one of the factors that enabled the Houthi to gain followers in the far north. Finally, the Houthi appear to envision a different relationship between formal politics and the tribes. The Houthi do not include tribal leaders in national leadership, though the current Houthi state is an ad hoc, wartime institution.

Local Tribes

Tribes are concerned with very practical local affairs, local security, and material benefit.[27] They are concerned with national issues only in as much as these affect the small tribal territory, though individual tribesmen may be committed members of national or international organizations such as the Muslim Brotherhood or the Baʿth Party. Tribesmen see themselves as equals, each fiercely independent, shunning any relationship that creates a dependency upon others;[28] and tribal leadership is consensual—a shaykh does not command members of a tribe, but must persuade them of his leadership. Al-Zaheri describes the relationship as one of "cooperation and mutual respect."[29] And Weir argues:

> Since leaders have no means of mass coercion, they therefore have to persuade their followers that their interests are threatened in order to galvanize their support. Strong, honest, and politically astute shaykhs with a good case and wealthy tribes are therefore better able to pursue inter-tribal disputes than shaykhs with poor, weak tribes and shaky pretexts. For every grievance pursued, therefore, many are ignored.[30]

Tribal customary justice is based upon collective responsibility and mediation to restore the peace, a system that conflicts with the state's ideas of the universality of law and equality of citizens. In this sense, tribes are small sovereignties that contest the state's power in the tribe's territory.[31] Tribes are small autonomous units suspicious of their neighbors, such that tribal society is fractured and does not constitute a unified political bloc of any sort. The tribes agree only to disagree. As Weir noted, "the bipartite division of the Rāziḥ tribes into 'naturally' opposed 'sides' is at the forefront of everyone's political consciousness."[32]

The ubiquity of tribes in Yemen is due primarily to their effective provision of local order and security.[33] Tribes are small societies that bind rural communities together for the promotion of mutual interests. In the past, tribesmen were agriculturalists. They prided themselves on their independence and autonomy, and were dependent upon no one, including for their own material needs. Tribesmen cultivated grains, and though they clearly depended upon markets for trade, they shied from commerce, which they looked down upon.[34] Those providing services to others, including merchants, were considered weak peoples. In tribal society, warrior tribesmen provide protection, and non-tribesmen living in tribal territory are dependent and receive protection from the tribesmen.[35] In Gerholm's account, tribesmen consider merchants "market rats."[36] The last half-century transformed Yemen's economy.

Agriculture plays a much smaller role in the total economy today, and global commerce has penetrated even the remotest villages. Currently, merchants are wealthy, and tribesmen have decided that commerce is no longer a despised occupation: "A large portion of the tribesmen have entered an ambiguous social category for which the previous separation between the tribesman and the market has broken down."[37] Rural Yemenis are occupied in agriculture, commerce, transportation, and construction, and are employed in the military and state. In the tribal far north, the vast expansion of lucrative *qat* cultivation has also buoyed the rural sector.[38] The transformation of the Yemeni economy coupled with the rapid increase in population have drawn Yemenis toward the city. In the countryside, however, the transformation of the economy has not undermined tribal social order (at least not yet), and land is still a central component of tribal identity.[39]

The local tribe is the fundamental political unit of tribal society. Tribes identify themselves relative to other tribes by genealogy; at the highest order, all tribes are related to a common ancestor,[40] and the divisions and relations between tribes are described by branches of genealogy. However, genealogy is only symbolic, and Yemenis recognize that members of a tribe are not all related by blood. Though a rare occurrence, members of a tribe can switch tribes if they feel their tribe does not back their interests, but doing so involves a move of residence. More commonly, people refer to a tribe as the "people of a region," a geographic reference to people living in a defined area.

Tribesmen's primary loyalty is to the local tribe. Tribes are subdivided into units sometimes called fifths, fourths, or thirds, and each subunit is made up of a group of villages, which is the smallest unit of Yemeni society where a single clan will dominate. The tribe is collectively responsible for tax collection, defense of the territory, and payment of tribal fines. The subunits of the tribe are assigned a proportion of the tribal levy according to a customary proportion, not always based upon relative population.[41] Among the roles of tribal shaykhs is the collection of funds and the representation of the tribe to the state or outsiders.

Tribal justice is based upon collective responsibility, retribution, and moral balance. In principle, members of a tribe are collectively responsible for the tribe. If a tribe member causes harm to someone from another tribe, the entire tribe is responsible.[42] Retribution restores the moral balance. Brandt notes that "a tribesman's honour can be impugned by attacks on any component of his honourable self, but three particular components are metonymically exalted to special iconic status: daggers, women and landholdings."[43] In practice, the threat of retribution spurs the offender's people to seek out shaykhs to mediate the conflict and negotiate payment to restore honor and balance. The duty of the shaykhs is to "solve people's problems," including dispute mediation, from which they earn income for their services.

The units at odds in any dispute is negotiated. Determining who are the offender's people and the victim's people is part of dispute negotiation.

Depending upon the nature of the conflict, subunits of a tribe, whole villages, or wider tribal confederacies may be at odds; this makes tribal society extremely fractured and easily manipulated from outside. The common assumption that tribes act automatically as a collective—a kind of group-think—does not hold in Yemen. Tribesmen evaluate the claims of a fellow tribesman and decide on their own whether to support his claims.[44] If the tribesman in a dispute has behaved dishonorably, fellow tribesmen are unlikely to uphold his claims. Villages within a subsection may differ in their interpretation of events, such that one village may support the tribe while another refuses. In Weir's study, "order-maintenance in Rāziḥ has marked voluntaristic and collective features, and there is a perpetual tension between the impulse to support family and clan, and the requirement to comply with the law."[45] Dresch, meanwhile, observes:

> [M]en may refuse to become involved in events that, abstractly conceived, concern them because they concern the name those men share. It is not unusual for sections of a tribe to refuse support to their "brother" sections at odds with another tribe, or even to turn on them and actively oppose them. Tribes are not solidary groups.[46]

The tribal customary order clashes with the state's system of justice. The state presupposes that individual citizens are equal before the law. The state administers justice according to the law and punishes offenders. In tribal custom, justice is negotiated by shaykhs chosen by the disputing parties.[47] There is no universal law in tribal society, though there are longstanding customs. Proponents of the state argue that shaykhs stand between the state and the individual and that justice in tribal society depends on the relative power of disputants, not the equal application of the law. Thus, "what is at stake is something akin to sovereignty."[48]

The local focus of tribes is important for understanding tribal behavior. Tribes are primarily small units of government concerned with local affairs. Members of the tribe may be distributed between different national political groups such as Islah, or the General People's Congress, or even the Baʿth Party; however, tribal behavior is not determined by political affiliations but by calculations of local interest. Tribes are "realists." When Ali Abdallah Saleh declared his rebellion against the Houthi in December 2017, the tribes allowed Houthi reinforcements to pass through tribal territory and defeat Saleh despite avowed loyalty to him. Tribes calculated correctly that Saleh's cause was lost.

Tribes are driven by very local considerations, not national politics. National and foreign interests attempt to use tribes, but the nature of tribal society tends to balance the influence of one outside power by another. Dresch notes that "since the war [civil war of the 1960s], the tribes' propensity to harbour opposing factions and at the same time contain their antagonism has often been in evidence."[49] At the scale of the local tribe, tribal social order provides an alternative means of justice that challenges state sovereignty, and tribes persist in Yemen in large part because they successfully provide local security and order in rural areas.

Tribal confederacies are alliances between sets of tribes. To secure their position relative to tribes around them, or to secure key economic relationships like access roads and markets, tribes contract strategic alliances with other tribes.[50] Alliances may be represented by shaykhs, but tribesmen have no obligation to an alliance only to the tribe. Currently, there are two famous confederations, or large alliances, in Yemen: Bakīl and Ḥāshid. In the past, there were others in the south and east of Yemen, but they became irrelevant and disappeared. In the far north, Bakīl and Ḥāshid maintain a long historical presence. These tribal alliances gather tribes into broader coalitions that give leaders of the confederacies considerable power. They cannot command tribesmen, but they can gain significant influence over a broader geographic area than their local tribe.

The influential shaykhs of the confederacies of the far north were instrumental in shaping the formal institutions of republican Yemen. They were the leaders of the tribal armies during the civil war and they parlayed their military importance into political positions in the government.[51] The leader of the Ḥāshid confederation, Abdallah bin Hussein al-Aḥmar, was Minister of Interior in the very first government under al-Sallal, and was speaker of Yemen's parliament until his death in 2007. The shaykhs' political interests lay in maintenance of the tribal system and their own positions atop that system.[52] In the civil war of the 1960s, republican shaykhs fought not only royalist forces opposed to the republic but also republicans who proposed a more state-centric model of government that would have reduced the role of shaykhs in government and in society. In the decades following the founding of the republic, the shaykhs' ability to gain positions in the formal state enabled them to steer the course of political development in their favor. Shaykhs ensured that reserve tribal fighters remained a powerful military force within the country, that tribal leaders and custom governed the tribes' territories, and that tribal shaykhs would remain powerful in the formal institutions of politics.

Shaykhs in Government: The Political Foundation of the Republic

The republican coup carried out by military officers in the imam's guard in 1962 was immediately backed by Nasser's Egypt. Within three days, fifty thousand Egyptian troops had arrived and taken command of both military and state.[53] Yemeni republicans recognized the political and military importance of the tribes and sent emissaries to important tribal shaykhs; however, the latter did not need much persuading, having suffered greatly under the Zaydi imams.

Under the Zaydi imamate, tribal shaykhs, though powerful, were assigned a lower social status. Zaydi Hashemites, descendants of the Prophet through Ali and Fatima, occupied the top of the social order as well as most official positions in the state and military.[54] In the social order, non-Hashemite religious scholars followed the Hashemites, and below them were shaykhs and tribesmen. The imams relied on the northern tribes for their power but relegated them to a lower social rung. The Zaydi imams used tribesmen for their military forces and manipulated tribes to gain their allegiance. To ensure obedience, the imams kept the sons of leading shaykhs hostage in the imam's quarters.[55] As the imamate unraveled in the mid-1950s, several tribes rebelled. The Hāshid, the tribes of the most important confederacy, rebelled in 1959, but its rebellion was put down and its leading shaykh, Hussein al-Aḥmar, was executed along with his son Ḥamid. As a result, Hussein's other son, Abdallah, became the most important leader of the tribal forces in the republic until his death in 2007.

At first, the Egyptians joined Yemeni republican leaders in seeking tribal support. The new republican government created institutions to incorporate tribal leaders and tribesmen, beginning with a Supreme Committee for the Defense of the Revolution, a tribal army led by 180 shaykhs, to defend the borders. The shaykhs were given the rank and salary of government ministers.[56] In April 1963, republicans included thirteen shaykhs in the Yemeni Presidential Council, out of a total of thirty-two members, and created an administrative system for the north composed of tribal leaders.[57] Tribal leaders had effectively replaced the Zaydi Hashemites in the administration of the north. The republican movement was divided between those who wanted to establish a republic governed by conservative leaders, including tribal shaykhs, and those who wanted to transform Yemeni society and minimize the influence of religious and tribal leaders.[58] As Dresch notes:

> [A]t the crux of this potential contradiction were the major shaykhs, whom urban nationalists (primarily, the young men who returned to Yemen after the

1962 coup) increasingly saw as a single interest group ... The major shaykhs, for their part, had little time for these *awlad shawari'* ("riff-raff", "street people") who lacked tribal standing and who preached the equivalent of permanent revolution.[59]

After initially supporting tribal initiatives, Egyptian leaders came to side with those who wanted to minimize tribal influence. But Yemenis chaffed under the domination of the Egyptians, and tribal, religious, and socially conservative republican leaders convened a conference in Amran in 1963, in the heart of tribal territory, to propose an alternative to the Egyptian-led government and to increase the role of tribal leaders. A second conference in the Sudan in 1964 suggested "a national conference in a Yemeni city attended by 196 representatives of the religious scholars, tribal leaders, military commanders," which eventually took place in Khamir in 1965.[60] After the withdrawal of the Egyptians in 1967, this conservative faction consistently won political confrontations with Yemenis wanting greater social change. In a critical telling moment in 1968, weapons bound for the Yemeni army were diverted to tribal leaders. Burrowes argues that:

> ... the pattern for the rest of the al-Iryani era was set in the al-Hudayda incident in March 1968 when conservative and progressive republicans fought over whether a new shipment of Soviet arms should go to tribal irregulars or to the more professional units in the regular army—it was the tribalists who won the dispute and got the arms.[61]

Between 1974 and 1977, the al-Hamdi regime tried again to push tribal shaykhs from the institutions of government and the military, but al-Hamdi was assassinated in 1977. Ali Abdallah Saleh came to power in 1978, representing the conservative faction again.

Tribal leaders rose to the top of Yemeni politics due to the importance of the northern tribesmen in military conflicts. Tribal leaders allied with conservative religious leaders in order to outmaneuver those who wanted to build a strong state and reduce the power of the tribal shaykhs and religious leaders.[62] The power of tribal shaykhs in official positions allowed them to chart the development of the formal institutions of the Yemeni state.

Tribal Shaykhs in Government

The sight of tribal shaykhs in government and in the military gives the impression that tribes dominate the government and that Yemen is a republic of *shaykhs*. However, tribal affairs are local, and in local affairs, each tribe strives to maintain its own autonomy and to balance the power of their neighbors. Tribal shaykhs are often interested in local material benefit, not ideology or long-term policy development: they align with whichever side pays the best; they do not constitute a political bloc.[63] As a group, tribal shaykhs in the republican government created institutions such as the Office of Tribal Affairs in the Ministry of the Interior, which channeled subsidies to their counterparts.[64] Representative of the new relationship between tribe and state in the republican era, the Office of Tribal Affairs subsidized the northern tribes rather than collecting taxes from them; the office also maintained a list of "official" shaykhs, and the state now determined who was a shaykh and who should be paid.

As a group, shaykhs also guaranteed that tribal administration would dominate in the north, and that the Yemeni military would employ them and their tribesmen. But beyond these efforts, tribal shaykhs compete for benefits. Since tribes seek to balance the power of neighboring tribes, state benefits channeled to the tribe strengthens the role of the shaykhs within that tribe because they can deliver material benefits; however, material benefits also create competition between the tribes. According to Brandt, "many shaykhs retained their tribal ties and values and imported their rivalries and enmities into the state."[65] By not representing a single political bloc, tribal shaykhs become prey for larger forces seeking to gain influence, such as political parties or the central ruler, and "many influential shaykhs of the area became easy targets for co-optation, allowing the young Yemeni republic to push its agenda without making substantial efforts at state building."[66]

The leaders of tribal confederacies are better able to represent general interests than smaller local interests, but the two large confederations—from which came leading shaykhs such as Abdallah bin Hussein al-Aḥmar, Mujahid Abu Shawarib, Amin Abu Ras, and Sinan Abu Luḥum—also compete for advantage. Weir found that:

> ... inequalities between tribes create particular needs and dependencies, and temporary or permanent inequalities in power, and these in turn provoke cooperation, compromise, or friction in different circumstances. Al-Naẓīr and Munabbih, for example, are large, wealthy tribes, with a consequent tendency to dominate others. Small, weak tribes offset this pressure, and strive to preserve their autonomy and maintain the inter-tribal balance of power, by making defensive alliances with other tribes.[67]

Bakīl and Ḥāshid are as much a part of tribal social order as small local tribes, wherein each competes and monitors closely the activities of the other. The upper echelons of tribal leaders in government come from these larger confederations, assuring that tribalism remained important in the republican state.

City Shaykhs

The entrance of shaykhs into state leadership changes tribal leaders. Tribal affairs are local affairs, and the role of the tribal shaykh is also local. Shaykhs make their reputations on their ability to solve people's problems and to bring prosperity and security. However, tribal leaders in cities are distant from the local tribe; and while they may have access to state resources, they may not be available to direct local tribal affairs. Brandt argues that "many shaykhs moved from their tribal areas to the capital, Sana'a, or stayed there over long periods of time, thus loosening their tribal ties and, consequently, losing their tribal influence."[68]

More significantly, city shaykhs may develop other interests in urban Yemen, transforming them from tribal leaders to businessmen, state leaders, or military commanders. Alley interviewed members of the central committee of the General People's Congress, the ruling party, noting that:

> ... a Presidential advisor suggests that the incorporation of tribal elites into the private sector was a deliberate attempt to change the nature of a shaykh's connection with his tribe. Before the 1980s, tribal involvement in business was unusual because it was considered shameful for tribesmen to engage in commerce. Now, the majority of young shaykhs are also businessmen. Some Yemenis openly worry that some combination of business interests, party affiliation, and movement to cities is changing, and possibly weakening, the relationship between shaykhs and their tribesmen.[69]

Dresch observed that "sons of other great shaykhs have emerged as businessmen and one cannot see them ever being shaykhs themselves. Their interests lie in real estate, commerce and a life based in part on Paris, London or New York."[70] Thus, it is striking that Amran, the governorate at the heart of the tribal north, and the seat of the al-Aḥmar family's reign over Ḥāshid, is very poor. If tribal shaykhs managed to detour state development towards their interests, tribesmen seem not to have benefited. Shaykhs' interests transform into broader economic or national (and even international) political interests to the detriment of local tribesmen.

The sons of Abdallah bin Hussein al-Aḥmar seem very much "city shaykhs." All are embroiled in the politics of the central state. Before the

Houthi ascent, Alley described their incorporation into the Saleh regime's system of patronage:

> The sons of the late Shaykh 'Abdullah al-Aḥmar have multiple points of access to the patronage system. For example, Hamid al-Aḥmar is deeply embedded in private sector patronage, while Husayn, Hemyar, and Hashem are included through the ruling party and/or the military/security apparatus. Hemyar is now the Deputy Speaker of Parliament and Hashem is a member of the Republican Guard.[71]

The Houthi have upended the al-Aḥmars' fortune. Hussein al-Aḥmar fought the Houthi from the family home in Amran, and famously tried to raise a tribal "popular army" against the Houthi as his father had done in the civil war against the royalists. However, Hussein lost. Wealthy businessman Ḥamid al-Aḥmar threw his weight behind the Islah Party, which his father also led, but bet on the Muslim Brotherhood against the Gulf states and lost. He is now based in Turkey.[72] Sadiq al-Aḥmar, the eldest, inherited his father's position of paramount shaykh of Ḥāshid and now sits in Sanaa a prisoner, in effect, of the Houthi. Hashem al-Aḥmar commanded until recently, with Ali Muhsin, the Saudi-backed Yemeni military in the eastern desert deployed against the Houthi. None play the tribal role that their father played; all are part of national politics, the global economy, and international intrigue.

The success of the tribal leaders in entering national politics may be their undoing, at least as tribal leaders. While they may remain powerful as individuals who ensure that the state does not interfere with formal tribal autonomy, they have also been transformed into members of the national elite that is driven by different concerns and interests. While the tribesmen and shaykhs who remain in rural areas have also gone into business and received the benefits of state patronage, their residence in rural tribal areas keeps them involved in local affairs—though Brandt shows that the legitimacy of these shaykhs is also challenged by growing inequalities in tribal areas.[73]

The rise of the Houthi has upended the dominance of tribal leaders. The Houthi depend upon the tribal north, but the Houthi assert Hashemite interests in leadership and not those of tribal leaders.

Martial Abilities—Tribal Militias for Hire

The success of tribal leaders in the republic is largely due to the importance of the martial abilities of tribesmen in the north.[74] During the 1960s, Egyptians, Saudis, and Yemeni republicans and royalists all turned to the far north to pursue their battles because the armed tribesmen were the main source of fighting forces for all sides. Each side bought influence with cash and weapons, and much of the civil war was fought in these territories. In the inter-Yemeni wars in 1972 and 1979, tribal fighters played key roles in the north, and during the civil war of 1994, each side tried to find backers in the tribal north. More recently, the Houthi wars of 2004 to 2010 were fought in tribal territory.

Tribal wars are distinctive: they are largely symbolic, small skirmishes, not wars of conquest and destruction. Ironically, tribal social order is designed to contain conflict, not exacerbate it.

> A war may be spoken of by those involved as being between two tribes, or even between Ḥāshid and Bakīl, but the men doing the fighting usually number dozens, and only seldom even hundreds, while the sets in whose names they fight comprise tens of thousands. Most of those who fall within the two opposed sets will take little or no part. But even small-scale fighting exemplifies the opposition between the two tribes and hence demonstrates those tribes' honor, which itself gives events their sense.[75]

Weir makes a sharp distinction between the warfare of states and that of tribes: tribal warfare is largely symbolic whereas the warfare of states aims to conquer territory and destroy opponents.

> There is no evidence that inter-tribal wars were invasive or attritional. Leaders had no "imperialistic" intention of conquering, colonizing, or annexing enemy territory, nor of vanquishing or slaughtering its inhabitants. Like other forms of direct action, wars took place between autonomous tribes in mutual respect of each other's political and territorial integrity, and with a shared concern to minimize casualties and achieve a speedy conclusion.[76]

While detailed ethnographies concur that tribesmen are not violent, that tribal wars are intentionally limited, and that the design of the entire architecture of tribal society aims towards containing violence, the wars in tribal territory have been very bloody. Estimates of the number killed in the civil war of the 1960s vary from 100,000 to 200,000.[77] While the numbers are significantly lower, the Houthi wars of 2004 to 2010 were also violent, as is the current war in Yemen.

The apparent contradiction—between tribes containing violence and those enacting it—resolves when tribal fighters are distinguished from tribal social relations. In the north, tribal fighters are warriors for hire. The tribesmen of the far north of Yemen distinguish themselves by their fighting ability. Tribesmen everywhere in Yemen, including in the weak tribes, carry guns and are very capable of using them since they are tasked with securing tribal territory.[78] Descriptions of the civil war and of Yemen's other wars always contain reference to tribal militias, irregulars, levies, "popular" armies, or mercenaries. Tribesmen in the north fight for a living.[79] Occupations of tribesmen in the north might include agriculture, transportation, commerce, construction, and warring. The last occupation, like the others, is not constitutive of tribal social relations, it is just an occupation.

The issue is complex. During the civil war, for example, tribes did lean one way or another—that is, either republican or royalist. Tribal leaders, particularly the leaders of the confederations who had wider influence in the north and in Sanaa, did command groups of tribal fighters in the war,[80] and tribes did fight each other during the war. But tribal wars—ones that involved tribal social relations in tribal territory—are different from the wars of states or political movements. Tribes fought in the civil war because they were paid in cash and in weapons that poured into the north from both the Egyptian side and the Saudi side. The bloodiest fighting, however, occurred not between tribes, but between armies, some of which were composed of tribal levies, militias, or mercenaries. According to Dresch, "the heaviest fighting between tribal levies thus took place in the Western Mountains, while on the plateau what would otherwise have been war *à outrance*, was consistently checked by the forms of tribalism."[81] When the money ran out, the fighting ended. The climactic siege of Sanaa by royalist forces intent upon wiping out the republic after the Egyptian withdrawal in 1967 ended in a republican victory. Lack of money sent royalists home. Subsequently, "the siege was finally raised by a column from al-Ḥudaydah which broke through by a combination of forces and persuasion; and the campaign ended with the collapse of royalist resistance around al-Matanah in Banī Maṭar when the royalist pay-chest was ambushed and the funds carried off."[82]

Thus, the paradox is that the power of the northern tribes is based largely on their martial abilities, yet tribal social order is designed to contain violence. The tribal role in violence is not so much tribal as an occupational role organized by outside, non-tribal forces such as royalists, socialists, republicans, Saudis, and Houthis.

However, the Houthi wars may have changed the nature of violence in tribal territory. Brandt notes how the rise of the Colonel Shaykh, a state-backed tribal shaykh incorporated into the state military, and the tribal militia, composed of more than tribal fighters, led to the erosion of tribal values and to the increasing brutality of the wars, creating what she calls "hybrid wars."[83]

A Tribal State?

Contrary to expectations, the Yemeni state does not oppose the tribal challenge to its sovereignty, but rather celebrates tribal custom. Ali Abdallah Saleh, the architect of modern Yemen, ruled as the Qajars did in nineteenth-century Iran. He played factions against one another, divided and conquered, and tied everyone into a large patronage network that he used to keep everyone off balance.[84] As we have seen, tribes in Yemen are ideal for such a strategy because they are small rural units, divided amongst themselves, and continually at odds with their neighbors. Indications are that the Houthi are little different, though due to their relative lack of resources for patronage, they tend to use more sticks than carrots, and do not pretend to elevate tribal leaders to national leadership.

Both Saleh and the Houthi preferred to perpetuate tribal social relations by relying upon tribal customary mediation to resolve issues between the state and tribesmen or tribes. When a conflict erupts between the state and a tribe, the Yemeni state prefers to use tribal mediation, appealing to shaykhs for arbitration to resolve the issue. Dresch described the state's approach in a local dispute in the north in the early 1980s: "The government arrested ten men from Bayt Marrān and ten from Khubbah, the latter on the principle that a section or tribe is responsible for what happens in its territory."[85] The state knows tribal custom and perpetuates it by its use.[86] Even contested elections are resolved in tribal territory by arbitration.[87] Following the collapse of the Yemeni Socialist Party after the civil war of 1994, Saleh's regime attempted to extend tribal social relations into the south.[88] Tribes reemerged in parts of the south for their own reasons, such as reclaiming confiscated land and providing local security as the state collapsed, but Saleh had the Office of Tribal Affairs subsidize hundreds of new shaykhs that he appointed. Saleh saw that the reemergence of tribal social order benefited his regime.

The Saleh regime has itself been called tribal,[89] because Saleh recruited his close relatives into the top security and military posts of the state. Saleh was from Sanhan, a tribe affiliated with the Ḥāshid confederation, but his rise to power was not because he was a shaykh—it was through the military. He was commander of the garrison in Taiz when he was chosen to lead the country. Saleh's patronage was diffuse and ecumenical, but his control of the very core of the security and military was extremely calculated: he placed his close relatives in all the key positions. This is a form of tribalism that has no equivalent in tribal custom, and might be considered a case of "ganging up," prohibited in tribal custom.[90] Instead, Al-Dhahery and Al-Sharjabi point to the fact that Yemeni leaders usually come from outside tribal society.[91] To overcome tribal rivalries, tribal society looks for a non-tribal, neutral arbiter. Yemeni history is replete with cases of outsiders coming to Yemen and integrating into Yemeni politics as a chief arbiter.[92]

States in the Informal Politics of the Tribe

Not content in preserving tribal forms of local government and playing on the divisions between tribes, the central regime also intervened in local domestic tribal politics to ensure regime dominance. Here, the regime intervenes in tribal informal politics by promoting loyal leaders. Thus, "while confrontations in the cities are submitted to tribal law, in the countryside tribal divisions are cross-cut and infested with state intrigue which seems to many the symptom of tribalism's weakness."[93] Initially, this entailed promoting shaykhs loyal to the republic, but patronage was also used to tie important royalist shaykhs to the regime. In this way, "the formative phase of the republic in Sa'dah was closely bound up with the emerging dominance of those shaykhly lineages who were rewarded for their loyalty during the civil war."[94] The central regime used rewards of government contracts, import licenses, and positions in the ruling party, the military, and the government to channel resources to key allies, which in turn enhanced the position of these men in local tribal society. Brandt cites the cases of relatively insignificant shaykhs and tribesmen, Faris Mana and Ali Husayn of al-Munabbihi,[95] who achieved new wealth and translated this into leadership positions within their tribes.

Brandt's meticulous detailing of the Houthi conflict hints at changes in tribes and the tribal order in the north. She argues that the state's interference in the domestic politics of tribes may in fact be eroding tribalism, at least in the far north:

> [T]he patronage policy of the republican government, particularly the Salih government, has not "nurtured" the local tribal system, but, on the contrary, helped to distort a functioning tribal order by elevating in importance positions of authority and economic favouritism, which have altered the character of tribal leadership.[96]

The distortion of tribal authority, Brandt argues, prepared the ground for the rise of the Houthi, who adeptly exploited the ill will created by the Saleh regime's policies among the tribes in the far north. Al-Sharjabi also argues that the republican regimes have transformed the relationship between tribesman and shaykh. According to recent survey results, tribesmen believe that shaykhs are more interested in their personal advancement than that of the tribe, and that the consensual nature of domestic tribal politics is eroding.[97] In addition, Brandt argues that warfare is changing tribal relations. Tribal custom mitigates against violence, and tribal society tries to contain it, but the recent Houthi wars have introduced a new level of violence that may transform tribal society in the north. Tribal warfare is becoming more mercenary, while also retaining a tribal element as well.

Conclusion

Tribes are small sovereignties that challenge the state in Yemen through the provision of a system of local government that conflicts with the state's own sovereignty. The ability of tribal order to provide local security and social stability in rural areas in the absence of effective state governance explains the persistence of tribes and tribalism in Yemen. But tribes do not rule Yemen. Tribal social order is fractured, with each tribe seeking to maintain its autonomy in a local environment surrounded by competing tribes. Thus, there is never a tribal political position. Tribal social order is easily manipulated from outside, such that non-tribal powers compete to gain tribal support, and tribal territory comes to reflect the divisions of outside society. Tribes are divided by sect, by political party, and by foreign influence—not out of conviction, but often motivated by material advantage.

Tribal leaders—shaykhs—entered government for the first time after the republican coup in the far north, a rebellion in part against the social hierarchy that disadvantaged shaykhs. These shaykhs parlayed their military importance to the republican government into a permanent position in the state. Tribal leaders in the state guaranteed that tribal order in the far north persisted and was not replaced by a state-centric model.

Ironically, the Yemeni state promotes informal power rather than formal power. The Yemeni state prefers to be the grand arbiter between many different centers of power in Yemen, pulling and manipulating the myriad factions of Yemeni and tribal society through a centralized but diffuse patronage system. Rather than oppose the sovereignty of the tribe, the central state encouraged it, preferring to rule over a myriad of divided small entities than to govern citizens directly. At the center of the patronage system was a core of Saleh's clansmen, which acted not in tribal fashion, but as part of a personal pact with the person of the president. Loyalty to a tribe differs from loyalty to the person of the president in a small elite core. The breaking of that pact by cultivating Saleh's son, Ahmad, for the presidency, was one of the factors in the unraveling of the regime in the Arab uprising of 2011.

The Houthi leadership is another type of non-tribal elite core based on the personal leadership of Abd al-Malik al-Houthi and some form of Hashemite (Zaydi) solidarity. The Houthi built a constituency in tribal society in the north by manipulating tribal factions. However, the Houthi also violated tribal social norms by introducing a new level of violence in tribal wars. The Houthi also do not include tribal leaders in top positions of their state. Though the Houthi state is an ad hoc arrangement during the war, the Houthi appear to promote Hashemite interests over those of tribal elites, and will likely alter the relationship between tribal leaders and the formal politics of the state when the war concludes.

3

ÇAY POLITICS

INFORMAL POLITICS IN TURKEY AND
VOTE MOBILIZATION IN ISTANBUL AND ŞANLIURFA

Michelangelo Guida

Introduction

Despite the fact that today's Turkish political parties emerged in the modern context, aside from formal campaigning, political parties must resort to a series of *informal* tools to maintain or gain consent. Among these tools is the exploitation of "kin-like networks" that survive and sometimes evolve in the rapid process of modernization and democratization. This chapter presents two examples of kin-like groups and their role in vote mobilization: the local elections in Üsküdar in the political campaign of 2009, and the case of the *birleşik oy* (communal vote; literally, "united vote") in the province of Şanlıurfa.

The first case is based on the 2009 electoral campaign in Üsküdar, one of the thirty-nine districts of Istanbul Greater Municipality. Here, the results of my fieldwork and a survey I undertook in Üsküdar and two other districts of the city clearly showed that the AK Parti's winning strategy was built on infor-

43

mal and intimate relations with voters, rather than utilizing media and formal campaign strategies. A chat and a glass of *çay* (tea) shared with *hemşehri* (fellow townspeople) and women's networks appear to have been much more influential than any media campaign strategy. As we will see in this case, voters did not even recall the official slogans of political parties.

The second case study shows the great capability of *ağa* (tribal chieftains) in mobilizing votes in certain districts of Şanlıurfa province, in southeastern Turkey. Chieftains' power originates from a mix of coercion, well-rooted values of *şeref* (collective honor), tribal loyalty,[1] as well as the capability to build ties with national authorities. It seems that the involvement of notables in the elections is also to some degree accepted by institutions; very few complaints against the chieftains and their manipulations of the vote are filed in court, and authorities are well aware of their role in vote mobilization. In this sense, despite the demographic, social, political, and economic transformations, tribal identities have not disappeared, but evolved into a functional and dynamic network of patronage. As such, an analysis of patronage and informal relations, as well as their influence on political mobilization, certainly helps in understanding political practices and informal practices in Turkish politics.

Turkey's first free and fair elections were held on May 14, 1950.[2] However, Turkey is placed in the third wave of democratization, because the 1980 military coup suspended and deeply changed the constitutional framework. It was not until 1983 that new elections were held.[3] New political parties were established, and completely new entities were formed with no relation to previous political parties. Anavatan Partisi (Motherland Party, ANAP established in 1983) and Adalet ve Kalkınma Partisi (Justice and Development Party, AK Parti established in 2001) dominated the political scene from 1983 to 1993, and from 2002 to the present, respectively. The period from 1993 to 2002 was characterized by volatility and political instability. New parties with deep roots in the pre-1980 political system, such as Demokratik Sol Partisi (Democratic Left Party) and Refah Partisi (Welfare Party, RP), were forced to adapt their methodology and ideology to a modernizing society.

All these parties had to radically change their campaign strategies because of the rapid change in the structure of the media.[4] For instance, in 1983, the ANAP was favored in the first televised debate on Turkish public television. The first private television channel began broadcasting a few years later, in May 1989. Today, 87 percent of Turks follow the news online,[5] and 47 percent declare that their main source of news is television.[6] However, when asked specifically about trust in the news, 46 percent of the respondents say that they do not trust it. Moreover, 50 percent have an overall distrust of social media, and 33 percent distrust television. Overall, distrust in the media is equal only to Greece, and is surpassed only by the percentage in the United States, where overall distrust of media is 40 percent.[7]

In this climate of mistrust, two loyalties appear to maintain their relevance and are the base for informal politics in Turkish politics: tribalism and *hemşehrilik*. As Eickelman stresses, tribal identity and kinship relations are something that local people create.[8] There are four main forms in which people create tribal identity in the Middle East (and also in Turkey). Firstly, anthropological concepts are created by observers for analytical purposes.

Secondly, tribal identity is the elaboration and use of explicit "native" ethno-political ideologies by the people themselves to describe their sociopolitical organization. Even if kinship and tribal identity often results in the imposition of unequal social relations in Şanlıurfa or even Istanbul, it appears to be commonly accepted through a validation process instigated by its democratic connotation and the mutual benefits obtained by involved agents.

Thirdly, tribalism and kinship are concepts used by state authorities for administrative purposes. The Ottomans favored tribes in many areas of the empire in exchange for military and tax collection services.[9] Since the introduction of democracy in Turkey, political parties also have exploited—and apparently strengthened—different forms of kinship, because influencing groups that are bound by different forms of identity is cheaper and easier than campaigning for the consent of individuals throughout the country.

Finally, implicit, practical notions held by tribespeople, which are not elaborated into formal ideologies, serve as a guide to everyday conduct in relations between larger groups. Alan Duben shows that despite urbanization or industrialization, an institutionalized system of wider kin relations persisted even in urban Turkey. Moreover, he noticed that because the city represents a much more hostile environment, there is a prevalence of a "kinship idiom" in urban spaces to a greater extent than in rural contexts:

> In the interstices somewhere between family, kinship and certainly inevitably impersonal encounters that individuals in Turkey try to place their interactions with each other in a kinship idiom, an idiom whose rules are familiar to them, rooted as they are in the kinship system and in a long history, and in place of which alternatives that we label the "public morality of a civil society" have not adequately developed.[10]

By "kinship idiom," Duben indicates a range of codes governing behavior, from genuine altruism to the pretension of altruism overlaying a careful calculation of interests. Interactions utilizing this idiom involve individuals who, in some cases, share certain social attributes, such as membership in a common sect or ethnic group. This concept recalls Eickelman's "closeness" (*qaraba*) of urban and rural Moroccans,[11] and also the Ibn Khaldunian concept of *'asabiyya*. These are ties of obligation between people with asserted and recognized ties of kinship, or ones that emerge through participating in factional alliances, patronage, and client relationships, or even through common bonds that developed out of residential propinquity. Consequently, affinity among kinspeople in urban societies can also be created in their daily lives without actual biological or marriage ties, to gain advantages through altruism in an alien social environment without social welfare provided by the state or collectivity. Thus, a person relies on this informal system of justice, which brings social security, interpersonal expectations, and intimate reciprocities.

The vocabulary used by Turks is also evidence of the kinship idiom. It is not by chance that an influential person or "protector" in a relationship of patronage is called, in Turkish slang, *dayı*—the maternal uncle, the most intimate relative outside of the nuclear family. *Hemşehrilik* (literally, "coming from the same town") is also a strong kin-like relation that uses a kinship idiom. The term has a very broad meaning: two people in the same district meeting one another will call each other *hemşehri*, as would two Turkish migrants from different provinces meeting abroad. A stranger with a similar social status can also be called *hemşehri*. Indeed, "the social function" of the term denotes more than a common origin, and is used "to construct a link so that the speaker is not anonymous anymore, and therefore make[s] it possible to relate to him so as to have a chat or offer a *çay*."[12] The term *hemşehri* is not used by villagers in reference to the village community, which is characterized by strict hierarchy, but is explicitly used in cities to indicate a group of equals willing to act collectively.

Ayşe Güneş-Ayata, in her study of Ankara's shanty towns in the late 1980s, shows that *hemşehrilik* is not simply the result of chain migration; it is not always exploited by new immigrants to find shelter or a job through this network. It is mainly used to gain an "identity" in the megalopolis. Moreover, this affiliation does not weaken in urban space. On the contrary, when interactions with "strangers" or "others" increase in the urban context, it is strengthened and preserved by the natives.[13] In the big Turkish cities, *hemşehrilik* networks are further preserved due to many choosing to live in the same neighborhood in order to be part of the coffeehouse culture, charity or "cultural" associations, sports clubs, and religious organizations (charity, educational, and mystical circles outside the state official religious administration) established by and for fellow townsmen.

To understand how the kinship idiom persisted despite the sociopolitical transformations of Turkish society, we should remember that Western civil and criminal codes, a large state bureaucratic apparatus, and modern mechanized workplaces were "transplanted" to the newly founded Turkish Republic, and the well-established, old personalistic networks frequently became intertwined with religious discourse. The older patrimonial personalistic codes, which can be traced back to social institutions such as the *futuwwat*, *ahîlik*, or *loncas*,[14] continued to be effective in the everyday lives of people, even in the public sphere.[15]

The state is termed *baba* (father) in Turkish colloquial expressions because the central state has always been perceived as the source of secure jobs, the fulcrum of national identity, and the provider of handouts. However, the Ottoman and Republican states have never been seen as close and intimate with society. On the contrary, in the 1990s, it was the RP that maintained a kinship idiom with its constituencies, and it began using local governments to deliver services impersonally to citizens—so successfully, in fact, that it gained loyalty from almost all shanty areas.[16]

Finally, the Ottoman and Turkish states have been characterized as "transcendental," namely superior and supernatural, dominated by a bureaucratic intelligentsia holding a different *Weltanschauung* (worldview), and interested in implementing policies to educate and modernize even if these reformist ideas were not shared by the majority of the population.[17] The transcendental state has been inevitably seen as distant and unapproachable, and consequently not an alternative to kin-like relations.

After these necessary definitions, we can move on examining our first case, local elections in Üsküdar.

Political Campaign in Üsküdar

The March 2009 local elections were held after the AK Parti national government had already ruled for seven years and had, in that time, curtailed public opposition to the military and the bureaucratic establishment. However, after an economic boom, Turkey began suffering from the international financial crisis. The party performed well in the elections, confirming people's positive perception of the party's achievements in national and local governments. Nationally, AK Parti obtained 39 percent of the votes—

seven percentage point less than in the 2007 general elections, and two points less than in the previous local elections—against 23 percent and 16 percent attained, respectively, by the opposition forces of Milliyetçi Hareket Partisi (Nationalist Action Party, MHP) and Cumhuriyet Halk Partisi (Republican People's Party, CHP).[18]

The AK Parti candidate for Istanbul Greater Municipality, Kadir Topbaş, confronted leftist-Kemalist challenger Kemal Kılıçdaroğlu, who gained national prominence by attacking the AK Parti with charges of corruption and a hint of populism just a few months before the beginning of the 2009 electoral campaign. Despite his failure to win in the local elections, his appeal made him so popular that, in May 2010, he became the leader of CHP when his predecessor was forced to resign after a sex scandal.[19] Nevertheless, in Istanbul, AK Parti's candidate obtained 44 percent of the votes against 37 percent of the votes obtained by Kılıçdaroğlu.

During the 2009 electoral campaign, I joined a team of researchers that followed the campaigns of the two main political parties—AK Parti and CHP—in three districts that are part of Istanbul Greater Municipality: Kadıköy, Küçükçekmece, and Üsküdar. After the March elections, we applied a face-to-face survey on a random sample of 2,914 people within the borders of these three municipalities.[20]

Kadıköy is a wealthy residential area that has been leaning center-left since 1989 and is also renowned for its nightlife and attractions for young people. Küçükçekmece is a former industrial area developed after the 1980s and hosts a large immigrant population from Anatolia. Üsküdar, with its 582,666 inhabitants (in 2009), was chosen as a study area because it represents middle-class, moderate voters in the megalopolis of Istanbul. Üsküdar was established as a Greek colony in the seventh century BC, but its population—as with all areas of Istanbul—generally has a history of internal migration from other areas of the country. Here, the district was controlled by the RP from 1994 to 2004, and since then by the AK Parti, which did not fear the challenge of CHP. Local CHP activists were uncomfortable with the strategy of their leadership on the national level, and with its choice to candidate in Üsküdar the businesswoman Sema Barlın, who conducted a rather dull twenty-day campaign, with few public appearances and a small budget. Twenty-nine percent of the votes that Barlın obtained were a combination of partisan and "secular" votes—one side of the deep polarization among Turkish voters.[21]

However, in the district, AK Parti was facing two possible threats: one coming from the heir of the RP, Saadet Partisi (Felicity Party, SP) candidate

Yılmaz Bayat, who had twice been mayor of Üsküdar and was praised for his successes in the administration of the district. SP's candidacy may have divided the center-right and conservative constituency, and, consequently, strengthened the opposition. The second challenge was represented by the fact that AK Parti did not nominate the incumbent mayor, who had become unpopular with his rigid positions and lack of dialogue with its constituency. In the 2009 elections, AK Parti candidate Mustafa Kara had focused his visual campaign on making his name familiar to, and popular among, voters, as well as on attempting to overwhelm SP's campaign, which was conducted with limited financial resources. AK Parti's campaign was successful, and Kara obtained a relative majority of 38 percent of the votes against SP's 20 percent.

Nevertheless, the results of the survey (see Tables 1 and 2), which we conducted immediately after the elections, exposed the ineffectiveness of Kara's formal visual campaign. Despite large economic and human investments in the campaign, nearly 80 percent of the sample in the three districts failed to remember any of the party slogans. In Üsküdar, just 27 percent of those interviewed remembered some of the slogans of the AK Parti's local candidate.[22] Thus, in this context, why do political parties allocate so many resources in visual campaigns if only a small proportion of the electorate remembers the slogans? Perhaps because parties need to maintain their presence in the streets and to visually overwhelm the competitors. Indeed, during the 2009 campaign, party loyalists draped main streets and squares with party flags and posters. Moreover, at the national level, rather than changing the electoral law, the AK Parti transformed political campaigning by increasing its own election spending so that minor parties in the center-right spectrum—some of which were prominent in the 1990s—were unable to contest the AK Parti's dominance.

During our research, no candidate or party official would reveal the exact figures of their election costs, and, in accordance with Turkish law, there is no obligation to publish these figures. However, the AK Parti campaign director told us that in the district of Üsküdar, the party hung flags across approximately 500 kilometers, and, among other giveaways, it distributed five thousand dianthus flowers. Giveaways are crucial when candidates and party members conduct house visits and when approaching people in the street. Moreover, the district branch of the party employed twenty full-time employees to hang flags and posters, and had between 500–600 volunteers, who received lunch, dinner, and beverages when working.[23]

Table 1: Do you remember any of the CHP slogans?[24]

	National	Greater Municipality	Kadıköy	K.Çekmece	Üsküdar
Do not remember any	95.2	85.5	66.2	97.3	95.1
Sakin Güç	7.1	0.4	0.4	0.2	–
Kadıköylülerin Selami var	–	–	32.7	–	–

Table 2: Do you remember any of the *AK Parti* slogans?[25]

	National	Greater Municipality	Kadıköy	K.Çekmece	Üsküdar
Do not remember any	57.7	79.7	79.9	84.4	73.2
Durmak yok yola devam	21.4	3.9	2.9	2	0.9
Büyük düşün	9.4	6.8	11.1	2.1	5.1
Sen İstanbul'sun büyük düşün	–	6.6	–	–	–
Sen Kadıköy'sin büyük düşün	–	–	4.4	–	–
360 derece belediyecilik	–	–	–	3.2	–
Sen Üsküdar'sın büyük düşün	–	–	–	–	17.3

Conventional campaigning appeared as largely ineffective. Indeed, the aim of the electoral campaign was to reach powerful networks based on personal relations—something that Jenny White defines as "vernacular politics."[26] That is, an autonomous, grassroots political process in which local and religious networks cooperate with political parties and civic organizations in a sustained social and political movement.

In White's study of the Islamist RP and Fazilet Partisi (Virtues Party) in the working-class district of Ümraniye (bordering Üsküdar), she noticed that what binds people together in the movement behind the party is neither ideology nor any particular type of organization; "rather, the movement is rooted in local culture and interpersonal relations, while also drawing on a variety of civic and political organizations and ideologies."[27] Consequently, RP owed much of its success to its ability to incorporate hybrid populations and to build on local community networks.

In the 1969 electoral campaign, Necmettin Erbakan, the founder of the Turkish Islamist political movement, brought some relevant innovations to electoral campaign strategies and strengthened his official campaigns with informal tools. In contrast to crowded rallies, Erbakan gave much more importance to small meetings—many organized in private houses—where the candidate might have more direct and personal relations with the voters. At first, Erbakan's party was helped by local activists, including the local imams and other preachers who had won the trust of the local people already.

In rural areas, there was a similar policy. Erbakan's party activists visited villages, delivered sermons about religion, and gave out gifts, including tape recorders and audio cassettes of Erbakan's speeches.[28] The obvious aim was to reach voters in remote areas who did not have electricity or television. Thus, Islamist parties invested in the power of "the gift"—a by-the-book implementation of Marcel Mauss' theory—aimed at building "intimate" relationships between the voter and the party, as well as instilling an obligation to reciprocate by voting for the party.[29]

When it gained local governments in the 1990s, RP also used municipalities and the party's structures, as well as powerful webs of informal politics—religious confraternities, religious movements, and *hemşehrilik* networks—to win trust among a larger section of the population. In the 2000s, the AK Parti adopted and meliorated RP's strategies. To gain access to these community networks, the RP first and the AK Parti later had to become "intimate" and adopt a kinship idiom. They did so by interacting with constituents on an individual level through known, trusted neighbors, building on face-to-face relationships, and situating political messaging within the community's idiom, cultural codes, and norms.[30] Despite the iconic nationalist and conservative attire of Islamist parties, *hemşehrilik* networks have imported into politics the contradictory evaluations and competing motivations of the different local communities empowered by informal processes.

The Islamist and conservative parties' electoral strategies have had an additional effect.[31] Firstly, they challenged the Jacobin, centralized, top-down paternalism of the political system, and aimed at empowering a new class of politicians and bureaucrats whom constituents perceive to be "just like us." The RP (initially) and the AK Parti (after the 2002 elections) generally shared the same community networks and idiom. Moreover, the widespread feeling of *mağduriyet* (of being unjustly treated) also helped and still helps in strengthening the constituencies' allegiance to the party.[32] Large sections of the "periphery" in rural and urban areas share similar feelings of being discriminated against because of their poor socioeconomic status or conservative worldview.[33]

Furthermore, there is also an important portion of the business world that shares the feeling of *mağduriyet*. During Erbakan's first electoral campaign in Konya, he was backed by the newly emerging conservative economic elites— ones who had been marginalized by the better-positioned economic and Istanbul's financial elites, who were much closer to the Kemalist apparatus and secular elites. Since 2002, this new "green capital" or "Islamic capital" has gained strength and large shares of the economy but remains resentful of past discriminations.[34]

Even if it can be defined today as a conservative party, the AK Parti emerged as the *yenilikçi* (reformist) wing of Turkey's Islamist political movement and inherited much of the cadre of the parties established by Erbakan and his electoral strategies. Indeed, President Erdoğan ameliorated the methodology of various political campaigns. In this way, the AK Parti earned the trust of a large constituency—bonded by a common sense of having been marginalized by the Kemalist state bureaucracy and mistrust of mainstream media, which has been allegedly controlled by the secular elites. In 1985, Erdoğan was appointed head of RP's Istanbul branch and improved the party's already well-functioning formal and informal electoral machine, extending it to reach all the sections of society that felt *mağdur* (marginalized). His first great success was winning the Istanbul Greater Municipality elections in 1994. His new strategy also included visits to brothels—going beyond Muslim taboos but embracing new marginalized social groups. An increasing number of activists were involved in the process, and more Muslim *tarikat* (confraternities) and *cemaat* (movements) were included in the broad ideological coalition.

The RP attempted to build intimate relations with voters, with strategies devised by the province director, who was considered to be the "brain" from whom all information and orders originated. For every single ballot box—in the 1994 local elections there were 15,596 ballot boxes in the province of Istanbul—there was a group of five activists registered for that box,[35] whose primary responsibility was to maintain good personal relations with the voters during the campaign. This organization permitted the party to collect data on voters and to establish relationships with each voter. Party activists had to collect feedback, complaints, and wishes, and transmitted them to the "brain" through the organizational chain of the party.[36] Particularly in the shanty areas, activists visited families and often delivered aid collected from the local business community or local authorities. Building trust between party activists and the public, Erdoğan was able to create a network of personal and informal idioms and a wide web of relationships between the party and the voters.

The RP and the AK Parti have acquired a huge advantage against their challengers thanks to their strategy to mobilize votes, with opposition parties failing to understand the importance of informal relations. Deniz Baykal, leader of CHP between 1992 and 2010, relied too much on media campaigning and ignored the idiom of the greater majority. In 1995, CHP's newspaper campaign advertisements featured a smiling Baykal who boldly encouraged people to fax their concerns to the party headquarters in Ankara. This was a significant miscalculation around access to fax machines and voter willingness to engage in such a non-interactive and cold relation with the party.[37] Baykal—as other Kemalist politicians before and after him—adopted an unfamiliar idiom, while no idiom was tailored specifically for the society in the rural setting or those with a rural background.

In 2009, the Istanbul AK Parti electoral structure included a person whose duty was to conduct public relations in every neighborhood and to oversee a coordinator for every ten ballot boxes. To support the ballot box coordinators, there were ten groups of nine activists, with each group responsible for a single box. Among the nine responsible for a ballot box, three were activists of the Gençlik Kolları (Youth Branch), three from the Kadın Kolları (Women's Branch), and three were experienced members of the party. Each member was responsible for several voters.[38] Activists also served as *müşahit* (observers) for the party on the Election Day. Moreover, according to the AK Parti's training instructions, "neighborhood and ballot box areas are the basic field for party activities. All the activities toward the voter must be done on this field with an 'active participation' and 'face-to-face/one-to-one' method."[39]

After acquiring voters' data, local activists visited them, checked their voter registration status, and established a new informal bond. Young voters are attracted through incentives such as concerts and the *Siyaset Akademisi* ("Politics Academy"), which introduces them to basic knowledge of political science and party ideology, and then inserts them into the party electoral machine so as to become part of a group. Women meet at tea parties and focus on mobilizing family members, frequently around charity activities.

Furthermore, activists are animated by the will to deliver a *hizmet* (a service on behalf of God and His community) and to strengthen their own networks. Working inside well-known community networks and using face-to-face campaigning gives a sense of empowerment to a largely excluded section of the population (women, youth, and religiously conservative activists). Voters, on their side, felt a sense of belonging and of being part of the political process thanks to visits by party members, symbolic gifts, and eventually material aid from the party itself or services that had been delivered by local governments because of party mediation.

In the 2009 local elections campaign, for instance, AK Parti's Üsküdar branch planned to knock on 50,000 doors, to distribute *lokum* (the traditional Turkish delight confection) or coffee sets during house visits, in addition to traditional election paraphernalia—70,000 pens, 2,000 men's ties, and bags and scarves bearing the party emblem and the name of the candidate.[40] Today, giveaways are widely used also by other parties; for instance, in the same election, the CHP candidate mayor in Küçükçekmece even handed out toothbrushes to symbolize his party's intention to clean up politics. However, as outlined in AK Parti training materials:

> ... the member responsible for the ballot box, and his aides, must hold one-to-one (face-to-face) meetings with the voters of the assigned ballot box, which the member is responsible for, and enlist the voters to join the party. To do that, party activists have to make periodic visits to the voters with leaflets and all other promotional materials.[41]

During an interview, Sinan Aktaş, the head of Kara's electoral campaign, took a phone call from an AK Parti branch member in Anatolia who was asking for suggestions on how to conduct a successful campaign; Aktaş replied: "One-to-one relations and keep him [the candidate] on the field."[42] Aktaş' strategy consisted of a campaign where candidates meet people, shake hands, and build personal relations with the constituency.

For months, Kara had several meetings with *sivil toplum kuruşları* ("civil society associations")—nongovernmental associations (NGOs) that usually represent kinship networks. Istanbul is now a megalopolis inhabited predominantly by migrants from different regions of Anatolia, and Üsküdar is no different. According to a survey conducted in 2008, 44 percent of the AK Parti constituency were born in the Black Sea region, as were 56 percent of voters' fathers. Only 26 percent of the constituency were born in Istanbul, and only 5 percent of voters' fathers were born there.[43] From a 2002 survey of Üsküdar's population, it is evident that Black Sea voters are overrepresented among AK Parti votes. In fact, only 30 percent of Üsküdar dwellers were born in the Black Sea region, while 33 percent were born in Istanbul.[44] People from the Black Sea are very active in building *hemşehri* networks and also are very active in the construction sector, both key to gaining votes and financing. It is not a coincidence that the party leader—Recep Tayyip Erdoğan—is originally from Rize, and Kara's predecessor in Üsküdar, Mehmet Çakır (2004–09) and successor Hilmi Türkmen (2014–present), both elected in the ranks of AK Parti, are from Trabzon, the largest city in the Black Sea region. It has also to be noted that in the 2019 local elections, and after twenty-six years of conservative and Islamist government in Istanbul Greater Municipality, a CHP candidate born in Trabzon's province was able to win.

However, Kara is originally from Kars, in Turkey's far east, and he had to gain the sympathies of the Black Sea networks. Consequently, he spent a great deal of his time visiting these *hemşehri* NGOs. For instance, on April 21, 2009, he visited the Bitlis Hizan Gayda ve Çevre Köyleri Sosyal Yardımlaşma Derneği (Association of Social Solidarity of Bitlis Hizan's Gayda and Neighboring Villages) in a very joyful and crowded meeting. Besides the stump speech presenting his program for the district of Üsküdar, he added anecdotes that highlighted his links to the region of Bitlis and his passion for its delicacies. However, beside the pleasantries, Kara was promoting the candidate to the district council from Bitlis who was supposed to become the real channel between the new mayor, the party, and fellow citizens in the area.

As a matter of fact, since Erdoğan became head of RP's Istanbul branch, the lists of mayor and local council candidates have been prepared with respect to the proportion of the population's place of origin, and with a fixed quota reserved for women and disabled people. At the same time, because 44 percent of AK Parti voters in Üsküdar are of Black Sea heritage,[45] in 2009, twenty-five of the forty-five candidates for the district council were also originally from the Black Sea region, whereas only six were born in Istanbul and seven were born in the Central and Eastern Anatolia regions. Eleven candidates were also involved in NGOs, many of them representing *hemşehri* networks. The candidates to the district council representing the Black Sea constituency were among the most active in the organization of events during the 2009 campaign. They worked hard to guarantee high attendance and for the presence of businesses that offered gifts, refreshments, and local cuisine to potential voters. Businesspeople are interested in participating because it gives them visibility among *hemşehri*s, and their support—probably also with conspicuous donations—of a candidate's campaign will likely help people in the the business community in their future bids to obtain permits (particularly building permits, which are a competence of the local council). This two-way clientelism is exploited by both businesspeople and politicians during their term. Voters support the party and their *hemşehri* candidate for a purpose; although voters are happy to see one of their own elected, voters also have the expectation that their candidate will be a link between the community and the municipality. The expectation is that the candidate who shares the same loyalty will eventually help the voter in the future, according to the dominant political philosophy of "who you know" or "having a *dayı* [uncle or *patronus*]" in the state apparatus.

The RP's—and even more so the AK Parti's—decision to rely on *hemşehris* is thus obviously strategic. AK Parti constituency and supporters are from the Black Sea, whereas people originally from Istanbul are more likely to vote for the CHP.[46] Moreover, the Üsküdar branch of the party organized festivals dedicated to different regions—*7 Bölge 7 Renk* ("7 Regions 7 Colors")—with entertainment and local catering. Each festival was dedicated to one of Turkey's seven macro regions and held in the biggest cultural center in the district. Obviously, the best organized event night was the one dedicated to the Black Sea region, held on February 28, 2009—a symbolic date serving as a reminder of the Kemalist military and the judiciary ousting of Erbakan government in 1997.

Finally, as we also will see in the case of Şanlıurfa, since the introduction of competitive elections, political parties have tried to exploit the already existing kin-like loyalties and idiom. Inevitably, this maintains informal relations with the so-called "civil society organizations" and the primitive loyalties beyond the formality of a campaign. However, the party leaders also have to maintain a solid coalition of networks after the campaign through great diplomacy and forms of patronage.

Communal Vote in Şanlıurfa

In a study published in 1962, Szyliowicz states that "kinship and family background were the decisive factors in village politics ... The world of the villager was a narrow one, bounded by the interests of his clan or family."[47] The author's conclusions were based on a study conducted in İçel province in southwest Turkey during the era of the conservative *Demokrat Parti* (Democrat Party, DP) (1950–61). Since then, İçel province has been greatly transformed by modern agriculture, industrialization, and internal migration, to a point that voting behaviors now follow completely different patterns. However, in the eastern provinces of the country, despite modernization, kinship and family appear to still be decisive factors in mobilizing votes.

The province of Şanlıurfa is an interesting example regarding the role of tribes. A brief analysis of the elected members of parliament from Şanlıurfa province, both in the Ottoman and Republican eras, shows us that members of the Cevheri family,[48] for instance, have been elected to parliament at least eleven times since the first free elections. Other leading local families like the Bucak and the Gülpınar were also able to show their capability to mobilize votes.[49] At the local level, these families are even more powerful.

An analysis of official results in the rural areas of the Şanlıurfa province may also show how many villages vote collectively (the so-called *birleşik oy*) for only one political party. These kinship ties remain, despite the fact that the province has seen a remarkable growth in population, from nearly 920,000 in 2007 to 1.98 million in 2017.[50] Expansion of education followed a similar pace and, for instance, between 2009 and 2017, female students in high school increased from 27,000 to 56,000. Moreover, Şanlıurfa has seen the most impressive urban expansion in Anatolia, with major infrastructure developments, and the expansion of the agricultural sector thanks to the *Güneydoğu Anadolu Projesi* (Southeast Anatolia Project) and the Atatürk dam on the Euphrates river.[51]

Nevertheless, the persistence of representatives of influential families among elected officials is evidence that tribal leaders (mainly Kurdish and Arab) in Şanlıurfa still have power in mobilizing votes for themselves and directing the voting preferences of entire local communities. Not only do tribal or religious leaders have the power of coercion over tribe members, but they also have a patron–client relationship with mutual benefits and a strong sense of affinity. Tribe members will support a specific leader or political view not because they feel forced or coerced; they may evaluate their bargaining position on a different basis than in other areas of the country. However, their decision-making can still be recognized as a process of calculating individual or collective interests within certain constraints.[52]

The agricultural economy of the area and state tenders are two dominant ecological constraints; for instance, the distribution of water in the fields and the award of state tenders can be maintained and enjoyed by all tribal members only if they manage to act collectively. The collective "action" is diverse and complex and it implies the cultivation of tribal networks, ranging from partnership in trade and agriculture to the exchange of brides between families and engaging in reciprocal visits and gift exchanges.[53]

Tribespeople, then, expect a range of patronage services from all influential notables affiliated with the tribe *ağa* (chieftain). Because of their leading position in the region's economy and society, chieftains have privileged access to political relations as well as to local and state authorities. Many chieftains run for local and national elections, and the strongest can also become a member of cabinet. Consequently, expectations are even higher of a kinsperson, including help in solving bureaucratic problems, getting privileged treatment in a hospital, or assistance in finding a job. Nevertheless, *ağa*s do not have a monopoly on the loyalty of their constituents; locals are likely to enter different types of loyalties based on the kinship idiom that is more successful in delivering benefits. Families like the Bucak are still territorial entities with strict control of their areas. However, many families that moved to the regional capital have lost their territorial strength and commitment to the territory, mainly because of their departure from the village, but also because other economic sectors—trade and, above all, the construction industry—are seen as more remunerable. State investments in expanding agricultural land and inheritance have also challenged the preeminence of chieftains' land ownership. Many families, though, have been able to maintain their influence by adapting to the changing social and economic environment.

The easiest and most straightforward way to understand the influence of the *aşiret* (tribes) on the electoral process is a detailed analysis of election results. Particularly in the districts of Harran (predominantly an Arab area) and Siverek (predominantly a Kurdish area), many villages vote en masse for the party chosen by the local notable. In the 2007 elections, of the 113 electoral boxes in the Harran rural areas, forty-eight were openly cases of *birleşik oy*; similarly, in Siverek, of the 186 boxes, fifty-one were cases of communal vote.

In previous general elections, the figures were more encouraging: of the Harran's 120 boxes, only seventeen were openly cases of communal vote, whereas of Siverek's 215 boxes, fifty-four were clear cases of communal vote. This system does not favor the dominant AK Parti alone, and it is not a recent phenomenon. However, the AK Parti's good electoral performance on a national basis and its relative stability have persuaded tribes to align themselves with the strongest actor on the local and national political scene. Moreover, in a political system with a dominant party, political affiliation to the AK Parti has a determinant role in the allocation of state tenders, particularly in the construction sector.[54] Nevertheless, in the 2009 local elections, AK Parti leaders boldly affirmed that people from Şanlıurfa would even vote for "Mr. Erdoğan's hung jacket"—namely, for whatever candidate the party nominates, even a dummy wearing Erdoğan's jacket—because of the undisputed commitment of the people to the party. However, the people of Şanlıurfa, outraged by the party arrogance, voted for Ahmet Eşref Fakıbaba, an independent yet popular candidate who ran without the support of any tribe.[55]

A primary example of communal vote can be observed in Çağlarbaşı village in the Siverek district (see Table 3). Here, the leading family is the Bucak clan, which has been affiliated with the Adalet Partisi (Justice Party) since the 1970s. The party was reestablished as the Doğru Yol Partisi (True Path Party, DYP) after the 1980 coup, and entered the 2007 elections as the new DP. Many members of the Bucak clan were elected several times to parliament and the *belediye* (municipality) of Siverek. At least twenty-one villages and some areas of the city of Siverek are controlled directly by the tribe, and many more prefer to get along with the Bucaks to avoid troubles.[56]

The Bucaks' power derived from their large estates (though no interviewee during my fieldwork could quantify it), coercion, and strong relations with the state—thanks to the *koruculuk* (guardianship) function in the name of the state against the terrorist organization Partiya Karkerên Kurdistanê (Kurdistan People's Party), and its gloomy relations with the deep state. The most renowned member of the clan, Sedat Edip Bucak, a three-time MP in the ranks of the DYP, was even involved in the Susurluk scandal that, in 1996, exposed links between the party, the police, and the Turkish mafia. The Bucak family was not able to solidify relations with the AK Parti, and in the June 2015 elections, Sedat Edip Bucak even ran for parliament in the ranks of the opposition party CHP. However, because of the political lockdown, dissent emerged within the family about some members' political affiliation.[57] The media reported that, after the disappointing electoral results in June 2015, the AK Parti convinced the Bucak family not to run for the opposition.[58] The AK Parti failed, however, to mobilize the vote in Bucak-controlled areas, as was also evident from the mixed results in the village of Çağlarbaşı.

In this last example, agricultural land and state relations provided strength to the tribe. According to many testimonies collected by the author, although the Bucaks have many armed men at their disposal, their control of local communities is very much due to the network of relations that the clan has and the sense of belonging that the tribal system provides. People feel necessary loyalty to the chieftain—or at least prefer not to challenge him—because the Bucaks can offer to the locals a strong networks and links with many sectors of the local governments and Ankara apparatus. Consequently, local people vote for the Bucaks, and any irregularities at the polls are often overlooked—not out of fear of the clan, but because the protection that the family provides might be necessary in the future.

Another good example of tribal capability to mobilize votes is represented by the Gülpınar family. Şeyh Eyyüp Cenap Gülpınar was a tribal leader and son of a Sufi shaykh who was executed after his participation in a Kurdish revolt during the One-Party regime (1925–50). Eyyüp Cenap Gülpınar was elected five times to parliament in the ranks of ANAP, and he served as vice prime minister in the last and short-lived ANAP government in 1991. His family's status is particularly strong in the southern area of Siverek's sub-district of Karacadağ. The elections results of the village of Gülpınar (see Table 3) demonstrate how the village supported the ANAP until the 2002 elections, when Eyyüp Cenap Gülpınar failed to be elected because of his party's electoral debacle at national level. He then shifted to join the AK Parti with his villagers' votes, subsequently becoming one of the parliament's vice presidents. He then handed the leadership of the tribe to his son, Mehmet Kasım, who has been elected in the ranks of the AK Parti three times.

The Kırvan (or Karavar) family, to which an estimated 100,000 people belong,[59] control the town of Büyüktepe, and have a long political history: they joined the War of Liberation (1919–23), were represented in the first parliament, and, in 1957, a representative of the family was elected in the ranks of the CHP. As the results from the town of Büyüktepe show (see Table 3), from the early 1990s, the Kırvans were loyal to the leader of the Islamist party, Necmettin Erbakan. Because of the party's poor performance on the national level, the tribe leader, Ahmet Karavar, was elected only twice to parliament, in the twentieth and twenty-first terms. However, his influence in Büyüktepe.lasted until the 2015 elections. In the 2011 general election, even if the SP obtained only one percent of the vote at the national level, it obtained a remarkable local performance. However, in the new political context after 2015, Ahmet Karavar's son, Mehmet, applied to become a candidate for the AK Parti in the 2018 general elections, but the party's central committee refused to support him. The result was that in two of the three ballot boxes in Büyüktepe (boxes 1101 and 1103), only the state officials on duty voted, whereas registered voters did not show up—a clear demonstration of voter disappointment.

In other examples shown in Table 3, it appears that all main political parties built relations with the local tribes; the CHP also seems to have a similar control of the southern area of Siverek, and the nationalist MHP performed very well among the Arab population in many villages in the district of Harran. In villages where there are no invalid votes, where participation is close to 100 percent, and where one party may score 100 percent of the vote, some irregularities can be assumed. However, thanks to the widespread *omertà* (code of silence), it is difficult to apply any form of penal action. While there is no real threat to villagers who do speak out, they risk losing their *şeref* (honor) in the community and being excluded, along with their families, from the social and economic life of the village. Political parties also appear well aware of the system, which offers them a comfortable way of mobilizing votes and thus a reason for not exposing it.

The actual mobilization of votes follows different paths. The most common approach is through the head of the village, who communicates his decision to the villagers or to the elders. All villagers are usually loyal and respectful of the decisions of the elders, or *ağa*s, and eventually participate in the practices of the common vote. In certain cases, it is the head of the village himself who casts votes in the name of all commoners. In this case, the officer in charge of the election box and the ballots will arrive at the village on the night before election day, and is usually hosted by the *muhtar* (head of the village). During the visit, among pleasantries, the officer—frequently a state official or a teacher from another province—agrees to let the head of the village cast the votes or agrees to an open vote. The officer will also cast a vote in the same box, which is why in many villages in Siverek and Harran all the registered voters' votes will go to one party, and only the votes from state and party officers (who are nonregistered voters but still eligible to vote) go to alternative parties.

If there is no politically involved *ağa* in an area, the heads of villages or family elders will try to reach an agreement with other *ağa*s in exchange for protection or material advantages. It may also happen that the head of a village reaches no agreement with the representatives of a party or local notable. A good example is represented by the village of Zincirliçay in the north of Siverek district (see Table 3). In the 2007 elections, out of 156 registered voters, only one voted—presumably the state official. In previous electoral contests, voters in this district aligned to the DYP, but in the 2009 local elections they opted for a neutral stand and split the votes among the AK Parti and the DP. The villages of Doruç and Parapara, in the district of Harran, showed how there is no ideological commitment to a party, and villagers switch their vote according to the party or clan that offers them more.

The Doruç example also shows the existing fractures in the powerful Arab Cumeyle tribe, which was split between two cousins: Mehmet and İbrahim Özyavuz. Mehmet was elected as mayor of Harran in the ranks of the MHP in 2009, and ran as a candidate of the AK Parti in 2011 and 2014. İbrahim was mayor of Harran from 1994 to 2009, was elected in 1999 as a candidate of the ANAP, and since 2004 has been elected as a candidate of the AK Parti. İbrahim Özyavuz appeared to have a particularly strong standing locally and

Table 3: Election results in selected villages of Şanlıurfa (1969–2018)

Elections	1969	1973	1977	1983	1987	1991
Çaylarbaşı (Siverek)						
Registered voters	387	393	468	321	488	550
Voters	285	199	420	277	470	534
Valid votes	274	187	420	277	436	532
First party/votes	AP/219	AP/108	AP/359	MDP/270	DYP/287	DYP/492
Gülpınar (Siverek)						
Registered voters	-	-	-	-	-	608
Voters	-	-	-	-	-	610
Valid votes	-	-	-	-	-	610
First party/votes	-	-	-	-	-	ANAP/610
Büyüktepe (Siverek)						
Registered voters	631	333	438	299	411	416
Voters	633	222	438	273	406	378
Valid votes	633	211	436	272	402	363
First party/votes	Ind./597	CHP/162 MSP/49	CHP/247 MSP/152	MDP/175	ANAP/274	ANAP/182
Parapara (Harran)						
Registered voters	200	178	201	111	260	262
Voters	200	180	201	111	251	262
Valid votes	200	180	201	111	251	262
First party/votes	CHP/198	CHP/151	MSP/180	MDP/110	ANAP/251	DYP/262
Zincirliçay (Siverek)						
Registered voters	-	-	-	-	-	139
Voters	-	-	-	-	-	139
Valid votes	-	-	-	-	-	131
First party/votes	-	-	-	-	-	DYP/95
Dedeköy (Viranşehir)						
Registered voters	119	110	109	112	127	125
Voters	119	79	106	103	127	117
Valid votes	119	79	106	103	126	112
First party/votes	AP/119	AP/67	AP/99	MDP/103	ANAP/116	DYP/108
Doruç (Harran)						
Registered voters	65	53	72	51	73	73
Voters	43	54	72	41	73	73
Valid votes	43	54	71	41	73	73
First party/votes	AP/24	DP/54	MSP/35	ANAP/40	ANAP/73	ANAP/72

1995	1999	2002	2007	2011	2015 June	2015 Nov.	2018
Çaylarbaşı (Siverek)							
545	788	901	578	665	605	582	558
543	792	911	576	644	481	451	411
543	788	910	576	644	463	441	384
DYP/543	DYP/785	DYP/900	DP/576	DP/644	CHP/328 AK Parti/87	MHP/194 AK Parti/184	AK Parti/254
Gülpınar (Siverek)							
825	934	966	507	419	455	465	461
842	945	972	512	415	425	460	445
842	942	971	512	413	423	460	444
ANAP/840	ANAP/935	ANAP/971	AK Parti/512	AK Parti/413	AK Parti/417	AK Parti/458	AK Parti/441
Büyüktepe (Siverek)							
557	599	519	488	545	575	569	594
558	600	521	490	537	454	557	479
558	598	521	488	536	444	555	176
RP/553	FP/598	SP/521	SP/488	SP/523	AK Parti/368 HDP/68	AK Parti/543	AK Parti/163
Parapara (Harran)							
276	301	463	449	342	478	498	548
269	296	459	420	340	473	493	538
269	296	459	420	340	472	492	538
Ind./269	DYP/294	DYP/426	AK Parti/363	AK Parti/340	AK Parti/255 MHP/186	AK Parti/478	MHP/305 AK Parti 217
Zincirliçay (Siverek)							
133	144	182	156	230	286	280	332
130	141	179	1	230	183	240	200
129	140	174	1	228	178	238	190
DYP/126	DYP/97	DYP/163	AK Parti/1	AK Parti/102 DP/97	AK Parti/75 HDP/68	AK Parti/185 HDP/30	AK Parti/127 HDP/46
Dedeköy (Viranşehir)							
207	185	186	167	225	285	290	321
203	184	184	166	216	283	291	268
203	184	184	166	216	277	287	264
DYP/203	DYP/184	Ind./183	AK Parti/136	AK Parti/215	HDP/129 AK Parti 128	HDP/131 AK Parti/130	AK Parti/142 HDP/109
Doruç (Harran)							
77	193	206	238	211	254	252	263
74	193	204	202	203	249	235	264
74	193	203	202	202	249	232	264
DYP/55	ANAP/193	MHP/179	AK Parti/200	AK Parti/153	AK Parti/142 MHP/100	AK Parti/211	MHP/161 AK Parti/93

Source: TÜİK (https://biruni.tuik.gov.tr/secimdagitimapp/secim.zul) and YSK (https://sonuc.ysk.gov.tr)

in the party, so much so that he likely influenced the election of his wife, Çağla Aktemur, to parliament in 2007, in the ranks of the AK Parti. However, in 2015, he switched political affiliation and became head of Şanlıurfa MHP branch. In 2018, he was elected to parliament in the ranks of the MHP and is currently in the party central executive board. In 2019, his son Mahmut was elected as mayor of Harran in the ranks of MHP with 55 percent of the votes. MHP entered the 2009 elections in coalition with the AK Parti, which did not present a candidate in Harran. The previous mayor, Mehmet Özyavuz, was forced to run for the DP—a marginal party at the national level—but obtained only 44 percent of the votes.

*Ağa*s can lose their capability to mobilize votes if misunderstandings emerge between local chieftains and the party central committee and, consequently, they lose their capability to deliver services to their constituency. In 2002, İdris Şıhanlıoğlu, the son of Mehmet Fevzi Şıhanlıoğlu, who was elected MP three times in the ranks of the DYP, failed to obtain a candidacy from his party. The DYP's Viranşehir and Ceylanpınar branches were closed, and the votes of the Şeyhan tribe went to another prominent member, Sebahettin Cevheri, who became an independent MP and entered the 2007 elections as an AK Parti candidate (see the example of Dedeköy village, which is controlled by the Şıhanlıoğlu family, Table 3).

Conclusion

Even if in other rural and urban districts of Şanlıurfa the phenomenon of communal vote is less remarkable, tribes maintain a huge influence on the electoral process. Circles of agnates, relatives, friends, and clients continue to dominate the public life of the province. As a matter of fact, Turkish public life in general is dominated by interpersonal, face-to-face relationships, and an idiom of informality. This was a system exploited by the Ottomans to gain legitimacy, and it has survived in many aspects in the Republican era, as Meeker rightly observes.[60]

Today, public life is characterized—if not dominated—by interpersonal relations. As we have seen, in both rural areas and also in a big and modern city like Istanbul, besides the formal conventional political meetings, parties opt for much less expensive informal door-to-door political campaigning, visiting families, businesses, and migrant associations, engaging in *sohbet* (intimate conversation) and a conversation over a glass of *çay*. The AK Parti is not the only political formation to conduct formal political campaigns and simultaneously exploit tribal or *hemşehri* networks, although it has tapped into them far better than others. However, in the 2019 local elections, the party failed to build a symbiosis between formal and informal campaigns. The party relied much more on a formal media campaign to exploit their dominance in the media. As a consequence, the party lost the Greater Municipalities of Istanbul and Ankara despite its coalition with MHP.

Moreover, the persistence of using the idiom of preexisting tribal, family, *hemşehri*, or community networks for access to public life is indicative of Turkish democratic attitude. At the same time, voters rely on these networks only if they are effective. Once these networks become ineffective and do not produce the expected results, individuals or entire groups may decide to switch to other more successful networks, which can be an alliance with another clan, a religious movement, or *hemşehrilik*. Thus, we can assume, as Meeker does, that these networks set aside ethnic and national identities (not a well-defined concept even in modern Turkey), communities, families, and tribes. Moreover, the gradual fragmentation of the tribal system has meant that clans opt for the strongest network without necessarily considering kin, whilst exploiting a kin-like idiom. Despite the fluidity of networks, however, there is compelling research indicating the power of the network and the perseverance of the kinship idiom, which also indicates that there seems to be a relative lack of individualistic culture in Turkish society.

4

DISSECTING THE SPATIAL RELEVANCE OF THE *DIWĀNIYYA* IN KUWAIT

AN INQUIRY INTO ITS "PUBLICNESS"

Clemens Chay

Introduction: The Spatial Expression of Dissent in the Gulf

The shift from an integrative community to urban anonymity has been a longstanding research focus in sociology.[1] According to contemporary urban sociologist Fran Tonkiss, two responses to earlier community forms—traditional societies governed by kinship ties and a sense of communal belonging—arise as a result of the modernizing and rationalizing push of urban processes. One is treating former community forms as a "non-urban" residue in the city; in other words, a social adaptation to new urban environments that transplanted older social and economic ties. The other is assimilation, understood as the erasure of both cultural difference and spatial divisions between groups to the extent that an individual is as "anonymous as anybody else" in the modern city.[2] At first glance, it may be tempting to regard Arabian Peninsula states as cities "unburdened by history" due to their respective rapid urbanization phases that led to the large-scale demolition of the pre-oil landscape.[3] Such a viewpoint subscribes to Tonkiss' second response, ascribed to anonymity. Yet it would be parochial to assume that anonymity is the core feature of today's Gulf city.

As architectural critic Mumford argues, the city remains "a related collection of primary groups and purposive associations," where people's purposive activities are worked out "through conflicting and cooperating personalities, events, groups, [and] into more significant culminations."[4] Pre- and post-oil urbanism in the Gulf has proven that social life, exhibited in both conflict and cooperation, has not been lost in the urbanization process. Governance in the Gulf is centered on the enduring paternalistic feature of its monarchies—in some cases, constitutional monarchies—and the post-independent state system that emanated from such a ruling style.[5] To this end, the relationship between the ruling family and the ruled is often the focal point of sociopolitical discussion.

Recalling the Gulf's pre-oil affinity with pearling, social unrest tended to be associated with disruption in such socioeconomic ventures. Spaces with "public" qualities in the Gulf port towns enabled the airing of grievances. The *diwaniyya* in Kuwait was a meeting place for the merchants, sea captains, and divers whenever an issue with maritime trade arose. Elsewhere in Bahrain, in December 1926, three hundred divers assembled in front of the British advisor's office in Manama and marched to the Al-Sakhir Palace in central Bahrain to appeal to the regent against the reduction of advances for the next pearling season, before regrouping and attacking the markets.[6] Returning to neighboring Kuwait, the town's main public square, Sahat Al-Safat, situated "at the landward end of the market," was not only the site where the palace guard regularly performed a Bedouin war dance to rally public support for the ruler, but also the venue where public punishment was meted out.[7] In the nearby bazaar, still known as Souq Mubarakiya today, the preeminent Sheikh Mubarak al-Sabah, the seventh ruler of Kuwait, like his predecessors, honored the social contract through his accessibility to the people by sitting regularly in public to address specific grievances. Various other sources have confirmed Sheikh Mubarak's aforementioned practice in the bazaar. Stanley Mylrea, Kuwait's first missionary doctor, described Sheikh Mubarak driving slowly through the streets "in a beautiful Victorian carriage drawn by two horses ... halting at the coffee-shop [in the bazaar] for a formal mejlis (council)."[8] As such, pre-oil urbanism in the Gulf witnessed the use of public space that conformed to Tonkiss' three ideal-types: 1) the square, representing collective belonging; 2) the café, representing social exchange; and 3) the street, representing informal encounters.[9] Crucially, the ability of public space to harness social resistance through its accessibility allows for the creation of what French sociologist Henri Lefebvre calls "counter-spaces," which are founded on the "primacy of *use*" and are criticisms of conventional sociospatial arrangements.[10]

Fast forward to present times, the general impression of Gulf cities is seen as feeding off a consumerist society. The overhaul of the physical landscape, followed by an "immense accumulation of spectacles," are steps to instill power in the built environment that has been made subservient to the goals of the capitalist economy.[11] With the physical landscape being a reflection of consumerist hunger, it is the state's ideals that are etched in space, and not necessarily the society's. As a result, citizens have had to take the initiative to re-appropriate public space in their own terms, as a "counter-space" to the state's creations, even if Gulf states are not known to be particularly sympathetic towards public dissent. Perhaps the two most intransigent states of the region—Saudi Arabia and the United Arab Emirates—have been watertight in their grip on society. For example, in November 2017, under the banner of anticorruption, eleven princes, four ministers, and dozens of other officials and prominent businessmen were arrested after Saudi King Salman Bin Abdulaziz ordered the formation of a supreme committee in a presumed campaign against corruption, but was actually a means to "limit individuals' ability to influence public opinion."[12] In a similar fashion, the Emirati authorities have clamped down on dissenting voices by issuing lengthy sentences to individuals calling for reforms, including Emirati academic Nasser bin Ghaith, and the internationally renowned human rights lawyer Mohammed al-Roken.[13] Elsewhere, in Kuwait, while demonstrators were convening on Tahrir Square in Cairo at the height of the Arab Spring in early 2011, a growing political opposition movement against the prime minister began in Al-Safat Square (until it was cordoned off), before relocating to the stretch of grass in front of the parliament building, which the opposition named Irada Square (Determination Square).[14] In February 2011, antigovernment protestors swarmed the Pearl Roundabout in Manama, Bahrain, in an outpouring of sectarian grievances.[15] Despite the authorities' decision to level the roundabout a month later, Khalaf contends that the memory, image, and symbolism of that public space remains "a critical element in unsettling the [Bahraini] state's once firm control on its image."[16] What is significant is that the continued use of public space to negotiate state–society relations remains; Kuwaiti historian Farah al-Nakib calls this act "restoring the urban commons,"[17] and in her book *Kuwait Transformed* she alludes to Lefebvre's "right to the city."[18]

This chapter departs on the premise that not only is space a manifestation of the social, but that the public aspect of space raises the possibility of alternative forms of spatial politics. In a situation where there is discontent, space is manipulated into a platform of expression, reflecting societal sentiment as mentioned previously. More than a mere physical form, space is what its users make of it. As urban sociologist Lewis Mumford nicely sums it up, "social facts are primary, and the physical organization of a city ... must be subservient to its social needs."[19] Even a smaller built environment akin to Kuwait's *dīwāniyya*—the subject of this discussion—a seemingly unpretentious reception room, offers a profile of power relations when it is employed in a public manner. Tonkiss explains that power relations are unfolded "both *in* and *over* space," tracing a line from the "ordinary" experience of urban individuals to wider conceptions of social inclusion and urban order.[20] More importantly, public participation inscribed in these spaces attests to Hannah Arendt's argument that "power springs up whenever people get together and act in concert."[21] This study centers on Arendt's concept of the "space of appearance," a physical space where public matters are allowed to be expressed and debated. Over the course of this chapter, the *dīwāniyya*'s publicness will be substantiated by numerous instances of its public use, which ironically stems from its ability to connect the private realm of the family to the public domain. While the advent of social media has undoubtedly provided an alternative channel for public expression, face-to-face interactions and encounters, as the *dīwāniyya* best exemplifies, remain an innate quality of the "public."

An integral part of Kuwaiti culture, *dīwāniyyas* have been frequently mentioned in scholarly work as spaces for politicking. In its most basic form, the *dīwāniyya* is a reception room where predominantly men sit together regularly to discuss issues relevant to them. From Kuwait's pre-oil landscape catering to a bustling port town, to today's suburbanized residential areas, the *dīwāniyya* continues to find its place in the urban landscape despite the demise of other built environments. This study explains how the *dīwāniyya*'s spatial relevance is attributed to its "publicness" and quality of enabling face-to-face communication that technology has failed to provide. Departing from a traditional understanding of public space, this chapter shows how the *dīwāniyya* straddles the public–private divide. The space's malleability has ensured its persistence, and its capacity for socialization has led to its use by different societal groups, including foreign diplomats. Crucially, this study shows how an informal and indigenous mode of grassroots diplomacy provides for an expression of public sentiment.

Kuwaiti "Exceptionalism" and the Dīwāniyya

Kuwait has often been singled out among the Gulf states, owing to its relatively high levels of political participation. The country's overtures to democracy have paved the way for academic, if not popular, discourse to cast a positive light on its governance as the liberal exception among other Gulf countries. Kuwait's democratization, which has dominated a large part of the literature on its politics, has gained considerable attention as scholars attempt to decipher the motives for and reasons behind this phenomenon. Salamé's contention that Kuwait's political system is a "democracy without democrats"—one that is able to "prohibit authoritarianism" and invite the "voluntary pluralism of open political competition"—offers a critical eye by disputing "the validity of the valorizing discourse of democracy."[22] Arguably the most referenced book when discussing Kuwaiti politics, Mary Ann Tétreault's *Stories of Democracy* invigorates the democratization discourse further by normalizing Kuwait's exceptionalism, arguing that it shares a "common functional experience" with the West by virtue of moving from "traditional" to "modern" political institutions and practices.[23] A more recent work by Michael Herb contextualizes Kuwaiti exceptionalism:[24] the 1962 constitution provided both an impetus and an opportunity for various actors (internal and external) to acknowledge the need for political participation, thereby setting off a path-dependent argument wherein the culture of public participation became widespread, and the National Assembly gradually became a well-entrenched institution.[25] Yet, for all the vibrancy of scholarly discourse on Kuwaiti politics, little room has been accorded to space and social relations, barring the pioneering works of Farah al-Nakib.[26] Nor has the move toward "modern" practices explained the evolution of traditional (and informal) means of politicking in Kuwait, which has been a fundamental feature of Kuwaiti society and politics.

A recurring topic in the discussion of Kuwait's political trajectory is the *dīwāniyya*,[27] whose spatial relevance as a reception room has often been historically associated with Kuwait's bustling maritime trade. Having acquired British protection, Kuwait's oceanic connections were forged with India as the "region's metropolis" and the "administrative hub of the British Empire in the western Indian Ocean," allowing the former to profit from the networks that run as far as East Africa.[28] The interconnected courtyard houses that made up the Kuwaiti pre-oil neighborhood, known as the *farīj*, naturally gravitated towards the shore. These houses were also home to a series of small spaces constructed organically in support of port urbanism. For instance, tidal *inga'* (jetties, singular *nig'a*) were found just outside of these houses. Privately owned, merchants who had the "ability to pay ... according to the number and size of the boats in his possession" used these jetties as workplaces where Kuwait's pearling fleet could moor and undergo repairs.[29] Intrinsic to the communal spirit of Kuwait's port town was the *dīwāniyya*, which was usually one of the rooms surrounding the courtyard, and equally part of the housing compound (see Fig. 4.1).

Affluent families may have been the owners of these *dīwāniyyas*, but whenever a problem arose between stakeholders of the pearl trade (merchants, divers, ship-owners, sea captains), the *dīwāniyya* was often used as a meeting place for conflict resolution. These *dīwāniyyas* were also key venues for the exchange of information. As early as 1906, the British political agent

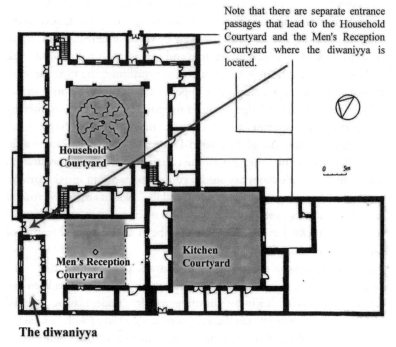

Fig. 4.1: An example of a floorplan typically designed for a pre-oil courtyard house.

Captain Knox, on his tour to the south of Kuwait, was invited to a *dīwāniyya* of the "father of the Koweit pearl merchants," Bishr bin Roomi, who requested information about the Ceylon pearl fisheries.[30] So vital were *dīwāniyya* spaces to Kuwait's trading activities that they were also established in Zanzibar and Kenya, where Kuwaiti merchants were stationed, as the former Minister of Higher Education Ali al-Shamlan, whose family background was heavily involved in the pearl trade, testified.[31] The above-mentioned spaces of "unplanned urbanism," as coined by al-Nakib, reflect not only functional diversity, but also a physical landscape "intimately linked to the town's port economy."[32]

More than a mere meeting venue, the persistence of *dīwāniyyas* must be explained in conjunction with governance and public participation. The Kuwaiti tradition, wherein members of the ruling family visit the *dīwāniyyas* of Kuwaiti families, continues today. Viewed in the formal–informal overlap of Kuwaiti politics, the *dīwāniyya* feeds into the narrative of a social contract between the rulers and the ruled. Kuwaiti citizens return the favor during the month of Ramadan when palaces of the ruling family are opened to the public, who deliver their well-wishes in much bigger *dīwāniyyas* (see Fig. 4.2). In 2014, upon visiting the A'soussi family *dīwāniyya*, which is open to the public on Sunday evenings, I witnessed the visit of Sheikh Muhammad al-Sabah, who casually told me how news still travels fast from the *dīwāniyyas* to the ruler's office. Elsewhere, I have argued that the *dīwāniyya* is not only an interlinked space and practice, but also a transmission of tradition that "perpetuate[s] a process of acculturation that [in turn] promotes, and to a large extent achieves social cohesion."[33]

More than acting as a social forum, the continued *dīwāniyya* tradition is significant as an outlet in which political debate and opinions can be expressed; in other words, the *dīwāniyya* remains relevant as a pressure point for venting.[34] Scholarly literature often mentions the use of *dīwāniyyas* for electoral campaigning. Tétreault argues that regular attendance at *dīwāniyyas* produces a significant amount of "face time."[35] This face-to-face communication in turn leads to the mobilization of voters by political candidates who host these *dīwāniyyas*. In another article, she identifies the *dīwāniyya*'s protected status as stemming from its ability to bridge "the public-private divide"—located within the private, family home and simultaneously open to the public.[36] Beyond the crossover between public and private spheres, the *dīwāniyya* uncovers the intertwined themes of the state and the family.

Fig. 4.2: The Al-Sabah sheikhs receive the public in the *dīwāniyya* of the Mishref Palace during Ramadan.

Delving into the period of Arab nationalism in the fifties and sixties, political activities in Kuwait were pursued under the banner of social activities, as political parties were outlawed.[37] Ahmad al-Khatib, a partisan of Arab nationalism and later a leading opposition figure in Kuwaiti politics, led the National Cultural Club while campaigning for public freedom by "visiting the *dīwāniyyas* in the area," which he admits in his memoirs to be the ideal method for garnering support.[38] The late emir, Sheikh Saad Abdullah al-Sabah, took it upon himself to visit various *dīwāniyyas* all across Kuwait in 1982 whilst he was crown prince. Puzzled by such a peculiar habit, Sheikh Saad's advisor questioned the sheikh, who later explained how city dwellers were concerned about the *Souq Al-Manakh* (stock market), whereas the Bedouins were more eager to know if there were available government subsidies channeled towards sheep feed.[39] Across different phases of Kuwait's history, the *dīwāniyya* has served its role dutifully under varying environments, whether for grassroots diplomacy, as a function room for maritime trade discussions, or for more contemporary political purposes. Its malleability reiterates the need to consider the dynamics of space and social relations in order to understand how its physical features are subservient to sociopolitical needs.

Moving Kuwaitis into the Suburbs

The discovery of oil in 1938 brought exceptional newfound wealth to the ruling family. By 1961, the International Bank for Reconstruction and Development, during its mission to Kuwait, found that oil production in that year alone "was 7 per cent of the world output and nearly 30 per cent of the Middle East," having increased exponentially since 1946.[40] These new economic realities financially empowered the state, which intervened heavily in all aspects of urban planning, with the 1952 Master Plan as the centerpiece of such pervasive spatial planning. Lefebvre labels such a spatial product of the state an "*oeuvre*" that "unmakes and remakes itself under our very eyes;" moreover, where "state bureaucratic rationalism" is involved, "a feeling of monotony covers these diversities and prevails, whether housing, buildings, alleged urban centres, organized areas are concerned."[41] The immense changes engendered by the master plan was described by Gardiner as follows:

> And so with Kuwait, ... the lengthy processes of industrial evolution are completely absent, and there is an extraordinary picture of one civilisation superimposing itself on another. Bedouin tents, mud-brick, the pearl trade, fishing boats, tracks; are superseded by oil, concrete, motorways, tankers, sophisticated structures—in a sequence of jumps that cover great distances in time like slides at a lecture depicting the story of Middle Eastern man from the Sumerian courtyard house of the third millennium to the apartment block or garden suburb of the mid to late twentieth century, all in the space of a mere thirty years.[42]

What is useful to our discussion on *dīwāniyyas* is the wider scheme for suburbanization under the 1952 Master Plan, which reshaped housing patterns drastically, and, in turn, had implications for the *dīwāniyya's* role since this space was integral to the architecture of the courtyard house. New neighborhoods were designed as "homogeneous residential areas, emphasizing detached single-family living on allocated plots;" the overall planning discourse contained "no expressions of the social values or norms these areas were expected to represent or promote."[43] As suburbs became enclaves that facilitate the distribution of services by the welfare state, they also drew social boundaries between different segments of the population, segregating non-Kuwaiti immigrants and formerly pastoral Bedouins from the rest of the Kuwaiti national population, while effecting a growing social distance between the townspeople and members of the ruling family.[44]

These socioeconomic inequalities resulting from state policies were compounded by the land acquisition policy (LAP), whereby the state purchased land within the town walls, enabling the relocation of families into the suburbs (see Fig. 4.3). Ghanim Alnajjar, whose doctoral thesis expertly dissects the LAP, showed how the scheme gave the ruling family "economic independence from the traditional merchant elite" by having the freedom to invest in stocks and real estate speculation, while also guaranteeing "the support of the most influential groups in society."[45] The state, led by the ruling family, bought these lands at inflated prices from the Kuwaiti families who stood to make a huge profit. Their future designated residences became relocated inland and away from the shore, and, instead of courtyard houses, these families are now owners of luxurious villas. The benefits did not stop here, though, particularly for the merchant families: they have since become agents for companies whose products are imported into Kuwait, and the accrued monetary benefits are distributed within the "family corporation."[46] What this means in today's context is that the *dīwāniyyas* hosted by the most influential families of Kuwait tend to be situated in the neighborhoods nearest to the old, pre-oil boundary wall, which is now torn down. As al-Nakib indicates, the neighborhood units bordered by the First Ring Road to the north and the Fourth Ring Road to the south were intended exclusively for Kuwaitis.[47] It comes as no surprise that my *dīwāniyya* exploits reaffirm the locations of prominent family *dīwāniyyas*: for instance, Shamiya (Al-Sager, Al-Marzouk families), Dasma (Al-Marafie family), Abdallah al-Salem (Al-Ghunaim, Al-Gharabally, Al-Jarallah, Al-Nisf families), Daiya (Al-Ghanim, Al-Roumi families), Faiha (Al-Mʻojil family), Nuzha (Al-Babtain, Behbehani families), Qadsiya (Al-Khaled family), and Mansouria (Qabazard family).[48]

With suburbanization, the *dīwāniyya* came to play an even more important role in maintaining the social fabric of Kuwait. Visiting a *dīwāniyya* enabled Kuwaitis to recover their "right to their city" by avoiding passive acceptance of the drastic, state-led physical changes to the residential landscape. This is a perspective that contrasts with the sense of powerlessness among local actors that many writings on the Gulf have underscored.[49] Oil wealth also made the *dīwāniyya* more affordable to citizens; while the car becomes a means of transporting Kuwaitis from one *dīwāniyya* to another, even enabling several *dīwāniyya* visits in one evening, and tens of visits per week. Commentators have remarked upon how, despite the dispersal of families as a result of urbani-

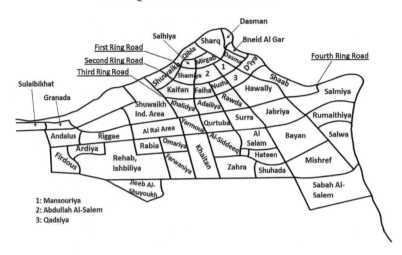

Fig. 4.3: Map of the Kuwaiti suburbs, with captions indicating the ring roads.

zation, the geographical zoning of Kuwait's residential quarters also translated into the "expansion of the *dīwāniyya* as an idea, as an institution."[50] In an attempt to maintain the interconnectedness between Kuwaiti families, Abdulrahman Khalid al-Ghunaim, a retired minister of communications, spoke about how he spearheads a fourteen-member executive committee selected from a pool of 150 extended Kuwaiti families that have their own *dīwāniyyas*.[51] According to al-Ghunaim, this committee seeks out the general opinion of different Kuwaiti families, and, acting as an "informal union," informs the ruling family of public sentiment. When Kuwaitis speak about the "official" nature of *dīwāniyyas*, they refer to the fixed day of the week when the said *dīwāniyya* is in session, a time when male members of the extended family are also expected to be present. The nature of the gathering remains informal, without a prior agenda, and visitors are free to drop in on the *dīwāniyya*'s "official" day. As *dīwāniyyas* become more affordable, they no longer need to be mere annexes to houses, but can each assume the form of a standalone building (see Fig. 4.4). Abdallah Qabazard, an architect by profession, explains this change in an interview:

> Until now, some *dīwāniyyas* are still annexes to the house. As time went by and some of the elders passed away, you have the heirs who take care [of them]. And if you split the ownership of that house with the annex, either they (the heirs) come to an agreement to keep it as it is, or to make the house as an annex.... The

family agrees that they would buy a [piece of] land, where they know their friends are having *dīwāns*, for example in Faiha, you see the Faiha *dīwāns* are almost close to each other.... The rest of the family chip in and make it a centre— a *dīwāniyya*—to the point where it is used for social events.[52]

As the target audience of contemporary housing shifted towards nuclear families (unlike the extended families in the pre-oil courtyard houses), the ability to afford a *dīwāniyya* became a gauge of wealth and individualism.[53] Al-Jassar, while echoing that the "identity and social position of the family is expressed through the physical aspect of the *dīwāniyya*," contends that the *dīwāniyya*, unlike the courtyard house, was "never viewed as a backward environment," hence the demise of the latter type of housing.[54] In all, the continued relevance of the *dīwāniyya* follows three principal reasons: 1) to act as an indicator of affluence; 2) to maintain links with the extended family; and 3) to enable regular contact between different families.

The Coming of a Digital Age to Kuwaiti Society

Speaking at the University for Foreigners of Perugia in October 2011, Kuwait's former Minister of Foreign Affairs Sheikh Muhammad al-Sabah

Fig. 4.4: The Al-Othman standalone *dīwāniyya* located in Abdallah Al-Salem area.

remarked how Kuwait is "one of the five leading countries in percentage of Facebook and Twitter users in the Arab world,"[55] yet reminded the audience that Kuwaitis are "traditionally modern:"

> Having been a sea-faring society prior to the discovery of oil, our forefathers set sail on the rough seas to make a living by trading with other societies ... Consequently, their exposure to different people, cities and religions instilled in them a strong sense of tolerance, which has been passed down from one generation to another. This sense of openness can be found even in our homes in what we call the Diwaniya [*sic*]. It is at such gatherings that any stranger can freely walk in at a given sitting and mingle and discuss politics, business and religion— no topic is ever off the table. Prior to the establishment of our parliament as we know it today, these Diwaniyas [*sic*] essentially were mini-parliaments scattered all over Kuwait ... Our Diwaniyas [*sic*] were our Facebook and Twitter, long before these social networking sites came into existence.[56]

Yet, there is no denying the impact of new social media on Kuwaiti society, ranging from the organization of social movements to facilitating *dīwāniyya* sessions. Al-Safat Square's historic role as an urban commons was "virtually revived" in the early 2000s when blogging became a mode of popular expression; the blog aggregate website that served as a directory for other blogs in Kuwait was known as "al-Safat," transforming the physical square into an "electronic agora" that is widely accessible.[57] In the spring of 2006, the Orange Movement (also known as Nabiha 5 or "We Want It Five") began with the idea of combatting corruption and redistricting, and ultimately pushed through a bill that reduced Kuwait's electoral districts from twenty-five to five. Besides campaigning through the movement's principal website, kuwait5.org, blogging was used to great effect:

> Bloggers covered the movement's activities and gatherings, writing about events and posting photos and video clips. Moreover, the bloggers urged their readers to participate in the movement. They announced upcoming events and connected protestors to each other online. In addition to promoting the movement, bloggers instructed Kuwaitis about their duties regarding the campaign ... Some bloggers formed the core of the movement or participated in the demonstrations.[58]

Tétreault, who described Kuwait's civil society as having "deep domestic roots and cosmopolitan branches reaching well beyond its formal borders," found that public space and *dīwāniyyas* also formed an integral part of the Orange Movement:

> Text messages were forwarded to friends of friends, and about 200 demonstrators wearing orange T-shirts and waving orange flags showed up in front of the

Sayf Palace, startling ministers as they drove in to their meeting and again as they came out. "The prime minister waved to us," one activist reported. "And we heard in diwaniyyas [sic] that they kept asking why was everyone wearing orange." Press coverage and word of mouth ensured that news of the demonstration would spread, sparking another rally the following week where more than 500 people gathered.[59]

What remains a constant, in spite of alternative media channels, is the relevance of physical public space. Beyond the symbolic nature of physical form, the city is not just "the setting of the struggle," but also "the stakes of that struggle."[60] Running against the dominant statist organization of space, the geography of protest and demonstration requires a tangible face, beyond the nonconfrontational facet typical of new social media. One interlocutor, Ameen Behbehani, mentions in an interview that opinions expressed through social media such as Twitter are highly discouraged by the emir; rather, *dīwāniyyas* are preferred for the expression of views so that any misinformation can be corrected immediately.[61] Such state intolerance proved to be true in 2013 when a youth activist was sentenced to five years in jail for insulting the emir on Twitter—an authority described as "immune and inviolable" in the constitution.[62]

The authority of the ruler, while considered sacrosanct, is equally important in determining the amount of civil liberties that Kuwaiti society enjoys. Between the ruler's choice of wielding the stick and dangling the carrot, Brumberg explains how liberalized autocracies akin to Kuwait endure because rulers "implicitly or explicitly allow some opposition forces certain kinds of social, political, or ideological power—but things must never reach a point where the regime feels deterred from using force when its [sic] deems fit."[63] Force exercised on *dīwāniyya* gatherings, however, has usually backfired against the regime. An attack on a *dīwāniyya* in 2010, followed by the beating of student protesters in 2011, had pushed the key swing bloc back into the opposition fold and, backed by street activists, "forced the hand of emir in accepting the resignation of the prime minister the very week he vowed never to do so."[64] Going further back in time, during the Monday *Dīwāniyya* movement,[65] the second meeting held at Mishari al-Anjari's *dīwāniyya* in Nuzha neighborhood district had to endure the presence of riot police with trained dogs that were dispatched to block access to the site.[66] Thereafter, then Foreign Minister Sheikh Sabah al-Ahmad (the late emir) invited five opposition leaders to his office on December 12, 1989, offering his apology for having forcefully closed the *dīwāniyya*, and reiterating the sanctity of the space.

As mentioned earlier, the *dīwāniyya*, situated within the confines of the home, is assured of its protected status. Articles 38 and 44 of the Kuwaiti constitution guarantee the formal protection of the home and, by extension, the *dīwāniyya*.[67] What differentiates new social media from the *dīwāniyya*, from a spatial perspective, runs along two lines: 1) the *dīwāniyya* is embedded in the family realm as much as it is in the public sphere, and its legal protection makes it a protected space unlike social media; and 2) the malleability of the *dīwāniyya*, and its historical and continued use as a space of socialization for all societal echelons, makes it more viable for grassroots diplomacy. In times of political crises—notably on two occasions when parliament was dissolved, in 1976 and 1986—the *dīwāniyya* "virtually replaced the National Assembly."[68]

A "Space of Appearance:" The Dīwāniyya's Involvement in Public Participation

Thus far, this study has uncovered the duality of the *dīwāniyya*'s publicness: 1) a space where the individual or the family seeks recognition and precedence; and 2) an associational space where "men act together in concert," and where power is derived from collective engagement and rational persuasion.[69] On point one, the *dīwāniyya* conforms to what Arendt calls a "space of appearance," where "action and speech create a space between the participants which can find its proper location almost any time and anywhere."[70] Just as the space of appearance is continually recreated by action, for the purpose of "discussing and deliberating about matters of public concern," the *dīwāniyya*'s malleability allows it to assume a public role.[71] However, when these activities cease, the *dīwāniyya* reverts to its functions of the family, making the public–political function "potentially there, but only potentially, not necessarily and not forever."[72] While the *dīwāniyya* has been the main reception venue for family functions, the townspeople also had the option of visiting the ruler in his *dīwāniyya*, as had been done in 1954 to protest against maladministration in city planning.[73] On point two, power, according to Arendt, "springs up whenever people get together and act in concert, but it derives its legitimacy from the initial getting together rather than from any action that then may follow."[74] Benhabib furthers explains the public dimension added to a space that is not "in any topographical or institutional sense:"

> [B]ut a private dining room in which people gather to hear a *samizdat* or in which dissidents meet with foreigners become public spaces; just as a field or a forest can also become public space if it is the object and location of an action

in concert, of a demonstration to stop the construction of a highway or a military air base, for example. These diverse topographical locations become public spaces in that they become the sites of power, of common action coordinated through speech and persuasion.[75]

In this manner, the *dīwāniyya*'s public involvement goes beyond its use as a primary site for electoral campaigning and other political activity; it also acts as an important *pre-political* platform that employs "speech and persuasion" to provoke action. Allowing dissent outside of a predetermined context, the "earmarking of particular *dīwāniyya* meetings" can have sociopolitical implications, and, in some cases, mass mobilization.[76] Musallam al-Barrak, a former politician and a household name, is known for criticizing government policies in his *dīwāniyya*. In 2013, when the criminal court found him guilty of insulting the emir, "thousands of supporters marched from Barrak's guest house [*dīwāniyya*] towards the central prison outside the town as a police helicopter watched from the sky."[77] More recently, after the November 2016 general elections, MP-elect Mohammad al-Mutair received twenty-one other newly elected MPs in his *dīwāniyya*, many of whom were known to be part of the opposition, in order to discuss nominees for various parliamentary positions.[78] By allowing Kuwaitis to act "together in concert," the *dīwāniyya* represents both the tensions and the interdependence between the state and the grassroots.

As the last section demonstrated, the *dīwāniyya* persists, despite the rise of new social media, owing to its ability to generate face-to-face interactions. Social media forms such as Twitter and Instagram may have extended an individual's reach and influence, but, in some cases, these virtual spaces still occupy a backseat, often acting as a means to invite audiences to one's *dīwāniyya*. One such example is Abdulaziz Jamsheer's Instagram profile, on which one can often find invitations to his *dīwāniyya* in Rumaithiya, where a prominent guest speaker often graces sessions.

Further societal changes are noticeable through the access to *dīwāniyyas* from a gender perspective. While social mores still form the basis on which the *dīwāniyya* remains a male preserve, it is a different story at the political front, particularly with the women's suffrage victory in 2005. The use of *dīwāniyyas* by female political figures as pre-political spaces has been deemed appropriate, even if Al-Mughni qualifies this breakthrough by pointing out that it is the upper-class women who have the luxury of such access, which "reinforce[s] rather than challenge[s] female subordination."[79] An interesting case study is that of Ghadeer Aseeri, a female parliamentary candidate who ran in the November 2016 elections. She has been active on Twitter and Instagram, often extending public invitations to what she calls her "mixed *dīwāniyya*."[80] In a personal interview with Aseeri, she revealed that holding her own *dīwāniyya* in the post-election period has allowed her to maintain political momentum. She noted that a *dīwāniyya* session where men and women are allowed to sit and discuss matters together is considered a step towards embracing the "new generation."[81] During the electoral campaigning period, she recalled how it was initially difficult to break through a predominantly male environment, but she later found that her candidacy was accepted in these *dīwāniyyas*, and attendees freely discussed day-to-day problems—what she calls "matters of the house" (see Fig. 4.5). While one can argue that Aseeri needed male support to enter the political scene, it is equally plausible that the *dīwāniyya* affords women the opportunity to be participants, rather than onlookers. Stephenson takes the argument further:

> The most significant aspect of elections, however, is their aftermath, the lasting effects of women's participation in them. Because *dīwāniyyas* (usually called *nadwāt* during the campaign season) were held to engage women during campaigns, this functioned to normalize their interaction with the space and the institution. In other words, women got used to going to formal *dīwāniyyas*, so the idea of hosting their own informal *dīwāniyyas* naturally progressed out of that experience, and was no longer an unthinkable or taboo idea.[82]

The *dīwāniyya* as an institution has shown itself to be politically enabling for both men and women, by virtue of the space's propensity to engage with the public. Véronique Bertrand-Galli, the second counsellor at the French embassy in Kuwait, said that when she visits *dīwāniyyas* with her female ambassador, they have always been treated hospitably as representatives of their country.[83] Indeed, the built environment of the *dīwāniyya* takes the form of a social theater where one has to see and be seen, and to hear and be heard—a space where actors can engage "in a debate over the general rules governing relations in the basically privatized but publicly relevant sphere of commodity exchange and social labor."[84]

The *dīwāniyya*'s spatial relevance must also be considered in terms of how it plays host to a series of different groups or "publics," largely allowing for their socialization. Social networks built through *dīwāniyya* visits still rest on family foundations, which involve status creation and maintenance. Here, networking is expressed through the "alchemy of consecration," which is endlessly reproduced in and through the exchange of congratulatory wishes, and the mutual recognition of family membership, all of which form the greater

Fig. 4.5: Ghadeer Aseeri making her rounds in *dīwāniyyas* prior to the November 2016 parliamentary elections.

Kuwaiti family.[85] Ramadan represents a high season for making introductions (particularly for diplomats) in *dīwāniyyas* that are useful at a later date, and for showing off visitor volumes, as well as, in some cases, for obtaining status boosters from prominent visitors such as sheikhs and foreign diplomats. The persistence of their *dīwāniyya*s in the present urban landscape serves as a listening post for the ruling family, who continue to monitor the economic grievances of not only the well-established merchant families,[86] but also of emergent families competing for the attention of those in power. The effects of Kuwait's state policies in the long run, including the redistribution of oil wealth, have also led to the formation of the intelligentsia, which, according to Halpern, are those "with knowledge or awareness to see that a social and political revolution is in progress, [and] form the largest and politically most active component of the new middle class."[87] Tétreault elaborates on the formation of the Kuwaiti middle class:

> It was not an investing bourgeoisie like the merchant elite (although a few families did achieve that status), but rather a group of prosperous, if wage-dependent, families that resemble middle-class populations in developed countries, including in their aspirations ... many monopolized by merchant-class citizens but others that were more broadly representative. Aided by the amir's drastic redrawing of electoral constituencies prior to the 1981 election to reduce the political weight of urban-based groups like merchants and Arab nationalists, Kuwait's "new men" ran for parliament after having cut their political teeth competing for positions on the boards of local cooperatives.[88]

This middle class, impelled by ideas and action, drove an environment of inclusive critical discussion, and, with the geographical omnipresence of *dīwāniyyas* in the suburbs, the "informal *diwaniyya* system" allows families to "demand an accounting from the Al-Sabah."[89] Not only are the traditional mercantile elites responsible for keeping the ruling family in check, the aforesaid middle-class families have now joined the ranks of the same *dīwāniyya* system in a bid to protect their interests. Former US Ambassador Edward Gnehm nicely summarizes the competing families behind the scenes of the *dīwāniyya*:

> The core families of the Sunni merchant elite remain the old founding families: the Al-Bahar, Al-Nisif, Al-Sager, Al-Ghanim, Al-Abdelrazzaq, Al-Rashed, Al-Roumi, Al-Nouri, Al-Hamad, Al-Abdulhadi, Al-Abdulghafour and others who recall the distinct areas of the old walled city of Kuwait where their ancestors settled. However, status among the Sunni elite is by no means static. Other Sunni families ... by virtue of their noble Arab stock, hard work, and business acumen, were readily integrated into the ranks of the merchant elite. Among these families are the Al-Duaij, Al-Shaya, Al-Ghannam, Al-Khorafi, Al-Othman, Al-Gharabally, Al-Marzouk, Al-Wazzan (Sunni), Al-Fawzan, and Al-Babtain. Many of the grandest diwaniya halls of Kuwait today feature a portrait of a father or grandfather who worked as a deckhand, water seller in the souq, or ditchdigger before accumulating family fortune.[90]

Moving away from the family scene, two other "publics" are worthy of mention: tribes and foreign diplomats. First, the *dīwāniyya* has been labeled as much a tribal custom of the desert tent as it is a built environment tied to Kuwait's formerly thriving port activities. In Kuwaiti historiography, where the seafaring activities take precedence over its hinterland trade, it is crucial to recall how the *dīwāniyya* is a tribal custom that was later transplanted in the courtyard house and internalized as a social practice. Even if the Bedouins tend to be a forgotten "public" vis-à-vis the seafaring portion of the Kuwaiti population, Kuwaiti historians, and indeed Kuwaitis themselves, seem to be in agreement that Sabah I (the first ruler) was chosen unanimously by tribal factions through the Bedouin custom of holding *dīwāniyya* sessions in tents.[91] Today, the retribalization of self also serves as a means of civic expression and familial association. This would mean having guests sit on the floor, and serving coffee and dates in a strict sequential etiquette (see Fig. 4.6). In a personal conversation, a member of the Thuwi Ziad clan, under the Otaibi tribal umbrella, acknowledged that certain tribal practices remain important today, such as having the *dīwāniyya* of the emir (or prince) of the clan for the purposes of conflict resolution, including the payment of blood money.[92] Spatially, suburbanization meant that families of Bedouin background tended to reside further away from the city. Bedouin settlements were also constructed in "separate areas" far away from the townspeople's suburbs, beyond the boundaries of what became the Sixth Ring Road (see Fig. 4.7).[93] It is therefore imaginable that the gulf between those with strong tribal affiliations and more "urban" people manifests itself in the form of different concerns.[94] In the periods leading up to

Fig. 4.6: The tribal-styled Al-Rashid *dīwāniyya* in the Sabah Al-Nasser area.

Fig. 4.7: Sheikh Mutlaq Aborgobh (second from left) of the princely Thuwi-Ziad clan holds his *dīwāniyya* in the Hadiya area.

parliamentary elections, clandestine tribal primaries continue to be conducted in *dīwāniyyas* as "an expression of tribal solidarity" and "normative trendsetters," in a bid to promote clan interests by electing fellow tribesmen to parliament.[95]

The second group of important players who attend *dīwāniyyas* are foreign diplomats, among whom the British and Americans have been particularly active. The regularity of diplomatic presence in *dīwāniyyas* indicates not only a willingness to engage with Kuwaiti citizens and their corollary customs, but also inadvertently highlights the benefits of the *dīwāniyya* as an indigenous diplomatic mechanism. Ahmad Alowaish, the political and media advisor at the British embassy in Kuwait, revealed that he urged the British ambassador to attend as many *dīwāniyyas* as possible in order to cultivate personal relationships and show the "British embassy's presence everywhere in Kuwait."[96] Barston, when outlining the diplomatic landscape, wrote that what constitutes diplomacy today goes beyond the "narrow politico-strategic conception" that it is the primacy of governments that dominate; rather, the practice remains equally defined by the agency of individuals.[97] Foreign diplomats therefore recognize that the official protocol of formal diplomacy must be complemented by the informal practices of the host country.

Former British ambassador to Kuwait, Matthew Lodge, said in a personal interview that the relationships forged in Kuwait are also reflected in the spaces that provide such networking opportunities:

> There is much more of a sense of collective interest, much more of a sense of a clear and confidently expressed set of multiple voices, not just in the political space, but commercially in the family. So there is a much wider conversation going on all the time. For me the diwaniyya [sic] culture...—and I have witnessed it firsthand for the last two years—is a clear manifestation of that. And it is fascinating to try and understand how that really impacts on decision-making in Kuwait ... What we really understand of the interrelationships between family and individuals, and within families, impacts on the work we are doing to strengthen and maintain the relationships.[98]

Indeed, as Neumann dissects the responsibilities of a diplomat, he emphasizes how the diplomat is required to juggle different "scripts of self against one another," including dovetailing what happens both inside and outside of a political entity.[99] The *dīwāniyya* presents various opportunities for the diplomat to fulfill his scripts by means of socializing with Kuwaitis, and often with people that one would not likely encounter otherwise. An economic officer at the US embassy in Kuwait shared how he had accepted an invitation to a *dīwāniyya* and met the CEO of Kuwait Flour Mills, someone whom he "had been trying to find an excuse to meet."[100] The informal atmosphere, coupled with the candidness of attendees, has been a push factor in easing diplomats into the *dīwāniyya* practice (see Fig. 4.8). Soft diplomacy, which encompasses the exertion of influence on public opinion, has been most definitely present in *dīwāniyya* visits by foreign diplomats. The Indonesian ambassador to Kuwait, Tatang Budie Utama Razak, notes that he has "to go to the *dīwāniyya* to discuss something related to his job scope," which ranges from meeting members of the royal family to promoting Indonesian culture and products.[101] As such, more than allowing for the conduct of local grassroots diplomacy, the *dīwāniyya* has proved to be a useful space for foreign diplomats to engage with the Kuwaiti public; in so doing, the mediating roles of the *dīwāniyya* challenge the conventional, top-down, statist paradigm of diplomacy. Activities in the *dīwāniyya* conflate a range of communicative practices, many of which bear the means of attracting and persuading individuals, and allow foreign diplomats to influence and be influenced.

Fig. 4.8: British diplomats on their *dīwāniyya* visits during Ramadan 2017.

Conclusion

Contending that technology is "no match for physically attending a diwaniyya [*sic*]," Winder argues that the *dīwāniyya* is "an essential setting in the story of Kuwait; there are just a lot more smartphones around."[102] That the *dīwāniyya* has been a core space and practice in Kuwait's past and present urbanism is testament to how the public face of space remains vital for Kuwaiti governance and the regulation of human flows and material resources. As explained in the introduction to this chapter, spaces that encourage collective belonging, social exchange, and informal encounters are crucial in any urban environment. The *dīwāniyya*'s publicness, as this chapter has shown, comprises all of the above qualities, with constant *dīwāniyya* visits being a means of consolidating kinship ties. Understandably, the recent COVID-19 outbreak has compelled Kuwaiti authorities to restrict gatherings, including those in *dīwāniyyas*, but the quality of publicness resurfaces in residential mobility patterns. Outside curfew hours, neighborhoods witness a 24 percent increase in activity, prompting urban planners to call for improvements in pedestrian infrastructure that cater to the public.[103]

Regardless, in the parliamentary elections at the end of 2020, some form of *dīwāniyya* campaigning was either restricted in numbers or held virtually. Competing and complementary social groups will continue to use the *dīwāniyya* as a release valve for airing grievances, owing to how the space is vaguely institutive compared with more formal institutions of power. This may present a means of managing dissent in neighboring Gulf states that is more viable than wielding the stick. On one visit to the Al-Thunayyan *dīwāniyya* in Jahra, an area known for having strong tribal linkages, an attendee who was the relative of a family from Saudi Arabia, repeatedly uttered "ḥuriyaa" (freedom) when I asked about the importance of the Kuwaiti *dīwāniyya*. Labelling the *dīwāniyya* as a subset of informal politics as this study has suggested, the activities within this microenvironment should also be seen as part of grassroots mobilization, community activism, and—specific to Kuwait—family-to-family involvement. As a space that operates between the family and public realms, the *dīwāniyya*'s malleability is a quality that has been often seized to mobilize the Kuwaiti public, or one of its "publics," resulting in its transformation into a "counter-space," particularly vis-à-vis the state and the ruling family. It would therefore be useful for future research to consider how specific groups, whether the tribe, merchant families, or the diplomatic corps, employ the *dīwāniyya* in their interests.

While some may label the *dīwāniyya* a "social theater," the space also presents life opportunities to its attendees. In particular, the space embodies an indigenous diplomatic practice that cuts across different levels of societal echelons. The average Kuwaiti, upon attending his family's *dīwāniyya*, has a realistic probability of meeting a member of the ruling family or an ambassador of a foreign embassy. The same can be said for a foreign diplomat during a visit to the *dīwāniyya*; while the act of mingling is expected in the confines of the room, such socialization means that the conduct of diplomacy is not a one-way exchange. Just as the *grande bourgeoisie* met with the nobility on an equal footing in the French *salons*, the *dīwāniyya* represents a space where the rulers and the elite meet Kuwaiti families, and other members of the public, as equals, offering a mediating role between different groups, and between state and society.

5

SHI'A-STATE RELATIONS IN QATAR

THE NEGOTIATION OF COEXISTENCE

Paulino R. Robles-Gil Cozzi

Introduction: Pluralism, Sectarianism, and Informal Politics

Religious difference exists in all societies and civilizations; diversity in interpretation, ritual, and understanding of the transcendental has been the norm rather than the exception. However, in order to build a strong identity or profile, societies, cultures, and states have often resorted to the projection of an official and unified religion that is integral,[1] in most cases, to the majority of the population. Notwithstanding, exercising religious difference translates into being part of a minority that may or may not, as such, be normalized into the general collectivity.

In the many efforts to prevent tensions and clashes among groups with different faiths, religious approaches, rituals, and confessional identities, the discourse and framework of religious pluralism emerges as a solid paradigm. Nevertheless, as a normative concept, it can only operate in secular, liberal, and often Western settings where religious denominations and sects are publicly recognized on equal terms and organized accordingly.

In the case of non-secular and illiberal environments, the absence of a formal framework of pluralism does not imply the nonexistence of religious diversity. Nancy Ammerman explains that religious pluralism as an empirical reality is the "normal state of affairs;" it is out there.[2] Relevant to this study is to acknowledge that, as a reality, religious diversity has existed for centuries in the Persian Gulf countries. However, the manners in which it has been organized and accommodated fit into the broader spectrum of informal politics.

The birth of nation states, especially young ones like those on the Arab side of the Persian Gulf, have necessitated the creation of strong identities based on a blend of racial, ethnic, and religious markers. In such a configuration, the smaller, different groups tend to be misrepresented or not represented at all. Such positioning has not necessarily pushed them to develop a separate collective consciousness opposed to the national majority or to engage in struggles for particular rights.[3]

Whatever the case, the sole empirical existence of religious approaches other than the official one is likely to be perceived as a challenge to modern nation states that have forged a narrowly defined and homogenous identity. Bender and Klassen, however, insist that not all religious minorities engage in a politicization of their identity.[4] In the same vein, not all majorities become "predatory." Hence, regimes, even if authoritarian, might pursue more nuanced forms of accommodation and negotiation, resolved in an informal milieu. In other words, the decision not to politicize a religious identity does not amount to giving up the particular needs or demands of a given group; rather, they are likely to be processed in an unexposed, private or semi-private space, without passing through the official channels or the public arena.

Yet, the debates on religious diversity and its possible arrangements in the Middle East are invariably affected by the sectarian phenomenon; the sectarianism prism of analysis has dominated the academic field and public deliberations in the region for at least the last three decades. From various disciplines, researchers have developed theories and explanations for the regional intersectarian dynamics, and some of them stress the role of the state as primordial to the sectarianization processes.[5] Toby Matthiesen and Frederic Wehrey focus on the regimes' instrumental use of sectarianism for political ends and explain how sect identity crosses other sociocultural stratifications.[6] Matthiessen notes that sectarian identity entrepreneurs are ultimately responsible for creating a sectarianized Persian Gulf. He argues that these entrepreneurs profit from the manipulation of sectarian divisions in society; and that their economic, social, or political positions often depend on the perpetuation and deepening of the boundaries between sects.

Other authors argue that sectarianism is unrelated to the regimes' role, and that the sect-state dynamics are not the result of oppressive top-down schemes, but a consequence of local conditions and subtle agreements among multiple actors. From an economics perspective, Justin Gengler uses the rentier bargain model to explain how regimes allocate revenues to guarantee support—and appeasement—from less favored social sectors.[7] Finally, for Adam Gaiser, sect identity is not fixed, but situation-specific; individuals and groups have the agency to regulate or reject the grand sectarian narratives and even contribute to processes of de-sectarianization.[8] Both Gengler and Gaiser provide useful explanations to understand the sectarian dimension in the case of Qatar, and the relations between the Shi'a, the state, and the public sphere.

Drawing from more than twenty in-depth interviews,[9] as well as government documents, NGO reports, online fatwas, media debates, extensive fieldwork, participant observation, and everyday conversations, the present study relies on both the human dimension of the sectarian experience and the non-institutional (tacit, informal) forms of accommodation. It assumes that informal politics appear wherever individuals—citizens and residents—have limited agency, and where groups have little or no representation. Thus, this study argues that Shi'a-state relations in Qatar are not mediated in the public arena and do not appear in formal political deliberations.

The Shi'i Social Fabric of Qatar

The presence of Shi'a in the land demarcated by the State of Qatar is neither recent nor strange. The fact that their identity is not formally represented, and has been wiped from school textbooks, does not signify that they have not been an intrinsic part of the country's past and present. Since the eighteenth century, the human profile of the territory has been diverse and has not corresponded exclusively to one tribe, ethnic group, or even a specific religious denomination or sect. In 1930, 20 percent of the population was Shi'i Persians.[10] This group of people was called 'Ajam, and soon became an integral part of the state formation and consolidation. They were not, however, the only Shi'i constituency in the region.[11] The Arab Shi'a, although a minority in most Arab countries (except in Iraq and Bahrain), have long been part of the social fabric of Gulf states. In countries such as Oman, the UAE, and Qatar, Shi'a have opted for a very low profile, perhaps as a result of their minority status or their fear of being perceived as a threat. Fuller and Francke write "in geographic terms, Shi'ism has in one sense remained on the peripheries of the Arab world, but in another sense, it lies in the absolute heart of the Persian Gulf ... Indeed, many Shi'a refer to the Gulf coastal region as the Shi'ite heartland, in which they live in a relatively consolidated fashion."[12]

Historically, there has been a strong presence of the Bahārna, an ethnoreligious group comprising the Arab Shi'a on the Eastern coast of the Arabian Peninsula. In their nativist narrative, they see themselves as the original inhabitants of an ancient Bahrain, considered a large area, going all the way from Basra—in today's Iraq—down to the Trucial Coast (in today's UAE and Oman), and passing through Bahrain and Qatar. According to Gengler, Shi'a in the Persian Gulf yearn for a time in which they were united in one nation called Bahrain, with abundant natural resources and devout to the Shi'i creed. Such a state of affairs would later be threatened by the Sunni conquest.[13] A second notable group developed in the Al-Ḥasa oasis and are known as the Ḥasawiyyīn.

The 1950s became a demographic shifting point due to the considerable influx of migrants who arrived in Qatar during the oil industry's expansion. Later, in the 1970s, the oil boom and the discovery of natural gas reservoirs led to a second wave of immigrants that massively populated the tiny peninsula, causing a significant demographic/population imbalance whereby Qataris became a minority in their own country. Such a position could have pushed Qataris to exert a preemptive mobilization based upon sectarian identity to preserve their status, but they did not. Rather, the regime opted for more discreet strategies to reinforce the Sunni character of the state— ones that did not involve the systematic discrimination or marginalization of the Shi'a. In other words, no laws or public rules have ever been enacted in which "sect" constitutes a structural or functional form of discrimination or differentiation.

For an external observer, the demographics of a tiny nation such as Qatar may appear simple to explain. However, the situation is complex because there is no information about religion and its distribution in official public documents. Despite the fact that there is a significant population that has a faith other than Islam,[14] and that within Islam there is a relevant minority in Qatar that adheres to the Shi'a branch, precise information is not accessible; the Shi'a are simply not represented in the official numbers.

The population policy of the Ministry of Development Planning and Statistics has adapted to the rapid reconfiguration of Qatar's population.[15] The ministry's technical committee formulated a new set of axes that provide a shallow description of the human profile of Qatar;[16] interestingly, none of the updated categories includes religion, let alone sect affiliation.[17] The official statistics are utilized to project the population in a framework of productivity and well-being, while deliberately omitting crucial information that could challenge the national ideal of a pure Arab and Sunni nation. This does not mean that the government ignores data regarding the religious picture of Qatari society, but the decision to not make it public is already telling of a deliberate tactic. It is likely that the state is trying to minimize the relevance of religious and sectarian denomination by withholding any informative publication that could fuel exclusivist discourses within social, religious, or political groups. In this case, the boundary between the formalities of public information and the selectivity of what remains hidden is blurry. This policy differs from that of neighboring countries like Saudi Arabia and Bahrain, which repeatedly mobilize sectarian identities for political reasons, as many scholars have explained.[18]

In order to get a sense of the number of Shi'a in the State of Qatar, I rely on primary data collected during the ethnographic research,[19] as well as certain secondary sources such as the 2009 Pew Research Center's survey on religion and public life,[20] which suggests that 10 percent of the inhabitants living within the State of Qatar—migrants included—are Shi'a. Furthermore, Martin Walker and Mehran Kamrava conclude that Shi'a comprise between 15 to 20 percent of the aforementioned entire population.[21] Considering that Shi'i sectors and individuals are seemingly not open about their affiliation, and that a large influx of immigrants came after 2010, then a figure of approximately 15 percent of the total population can be considered an acceptable approximate figure.

Shi'i communities in Qatar are heterogeneous; they are constituted of Qatari nationals, long-established migrant families—whose members may or may not have Qatari citizenship, depending on their time living in the country—and recently arrived foreign residents. They belong to different national and ethnic groups (Pakistanis, Iranians, Bahrainis, Lebanese, Iraqis, etc.), have different social statuses (citizen, expatriate, and immigrant),[22] are part of contrasting social classes, and are likely to experience various degrees of state inclusion/exclusion. In any case, the relationship these communities have with the state often remains outside the political arena. In certain cases, however, they are evident in other key fields, such as the economy. For instance, the Shi'a of Persian origin who arrived in Qatar at the beginning of the twentieth century were often prosperous merchants who spoke Arabic and were integrated into Qatari society by becoming citizens. They benefited—as many

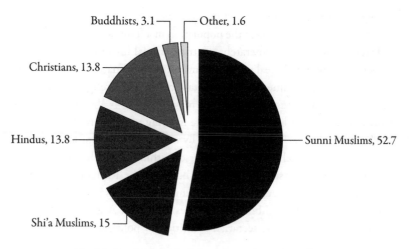

Fig. 5.1: Breakdown of religious denominations in Qatar.

other ethnic groups have done—from the well-known "Law No. 2 of 1961 on the Qatari Nationality."[23] The law is crucial, as it shows how, historically, being a Qatari did not depend on ethnic or sectarian origin, but rather on one's contribution to early state-building processes through regular and continuous residency in the country before 1930. The Arab Shi'a (Bahārna), for instance, arrived in Qatar much earlier than the Persians. As for the non-Qatari Shi'a, they are also diversified across ethnolinguistic lines, with most belonging to lower socioeconomic strati in comparison to the nationals. Although a small number consists of successful expatriates (from Lebanon, Kuwait, Azerbaijan, Iran, and even Iraq), most are part of the wider workforce industry—from India and Pakistan—and are referred to as low-income migrants.

Religious Life: Space, Authority, Rituals, and the State

Space

Qatar is a country with a strong Islamic Sunni profile and identity. The state entity that manages religious life is the Ministry of Religious Affairs and Endowments (Awqāf) and it is the only institution that formally designates a place for the Shi'a branch of Islam. In 2005, the ministry created a small Ja'farī court that deals with issues such as marriages, inheritance, divorce, and other religiously sanctioned matters of everyday life.[24] Nonetheless, there is no public information about the number of Shi'i mosques, *ḥusayni-yyas*, or religious centers or where they are located in Qatar. Similarly, their religious authority structure and the features of their ritual life in the country are not found in any existing document, file, report, or official website. In other words, everything indicates that the Shi'a-state relations are neither formal nor public; instead, their negotiations are held behind the scenes. In what constitutes an intriguing overlap of formal and informal politics, while led by public figures or recognized authorities, their identity during such encounters is not disclosed. It was only through extensive fieldwork and ethnographic research that I could determine a general picture of Shi'i religious life within Qatar's borders.

There are few religious spaces shared by both Qatari and non-Qatari Shi'a, but the most important is the Al-Buhārna Mosque and its sister mosque, Imām al-Ṣādiq, both of which are in Doha's Hilāl neighborhood. The former is the only Shi'i mosque that features live *khutbas* (Friday sermons), which are delivered by the single Shi'i imam—currently Sheikh Shaker Ali Yusuf—and approved by the Awqāf for that purpose. The latter mosque reproduces the sermon simultaneously through an indoor audio system. Next in importance and number of attendees are the Bukshaisha Mosque and the Zain ul-Abidin Mosque, both in the Al-Mansoura neighborhood. There are an additional three Shi'i mosques—the Jahramiyya Mosque, the Muhammad Ṣafār Mosque, and the Bahramī Mosque. Thus, there are at least seven Shi'i mosques in total in Qatar today. A curious feature of Shi'i mosques in Qatar is that the tops of their minarets are lit at night in green neon. According to most interviewees, this characteristic is neither the result of a religious norm nor compliance with a law or official guideline. Rather, it is yet another result of an informal convention; a custom serving the purpose of identifying a Shi'i mosque without compromising an explicit identity or association that could put the regulars at some form of risk.

Furthermore, there used to be some twenty *ḥusayniyyas*—also named *ma'tams*—which are ceremonial halls for the performance of Muharram rituals scattered across the country. Most of these were shut down immediately after a bomb blast—claimed by the Islamic State of Iraq and the Levant—in a Kuwaiti Shi'i mosque in 2015 killed twenty-seven people and wounded 230. The result was a robust securitization of the seven mosques and the four *ḥusayniyyas* that were allowed to remain operational, albeit under intense surveillance. Most interviews revealed that there are often at least ten plain-clothes intelligence agents at these religious places. In addition to metal detec-

Fig. 5.2: Bukshaisha Mosque.

tors, several CCTV cameras are located both in the inner and outer areas of Shiʻi spaces in Qatar. During peak dates of the Shiʻi Muslim calendar, the state takes additional measures, with security controls set at all entrances, including metal detector arches and guards with handheld scanners.[25] According to my interlocutors, during each of the three core days of Muharram rituals there are plain security vehicles outside as well: "If anyone drives in circles they will certainly be detained and questioned," an interviewee warned.[26]

The Al-Buhārna Mosque complex also houses a *ḥusayniyya* for the performance of mourning rituals,[27] which is mostly attended by Arab and ʿAjami people. The Jahramiyya Mosque is the only other mosque that is also used for *maʾtam* performances attended mainly by Iranians. Additionally, two other *ḥusayniyyas* operate actively in Doha: the Imāmbārgāh, which is run and attended by the South Asian community, and the Kuwaiti *ḥusayniyya*, frequented, as its name suggests, by Kuwaitis.

The vast majority of Shiʻa in Qatar belong to the Jaʻfarī school of thought and jurisprudence; and in the case of Qatari Shiʻa, they are all Twelvers. Since the Al-Buhārna Mosque and the Imām Ṣādiq Mosque (indirectly) are the only

Fig. 5.3: Al-Buhārna Mosque.

places permitted to deliver Friday sermons, they serve all the Shiʿi communities, regardless of their ethnicity or legal status. However, for Muharram rituals and other religious festivities, these two mosques are attended mainly by Arabs and ʿAjamis, whereas the other ethnocultural subgroups gather in their *ḥusayniyyas* or in the *majlis* (council) of a private home.

The COVID-19 pandemic's effect on religious spaces and rituals posed a challenge to the Shiʿi groups and communities in the Persian Gulf who have feared that public health policies, enforcing social distancing, and preventing ritual gatherings could actually suppose veiled sectarian forms of exclusion and discrimination, as has occurred in both Saudi Arabia and Bahrain.[28] The fact that Iran became the initial coronavirus hotspot in the region was used by some Sunni governments and media outlets to stigmatize and further alienate their Shiʿi populations.[29] The 2020 Ashura (Muharram) commemoration came as a litmus test: while mass polemic gatherings took place in Iraqi and Iranian shrines—despite strong warnings against this—the Shiʿa in Qatar unanimously abided by the strict measures imposed in the country and the specific informal requests banning congregations at the *ḥusayniyyas* and

Fig. 5.4: Inside Imām Al-Ṣadiq Mosque.

maʾtams, hence no rituals were held. COVID-19 is the most recent example revealing a *de facto* communication between the Shiʿa and the state in everything related to national security aspects, such as handling a pandemic.

Authority

The local religious authorities of Shiʿi Islam revolve mainly around two figures, the most prominent of which is Sheikh Shaker Al-Yūsuf, the head of the Jaʿfarī court at the Awqāf. He is a Qatari national, originally from eastern Saudi Arabia, who trained in Najaf, Iraq. The fact that Twelver Shiʿism has a religious structure with clear hierarchies and an established clergy system facilitates the identification of a centralized channel with whom to deal and accord, especially in the case of this small, sensitive minority. Therefore, Sheikh Shaker—as he is called by the members of his community—becomes the single figure through which the Qatari government monitors the content of sermons.

The second figure in seniority is Sheikh Habīb. His grandparents are from Oman, but he was born and raised in Qatar. Habīb is now in charge of several Shi'i mosques and engages directly with the communities attending them. However, he does not have the Awqāf approval or permission to deliver sermons on Fridays—not even if Sheikh Shaker is sick or out of the country—let alone to deal with jurisprudential matters for the community. Rather exceptionally, Sheikh Habīb did not receive his religious training abroad, as he had the privilege of being instructed in Doha by two senior imams who are now deceased: Syed Abdullah and Sheikh Meqi.

Since Qatar does not permit the establishment of religious Shi'i seminaries, and since all the senior qualified figures have passed away, those Shi'a hoping to acquire religious knowledge must travel to *ḥawzas* (seminars) in Iran or Iraq for instruction. Most Qatari Shi'a—both Arab and Persian—seem to follow the Marja'-e-Taqlīd (Source of Emulation) of Najaf led by Ayatollah 'Alī al-Sīstānī.[30] By contrast, only a fraction of the Iranian Shi'i community that migrated to Qatar sometime over the last decade follows the Iranian *marja'iyya* (religious authority; source), or figures such as Ayatollah Taqī Behjat and Ayatollah Ali Khamenei. The affiliation of Qatari Shi'a of Persian origin—and, increasingly, Iranians settling in Qatar—to the Iraqi Ayatollah 'Alī al-Sīstānī rather than to Iranian ayatollahs is noteworthy; it highlights the extent to which this sub-community has disconnected Shi'i religiosity from ethnic and linguistic affiliation as part of their Qatari integration strategy. According to a few informants, following a non-Iranian religious authority is in many cases a deliberate decision—a preemptive measure to avoid being associated with Tehran and accused of being a fifth column of the Islamic Republic of Iran, which is a common accusation and prejudice about Shi'a in Arab countries (Qatar not being an exception).

Furthermore, the two Shi'i imams in Qatar follow Ayatollah 'Alī al-Sīstānī, so it is understandable that their communities adhere to his *marja'*. On the other hand, South Asian Shi'a—who are historically independent from the former groups—tend to follow local religious authorities from Pakistan, such as Ayatollah Ḥusayn Najāfī (also known as Dhakoo of Sargodha) or Ayatollah Bashīr Najāfī, and develop religious practices shaped both by their respective *marja'iyya* and by their cultural contexts.

Rituals and the State

State surveillance in mosques and *ma'tams* aims not only to control potential security threats, but is particularly attentive to the content of sermons, lectures, and community discussions. Haidar describes life in the Shi'i mosques as strictly ceremonial and liturgical, never political and never addressing topical issues. Ja'far, a 25-year-old Qatari who graduated from an MBA program in the United States and holds a leadership position in the Doha headquarters of a global bank, confirms Haidar's statement by noting that Sheikh Shaker "sticks to a strictly religious discourse; he avoids politics by all means. He is neither a political nor a public figure."[31] In my numerous visits to Masjid Al-Buhārna for Friday prayers, and some of the *ma'tams* for Muharram rituals, political issues or public affairs were never raised. In many other countries with Shi'a populations, the mosque is a place where politics intermingle with the sermon; in Qatar, however, there is an informal agreement to avoid politicization of public affairs in Shi'i spaces.

Furthermore, the state restricts access to foreign Shi'i religious leaders, very few of whom are allowed to enter and preach in the country. Shaykh Hassan al-Ṣafar from eastern Saudi Arabia was one of the few foreign religious authorities—if not the only one—who had been granted permission to visit Qatar and deliver speeches until the 2017 blockade. Just recently, the Ministry of Interior, in coordination with the Awqāf, began to allow for the temporary entrance of a small number of Shi'i foreign authorities to assist during rituals on specific dates.

When it comes to attendees, Muharram is the peak of the Shi'i religious calendar and is top priority for many Shi'a, who take the day off work on the tenth of Muharram and sometimes the surrounding days; they either make an excuse or openly say that they have an excusable and mandatory religious duty. In many workplaces and schools, the administrative staff are aware of who is Shi'i, and they will likely allow for their absence on that occasion or choose to overlook it. Most of my interviewees agreed that this is one of the tacit agreements and unwritten concessions that has prevailed in Qatar. The confidence and determination of the Shi'a during Muharram can also be explained in the terms that Sabrina Mervin has used to describe that core commemoration:

> These rituals ... enable the individual to express emotions that they have to contain during the rest of the year, while enabling them to focus on themselves while connecting with the group. It enables the group, on the one hand, to connect with the transnational and globalised Shi'a community, and on the other hand, to negotiate its place as a (most often minority) community within the state.[32]

All Shi'i rituals remain indoors and are restricted to mosques, *ḥusayniyyas/ ma'tams*, and private *majlis* sessions. Muharram rituals, which in other contexts entail street processions, decorated caravans, and boisterous representations of Husayn's martyrdom, are forbidden in Qatar. Nevertheless, Sheikh Habib justifies such "politics of silence," arguing that processions and scenic performances are rather specific cultural expressions of the religion, though not religious duties in Shi'ism as such. "There is no need to change the situation here; there is an agreement from the beginning, it is better not to make noise," he remarked.[33]

While Shi'ism tends to be associated with overt expressive public performances, often crafted in an idiom of political resistance and "struggle against oppression," Shi'a in Qatar have either rejected the politicization of religion or kept their political sentiments to their private lives. The confection of the nation's Sunni brand entailed negotiating the permissible and the avoidable in public space. This has neither been the result of a public and deliberative process, nor resulted in a detailed, coercive normativity. Instead, accommodative practices have created a culture of "discretion of difference," one which is abided by effectively. A similar situation occurs with other religions such as Christianity, Hinduism, and Buddhism, whose religious communities have adjusted to a low profile and given up public displays of religiosity. In the case of Christianity, its different denominations have been assigned spaces in the Doha Religious Complex, and their rituals are performed regularly inside the complex's walls.

We can, however, find more straightforward positions from an official institution towards Shi'ism, which can be traced to the Ministry of Endowments and Religious Affairs. Although not a power structure, the Qatari Awqāf has an impact in different sectors of the society that consult it through the online website "Islamweb."[34] Inquiries seeking a position about Shi'ism have been responded to in the form of fatwas, most of which show a condemnatory tone against the beliefs and practices of Shi'a. Notwithstanding, those fatwas are non-binding, do not incite violence, and have not had a recorded effect on people's behavior towards Shi'i minorities.

It is important to note that, after an extensive search online in the English language section of the website, only ten fatwas (responses to inquiries from individuals) about Shi'ism were found. The last inquiry was dated back in December 2013; there were two from 2011, three from 2007, two from 2004, and two from 2003. Although the issuing of fatwas can be an indicator of the mainstream position of Sunni Islam in Qatar in respect to Shi'ism, it does not amount to the official position of the state, since the government is not linked to a religious establishment, and the 'ulamā' (Muslim scholars) in Qatar do not have a say in political decisions.

Furthermore, the Shiʿa in Qatar have a very high degree of independence compared with communities in neighboring countries, which are actively engaged in transnational networks. When asked about this, most interviewees confidently assured me that Qatari Shiʿa do not have ties abroad—or, if they do, they are fragile. On this point, I asked Mahmud, an Awqāf member, if the Shiʿa in Qatar are engaged in activities to support Shiʿa abroad. He underlined that solidarity actions towards Bahrain or other Shiʿi transnational communities facing disadvantages do not exist: "transnational Shiʿism does not impact inside Qatar."[35] In the same vein, 22-year-old Masuma, a Qatari woman who studies at a US branch college in Education City, expressed that she and her community often feel sorry for the Shiʿa in Bahrain and eastern Saudi Arabia, but at the same time are conscious of the limits of expressing public solidarity: "Making *duʿāʾ* is the best we can do, and God knows best."[36]

Accepting surveillance of mosques, controlling the access of Shiʿi foreign figures, listening to state-sanctioned sermons, banning Shiʿi religious institutions, defining the boundaries of rituals, or requesting a leave of absence from work on special occasions are all examples of unwritten yet official and binding accords between the Shiʿa and the state—breaching any of these agreements would be costly for the Shiʿa since the state will not fail to enforce. Such realities point again to a symbiotic relation between formal and informal politics in Qatar. To a great extent, and since formal politics are public, it is the degree of secrecy or covertness that often determines the condition of informality.

Navigating the Available Narratives

Despite the common reading of Qatar as a homogeneous and conservative country, a deeper look reveals a repertoire of existing discourses which have ultimately enabled different groups and individuals to live their lives more confidently. The simultaneous coexistence of apparently antithetical perspectives, such as Wahhabism and secular modernity, informs us that a diverse range of shared meanings cohabit in the same country. The need for self-assurance and domestic legitimacy in a conservative and religious society overlaps with Qatar's ambition to present itself as a competent global player of the twenty-first century. The present study explores four main narratives that may appear in tension, and presents alternatives to communities with different ways of thought, without jeopardizing the dominant Qatari status quo.

Qatari Wahhabism

Qatar publicly reinforced its Wahhabi profile in December 2011—the same year that the Arab Spring began—during the opening of the state mosque named after Imām Muhammad Ibn ʿAbd Al-Wahhab. The speech of Emir Hamad Bin Khalifa Al-Thani stated:

> We named the mosque after the great reformer Imam Muhammad Ibn Abdul Wahhab in honour of the Muslim scholars, who still carry his thought and call for revival to serve Islam and Muslims ... His walk all through life in the path of light spread throughout the Arabian Peninsula, guides people to the right path according to the Holy Quran and Sunnah, removes confusion from the minds and deviations that confounded souls.[37]

Although the emir "made a point of using the Wahabi term as a descriptor in public ... his director of communications at the time believes he did so to make clear to Saudi Arabia that Qatar alone would dictate the terms of its religious practices and the vocabulary used to describe them."[38]

As for the official statement issued by the Amiri Diwan, the seat of rule of the State of Qatar, it specified that the naming of the mosque was the "State of Qatar's intention to revive the Nation's symbols and its cultural values."[39] Other accounts suggest that Sheikh Hamad bin Khalifa sought to strengthen Qatar's regional influence and to create commonalities with neighboring Saudi Arabia. What the emir really meant in his discourse is not obvious, not even to Qataris, but it surely was not about excluding Shiʿa or promoting religious militancy among citizens or residents.[40] Instead, it was a move for Qatar's self-projection and perhaps a sophistication of its foreign policy discourse. The undeniable fact is that the Wahhabi ideology in Saudi Arabia has provoked animosity, violence, and systematic discrimination against the Shiʿi population—especially in the Eastern Province. Thus, the question is why this visible Saudi-Wahhabi anti-Shiʿism has not emerged in neighboring Qatar.

Qatar's projection of a different approach to Wahhabism is rooted in the DNA of the Qatari state. Since its founding, Qatar was determined not to emulate the Saudi kingdom. "Privately, Qataris distinguish between their 'Wahhabism of the sea' as opposed to Saudi Arabia's 'Wahhabism of the land.'"[41] Years before, Fromherz called it "Wahhabism-lite;" a form of engagement with the past—a profile that allows the national project to be shielded from foreign ideological influences and, at the same time, provides flexibility and much fewer constraints at a social level.[42] On the ground, most of the Shiʿi interviewees in Qatar acknowledge in one way or another that Wahhabism in

Qatar is quite distinct from that of Saudi Arabia. Some confessed that, before arriving, they had a preconceived idea of Qatar as being a harsh and strict country—in religious terms—but what they encountered was different, and better than they expected. As for the Qatari Shiʿa specifically, they argue that they have never perceived Wahhabism as a religious threat, rather as a cultural means resorted to by the state to connect with the past.

In relation to the state and to society, Qatari Wahhabism has its own independent agenda. Unlike Saudi Arabia, the Qatari state has not allowed the Wahhabi establishment to occupy a sphere of power, as evidenced by the fact that the figure of Grand Mufti does not exist.[43] The government coordinates and controls its ʿulamaʾ to guarantee congruence in the messages of sermons and public lectures, and creates projects that combine powerful Islamic symbols with Qatari heritage.[44] In this vein, Wahhabism belongs to a repertoire that is mobilized to create a profile, a projection, and a sense of tradition, but not as an ideological state weapon to discriminate against Shiʿa.

The Abode of the Dispossessed

The Wahhabi narrative, albeit nuanced in the Qatari case, gives an impression of an exclusivist worldview that intertwines with the nationhood narrative, creating a discourse that prevents certain forms of belonging to root, and prioritizes a selective sector. Nevertheless, Qatar has for a long time been a magnet for foreigners, who join the Qatari national project regardless of the impossibility of them fully belonging to it. At the end of the day, Qataris have guaranteed their country for themselves and have secured a specific national identity—which is nonnegotiable—regardless of their position as a numerical minority dependent upon others. Today, Qatar is inhabited by 2.7 million people,[45] of which only 11.6 percent of the population is native and 88.4 percent is foreign residents.[46] Having such a large presence of migrants requires having narratives other than exclusivist, in view of the fact that migrants must also feel welcomed and part of the general picture.

Among the discourses of openness and the portrayal of Doha as a global city for everyone, an old narrative has recently reemerged depicting Qatar as a "House for the Prosecuted" or an "Abode for the Dispossessed." It is based on the poem attributed to the father or "founder" of the nation, Sheikh Jassim al-Thani (d. 1913), in which he nicknamed Qatar "Kaʿbat al-Maḍiūm"—which could be translated as either "refuge" or "asylum."[47] Some historical accounts reveal that the small peninsula was attractive because it was not hostile to those seeking shelter from turbulent situations. Fromherz points out that the territory was the "perfect place to escape" and a "magnet for exiles ... who have used [it] repeatedly as a base for what the British called 'piracy' or for angry power-plays between surrounding sheikhs and Emirs."[48] He argues that both political and religious dissidents from the wider Muslim world have found shelter in Qatar. In the same tone, Ramy Jabbour explains that, at the dawn of the twentieth century, Qatar hosted "regional banished leaders, fleeing criminals, and exiled political figures."[49]

The philosophy of being a welcoming *Ka'bat* was endorsed and reiterated by Emir Tamim Bin Hamad Al-Thani when he stated that Qatar "has sided with the Arab people in their desire for freedom and dignity, and against corruption and tyranny," and it will remain "the Kaaba of the oppressed."[50] The phrase was seen displayed on banners, in the context of the Gulf Cooperation Council crisis, when Qatar was under siege by four blockading states. The extent to which the Shi'a in Qatar feel at ease as a result of this revived philosophy remains unclear, but it is a political statement that weakens perceptions of Qatar as a monolithic and exclusionary nation, as most conversations with Shi'a in this study revealed. Be that as it may, while the state formally embraces a Wahhabi identity, it informally projects and exercises an

Fig. 5.5: A few months after the blockade on Qatar was declared in June 5, 2017, a sign was placed on a roadside stating "*Ka'bat al-Maḍīūm*" (abode for the dispossessed).

increasingly tolerant profile that allows for otherness to coexist, albeit through state-operated accommodative practices.

Nationhood and Citizenship

Qatar has undertaken various efforts to delineate and build a national identity to create internal coherence and guarantee legitimacy of the state. Old tribal rivalries, antagonism between nomad and settled people, a history of slavery, the existence of Shiʿa communities, and the trend of a greater influx of foreign cultures due to migrants, are all sensitive topics that have challenged the idea of a united nationhood. Most interviewees agreed that the most evident divide in Qatar is that between a Qatari and a non-Qatari—and, of course, within that split many others emerge. Within the Qataris, a dividing line that deserves special attention is that between a *mūwāṭin* (citizen) and an *al-Qatari al-aṣlī* (national).[51] The former have their rights outlined in the Constitution, whereas the latter also hold the dominant characteristics that the exclusivist national discourse propagates, including having pure Arab blood and belonging to Sunni Islam.[52] Qataris occasionally distinguish between who is a "Qatari-Qatari" and who is just "Qatari"—i.e., a citizen but not national.

"Creating" a nation has its own paradoxes, as there are a number of neo-traditional assumptions and central myths of Qatari origins that "support current power and social structures in Qatar in ways that obscure history."[53] As Cooper and Exell put it, "the state agenda focuses on creating unity through concealing cosmopolitan pasts in favor of a unified national narrative of a pure Arab past."[54] In his multiple studies on sectarianism in the Persian Gulf, Gengler points out the impossibility of a united citizenry in the region as a result of "official narratives [that] reflect the ideal of the Sunni Arab tribesman."[55] The outcome of this nationalistic scheme is the exclusion or marginalization of those citizens without tribal ascription or Arab ethnicity and those belonging to a branch of Islam other than Sunni, let alone those who are not citizens. Yet, recent evidence shows a more nuanced scheme of belonging in which multiple accommodations and overlapping identities transform the dichotomy into a more fluid boundary. For instance, the distinction between *badū* and *ḥaḍar*—Bedouin desert dwellers of nomadic origin, and coastal settlers and merchants, respectively—prevails among Qataris who still evoke some forms of rivalry.[56]

Other dividing lines include, but are not limited to, the categories of Muslim/non-Muslim, expatriate/migrant, convert/Muslim-born, short-term/

long-term resident, monotheist/polytheist,[57] Khaleeji/non-Khaleeji, etc. A telling case is that of the central landmark of Qatar—its famous souk—and how it was renamed during the peak of the sectarian fever that engulfed the region after 2005. In his oft-quoted book, *The Shia Revival*, Nasr refers to the presence of an "Irani Bazaar" at the heart of Doha as a way to underline the Shi'i presence in a Wahhabi country, since most of the merchants and shop owners were Persians.[58] However, the famous bazaar, also known as Souq al-Farsi or Persian Market, was remodeled in a more Khaleeji fashion (Gulf fashion) and its name was changed to Souq Waqif (standing market),[59] "as an attempt by the State to replace any symbol of Persian culture with an Arab 'Khaleeji' culture."[60]

Although the formal citizen/non-citizen legal distinction does manifest systematically in all aspects of Qatari public life, degrees of inclusion/exclusion or determination of boundaries and roles, do operate informally within the "citizen" category, such as the customary ban for Qatari Shi'a to hold high executive posts in politics and customs, or to belong to the military, etc.

Secular Modernity

An alternative narrative is also being mobilized: one that looks toward the future and far beyond national boundaries. The Qatar National Vision 2030 represents Qatar as a modern society working for future generations. Despite constant references to the role of Islam and traditions and a way to preserve identity, the general objectives and descriptions of how the project will be implemented are framed in a rather secular language. The document acknowledges the tradition–modernity dichotomy, yet instead of presenting modernity as a danger to traditional values, it persuades the reader to understand it as an opportunity. The official vision of the future stresses that "it is possible to combine modern life with values and culture."[61] It addresses the heavy influx of foreigners—which is seen as a necessity—and promises accommodation of their cultural rights and guarantees the protection of personal freedoms.[62] At the same time, it shows commitment to the preservation of religious values, as well as the central role of the family.

Moreover, the active engagement in educational projects and the major objective of developing a knowledge-based society and economy is what ultimately underlies the modernizing reforms in Qatar. Such a projection can be read as a secularizing path towards modernization that becomes another narrative available to Qataris and non-Qataris alike—which is certainly nonsectarian. Developing a secular state appears as a solution wherever the "religious other" entails forms of tension or is perceived as a threat to the nation.[63] At first sight, a secular modernity seems to be a viable option for complex societies like the Qatari one; nevertheless, the extent to which secularization as such becomes an appealing narrative is uncertain.

In any case, the persistence of misconceptions and prejudices towards the Shi'a have pushed many Shi'a youth to prefer socializing in spaces where a more secular mindset prevails. They also seek spaces where pluralism is a tacit value—or reality—and people from different faiths, or even of no faith, gather in amicable spaces stripped of religious-based conversations, normativity, and practices. Four of the Shi'a that were interviewed were enrolled in bachelor programs of different universities in Education City when this fieldwork was conducted. The four agreed that they felt much more confident within the campus, and have developed social networks with more secularized—and who they deemed "liberal"—young people. They see in Education City a space of tolerance, openness, and inclusion of diversity where many ways of living and thinking converge. Furthermore, the urbanization of Doha is increasingly habilitating modern and secular spaces where the Sunni Islamic ethos is not a driving force; instead, a liberal ethos is commonplace.

Narratives as Informal Politics

As a nascent nation, Qatar is concerned with both guaranteeing domestic legitimacy and with the ways in which it is perceived abroad. Therefore, it has broadened the spectrum of narratives in order to cater to, on the one hand, native citizens and religiously conservative expatriates, and, on the other, to the internal "others"—such as the Shi'a—and to international players who are paying increasing attention to the small burgeoning emirate. In apparent contradiction, these four narratives—Wahhabism, secular spaces, exclusive citizenship, and an "abode for the dispossessed"—serve the purpose of helping the multilayered process of accommodation of difference. Shi'a, especially non-Qatari ones who constitute the vast majority of the Shi'a in Qatar, perceive that there is an increasing pluralization of Qatari society and a corresponding openness reflected in viable, alternative discourses whereby the notion of an Arab Sunni hegemony is challenged. Sajad,[64] a Shi'i Pakistani journalist, argues that "Before that world [cup] event happens, Qataris won't raise unnecessary tensions." On the contrary, the conversations that surface around the 2022 topic mention the potential of the event as a catalyst of tolerance, since it entails the prerequisite of an open-minded environment willing to host a tremendous diversity of cultures and worldviews.

In the same vein, members of the Al-Thani royal family have played a significant role. In most international events hosted, they pursue an agenda of displaying contemporary values related to a global type of citizenship. When asked about the country's leadership, all my interviewees with no exception praised the role of the royal family in one way or another.[65] Masuma recalls that when Sheikh Tamim Bin Hamad became emir, "he came with a discourse of non-discrimination." Here is an excerpt of his inaugural speech:

> We are a nation, a people, a cohesive society and we are not a political party. Therefore, we seek to maintain relations with all governments and countries. We respect all the sincere and influential political currents in the region, but we do not count against one another. We Muslims and Arabs respect diversity in doctrines. We respect all religions in our countries and abroad, and as Arabs, we reject the division of Arab societies on sectarian grounds, because this affects their social and economic immunity and prevents modernization and development on the basis of citizenship irrespective of religion, doctrine, and sect.[66]

Most Shiʿa groups and Shiʿi individuals in Qatar are hopeful that the profile of broad-mindedness and the narratives of tolerance that the royal family members project can be a determinant factor to accelerate Qatari society's embracement of pluralism and diversity. On the occasion of the 70th session of the U.N. General Assembly, the emir addressed the issue of sectarianism in the reported statement:

> At the level of the region there are various creeds and religions, but there is not, in my opinion, a Shitte-Sunni [sic] conflict in essence, but rather differences that are triggered by the political interests of countries, or the interests of political and social forces that foment internal sect-centric prejudices.[67]

The emir's words can be read as both a call for unity and as a sign of his country's disinterest in replicating the sectarian politics so widespread in the region. In the same vein, while such a declaration is inserted in a broader narrative that counters the idea of a top-down process of sectarianization, it is challenged by the official promotion of a homogenous nation with dominant features.

Containing the Arab Spring in Qatar

Qatar's role during the 2011 Arab uprisings is often discussed with regard to its foreign policy positions, mediation, and actions. Whereas Doha supported social movements against authoritarian regimes in North Africa, it was part of the Peninsula Shield Force that suppressed the mainly Shiʿi Bahraini revolt against the Sunni establishment. It must be said, however, that the demonstrations in Manama were sparked by economic and political exclusion—and not necessarily because of sectarian sentiments—that affected the Shiʿi majority. In fact, they drew inspiration from the impoverished Sunni youth who lack opportunities in North Africa.

Qatar's rhetoric in the cases of Egypt and Tunisia was easy to maintain since the events taking place there were by no means a potential hazard for Doha's stability, whereas the uprising that threatened a neighboring regime implied a far more important risk.[68] This was in part due to the sectarian tones of the Bahraini turmoil, which could easily jeopardize the entire Persian Gulf's delicate Sunni–Shiʿi balance. Qatar was certainly not concerned about its domestic economic conditions—since the per capita income of citizens was among the highest in the world—but what worried the regime was, rather, potential sectarian agitation.

The Shiʿa in Qatar, with a long quietist tradition, a rather weak transnational connectivity, and a strong allegiance to the regime, surely did not represent a threat. Nevertheless, a small incident did take place. One of this study's key informants intimated that, in previous years, Sheikh Shaker had some trouble with the government as a result of his public statements and actions. The sheikh's actions led to his disqualification as a religious authority in Qatar. The informant elaborated that the sheikh had conducted a fundraising campaign for Shiʿi communities abroad (most likely Bahraini) without the knowledge of the Awqāf, and without an official permit from the government. This is particularly sensitive since all charitable activities and fundraising campaigns are tightly regulated by the state, and all initiatives of this kind are obliged to request an official approval by the Regulatory Authority for Charitable Activities; any donation made without its knowledge constitutes a serious offence in Qatar.[69] In this particular milieu, only formal politics operate, and any attempt to go under the radar may have serious consequences. Qatar is certainly a big donor state, and encourages charity projects, yet never at the expenses of its national strategy.

Although I could not confirm that incident, two of the sheikh's relatives claimed that such an explanation was given by the government in order to disguise the real problem, which originated during a sermon back in 2012. The local Shiʿi community was already upset over what was happening to Shiʿa in eastern Saudi Arabia and Bahrain—the contagious effect of the Arab uprisings—when, in one of his sermons, Sheikh Shaker described a Lebanese *shahīd* (martyr), apparently a member of Hizbullah, as an exemplary man, and asked the attendees to make *du'ā'*—Islamic supplication prayer—for him. This immediately caught the attention of undercover agents who reported the sheikh to the intelligence services. In addition, he was accused of holding two passports, Qatari and Saudi, which may have signaled suspicious activity. The sheikh was called to court and was prevented, for some time, from delivering sermons to the Shi'a in Qatar.

This was a tipping point: blocking and detaining Sheikh Shaker infuriated some of the active members of the community, who called for a *thaura* (revolution) in Qatar. The sheikh's relatives recounted that some Shi'a in Qatar perceived the measure taken against their leader to be akin to the type of oppression and constraint that their Shi'a counterparts in Bahrain and Saudi Arabia were experiencing; they believed it was the right moment to react. Sheikh Shaker's reaction to the calls for a *thaura* was that of calmness and restraint; he firmly requested his community to be rational and to reject the desire for turmoil. The sheikh succeeded in calming them down, and this achievement—by no means a minor one—pleased the government and the Awqāf, who saw the sheikh as a major asset for Qatar's stability and the prevention of a sectarian problem.

Partners in One Nation: Economic Prosperity and Political Loyalty

Co-Building the State

Despite the erasure of their identity markers in official Qatari history, there have been prominent Shi'i Persian merchants whose skills have contributed to Qatar's development and who have thus secured a legitimate role and space for themselves in Qatari culture. Long before the oil boom, they were co-opted by the Sunni rulers in order to gain their essential support.[70] Later, during the oil era, these Shi'a had exclusive access to state contracts, were exempt from taxation, and were granted legal protection in exchange for not meddling in public affairs. "Traditionally, the Arabized Persians have stayed out of politics ... the evidence suggests that they court the favor and protection of the state, and their trading interests favor a stable status quo."[71] In other words, the successful Qatari Shi'i families have carved a path within the hegemonic system and guaranteed for themselves a dominant role in the economic and business world of Qatar, although without formal recognition of their key role in the country's development.

The case of the Al-Fardan—originally, a Shi'i Persian family—is possibly the most well-known. They have "dominated Qatar's luxury sector for decades.

Patriarch Hussain Ibrahim Al-Fardan is the driving force behind one of the most successful and powerful family-owned conglomerates in [the] region."[72] Their Shiʻi identity has not prevented them from flourishing and dominating many business circles in Qatar or from maintaining a close relationship with the ruling Al-Thani family, as crystallized in Sultan Al-Thani's marriage to Husayn's granddaughter. Furthermore, the Al-Fardan patriarch named his son Omar and his daughter Aisha in what many commentators conclude was a move to please the royal family and to show the willingness to counter any sectarian dimension to their role in Qatar.

Shiʻi individuals and groups in Qatar have relinquished public rituals, overt sect-identity markers, privacy in mosques and *maʾtams*, and even some political rights—in the case of the Qatari Shiʻa. They also claim to privilege the national guidelines and status quo over their sect particularities. "It's for our own safety, we all agree; it's for the *maslaha* [public interest]," an interviewee comments. The idea of the *maslaha* as a religious term and resource is recurrent among many of the Shiʻa when asked about surveillance of the community and security measures at mosques and *ḥusayniyyas*. They concede that giving up their assertiveness has the higher purpose of stability, integration, and consolidation, as well as community welfare. In this sense, we can say that prioritization of the *maslaha* is the basis for Shiʻi quietism in Qatar, and the essence of their strategical relation to the state.

It must be said that the ongoing economic dislocations resulting from the COVID-19 pandemic have not affected the specific type of relation between the Shiʻa and the state in Qatar. Contrary to many other countries where the new realities have been used as a pretext to affect sociopolitical arrangements in detriment of minorities and marginalized groups, the termination of thousands of employees in different sectors in Qatar has not been conducted on a sectarian basis. Although prone to instability, the current circumstances demonstrate how resilient and enduring the Shiʻa-state equation is in Qatar.

The Gulf Crisis

It is generally possible to say that the Qatari nationalist project has been successful and, at least outwardly, it appears that the emir enjoys a great deal of support from the public. The Shiʻi communities are no exception, and were part of the intense campaign to show support to the Qatari regime after the blockade started in June 2017. During my fieldwork with Shiʻa and in Shiʻi environments, I observed the many vehicles, facades of public buildings, walls of private homes, mobile phones, and so on, decorated with stickers and banners depicting the iconic "Tamim the Glorious" ("*Tamīm al-Majd*" design by Ahmed Al-Maadheed) graphic, as well as captions backing the royal family. Whether nationals or residents, many Shi'a did not hesitate to side with Qatar and make sure everyone noticed. Of particular interest is the main wall next to the entrance of the Mosque al-Buhārna, which is covered with a banner that exclaims: "For You the Nation, oh Qatar! For Us the Promise that with Tamim the Glorious we go forward and never go back!" Sunni mosques in the country do not display signs of support for the emir; they are in no need to underline their sympathy with the regime.

This manifest patriotism on the part of many Shi'a can be read as a strategy to safely earn visibility; they go around the city, gather in their sacred spaces, and perform as citizens, while enthusiastically siding with the state in moments when loyalties are tested; it can be deemed as a smart exercise of public informal politics.

Fig. 5.6: A sign on the wall of Al-Buhārna Mosque that reads: "For the Homeland, for you, oh Qatar, you have a covenant from us, that we shall walk with Tamim (the Glorious) with no retreat" ["Lil waṭan, laki yā Qatar, minnā 'ahd ma' Tamīm (al Majd) nasīr wa mā nirja' warā"].

There was a general consensus among the participants in this study that the conditions in Qatar have relaxed towards the Shi'a in recent years. Haidar and Sajad—my main facilitators and guides to the Buharna *ma'tam* and to the Imāmbārgāh, respectively—note that since the blockade, Shi'i scholars from abroad have been given permits to enter the country on special occasions to provide liturgical services. Such is the case of the Muharram commemorations of 2017 and 2018, when some Iraqi and Indian religious figures were allowed to enter the country.[73]

The Martyrdom of Imam Husayn—which is dramatically evoked every year—tends to include public discourses related to ongoing political circumstances of injustice or oppression. At the Buharna *ma'tam*, the most significant moment of the 2017 mourning speech by the Iraqi cleric was his closing statement. He thanked and eulogized Emir Sheikh Tamim Bin Hamad Al-Thani for his efforts in keeping Qatar standing strong in the face of the blockade. The Iraqi cleric mentioned the emir's full name at least three times and praised his achievements in keeping the country open to the world and away from sectarian discourses. The cleric even referred to the well-being of the Shi'i community and wished a long life to the emir and his family. A similar situation occurred at the Doha Imāmbārgāh with an Indian guest cleric, who dedicated his opening words to the emir. The Indian cleric praised the emir and the way he has opened the country's doors to the Shi'i community. The cleric also commended the emir's resilience in facing and managing the ongoing crisis, and made a brief *du'ā'* for him, which was followed by the crowd.

Sajad, my gateway to the Imāmbārgāh, explained that the ongoing crisis in Qatar has allowed the government to loosen its grip on Shi'a; "at the end of the day, they want to make the people happy." Although political issues are not usually raised in Shi'i spaces in Qatar, the paradox is that the only political content manifested in these recent years is that of loyalty to the state. I conclude that, in the last years, *'āshūrā'* in Qatar is also a form of endorsement to the Sunni regime.[74] In this sense, the Shi'i communities in Qatar have smartly escaped the forces and narratives that try to essentialize sect affiliation with specific modes of behavior and political contestation.

Conclusion: Peace and Coexistence as Priorities

When exploring the relations between the State of Qatar and its Shi'i population, one must understand that Shi'ism has existed in the small peninsula since at least two centuries before the founding of Qatar as a nation state. Shi'i presence has always been an integral part of the country's social fabric, and it is only in the wake of modern nationalism that the regime defined a homogeneous profile for the country. This formal self-projection is certainly a conservative strategy, but it is not a norm that systematically excludes difference. Nevertheless, a significant minority like the Shiʿa has its own particular type of interactions and arrangements with the state. With the exception of the Jaʿfarī office at the Awqāf, all the accords to fit Shiʿism are informal, yet effective. The agreements made with the Shiʿa and the processes designed to reach them have become a custom—an unwritten set of social norms; they suit the distinct Qatari way of dealing with minorities, which is rather discreet, private or semi-private, and even tacit.

In Qatar, social and religious heterogeneity is organized, but not in a liberal scheme where mobilization processes and struggles for representation are the preamble to a diversified public space. Rather, a formal and homogeneous national narrative prevails, while difference is accommodated informally. Without compromising its core values and rituals, Shiʿism is sheltered in a way to fit Qatar's priorities, but not in the form of an identity movement—as it would be in the case of some Muslim communities in Europe, North America, or India. In their integration or normalization process, the Shiʿa in Qatar seem to have generally agreed upon neutralizing their outward identity markers. This does not mean that the Shiʿa develop and manifest in clandestine settings or that their collective activities are illegal; conversely, the type of agreements reached with the state gives the Shiʿa both protection and guarantees, insofar as they abide by the boundaries determined by the state. In addition, whenever issues emerge, they are discussed on the sidelines, not at the center of the political stage.

The rentier state also plays a crucial role where the unemployment rate of Shiʿa in Qatar is close to zero.[75] As long as the Shiʿa are content economically, it is likely that they will neither demand a space for themselves in the political terrain—at least in the case of Qatari Shiʿa—nor organize themselves as a pressure group—in the case of migrants. The paradox is that, in Qatar's expanding and thriving economy, having a prominent role in the business and the financial sector is already a form of power. In other words, the Qatari Shiʿa might have given up their political role, but not their actual influence. There is no better way to guarantee protection of and inclusion into the establishment than being key partners of the regime in the state-building process.

Finally, after exploring the different sectarian theories, we can conclude that there are definitely sect-based differentiations, and spaces and roles reserved for Sunnis only. However, it would be inaccurate to claim that there is a top-down sectarianization policy, that social groups fuel sectarian sentiments, or that there are risks to sectarian stability or peaceful coexistence. Both the Shiʿa and the State of Qatar have consolidated a collaborative scheme that purposely escapes the grand sectarian forces of the region, and rejects being a part of such divisive narratives.

PART II

DIVERGING FORMAL
AND INFORMAL POLITICS

6

THREATENING URBAN INFORMALITY
IN THE MIDDLE EAST

Deen Sharp

Introduction

Urbanization is always embedded within struggles over social power. Who gets to build what, where, and how are political, social, and economic questions that can have far-reaching spatial and temporal consequences. It is through this understanding of the connection between social power and the processes of urbanization that we should comprehend the vast building projects that have been announced, planned, and started throughout the Middle East.

Since the coup in Egypt in 2013, for instance, the military government of Abd al-Fattah el-Sisi has pronounced its intention to build a startling array of construction projects, including 5,000 kilometers of new roads, eight new international airports, modernization of existing cities, and the further construction of new desert cities.[1] These plans by Sisi's government have not just remained on the drawing board. Forty-five kilometers from Cairo, the government says it has 200,000 workers constructing the country's first "smart city," the new administrative capital, intended to house 6 million people and occupy an area slightly larger than Paris.[2] On a visit to Cairo in 2018, I saw for myself the traffic of construction workers and machinery commuting to the new capital, and I talked to architects who were excited by the new opportunities this mass building project brings.

In addition to the large-scale city-building and infrastructural projects, the Sisi regime has also announced another major intervention into the urban fabric, namely the elimination of "informal" urban areas. The Sisi government's Egypt Vision 2030 has promised to "eliminate informal settlements and insecure areas."[3] The Sisi regime has given the Informal Settlements Development Fund (ISDF), established in 2008, renewed resources and power to begin this program of elimination. As the ISDF executive director stated to *Daily News Egypt*, "by 2030, Egypt will be completely slum-free, and all unplanned areas will have improved, in addition to all informal markets. In 2030, Egypt will be reshaped."[4]

It is unclear what the Sisi government considers to be informal, or what it deems to be slums. In the Maspero Triangle area in the heart of Cairo, where there has been a long, ongoing battle between the government and residents, the Sisi government reduced the entire neighborhood to rubble (see Fig. 6.1). The government forcefully evicted the residents in 2018, relocating many of them to another housing project an hour's drive away.[5] It is quite deliberately a spectacular and highly visual declaration of intent in the heart of the capital, articulating the extent to which the Sisi regime will go to reorganize the material and spatial life of Egypt. Unsurprisingly, the response from impoverished communities has been to create their own housing solutions, adding to informal settlements elsewhere.

The war against informal settlements and eliminating them should be cause for concern internationally. According to a 2016 Office of the United Nations High Commissioner for Human Rights (OHCHR) report, about 14 million households in Egypt were living without secure tenure, and 51 million people were without access to a formal sanitation network.[6] Sanitation networks are a good indicator of integration into urban systems, as they are among the most expensive basic urban services to install. Sisi's war against informal settlements is even more worrying in a regional context, in which not only are the processes of urbanization intensifying—and with it increases in informal urbanization—but the many conflicts in Libya, Yemen, Iraq, Sudan, and Syria have meant many inhabitants in the region need improvised shelter across the region.

Fig. 6.1: The Cairo district of Maspero after the destruction.

While this chapter emphasizes the issue of targeting the urban poor through the concept of urban informality in Egypt, I also use examples from across the region. It is a concept through which many governments in the region have displaced and dispossessed certain urban communities. The weaponization of urban informality and the many contemporary urban dynamics that gave rise to this category is part of a region-wide phenomenon. The rhetoric around urban informality throughout the Middle East often serves as a proxy for other social conflicts around class, politics, and religion. Governments have displaced and dispossessed communities of their right to the city through the rubric of urban informality.

In Turkey, for example, informal settlements are known as *gecekondus* (literally, "built overnight"). As part of the Urban Transformation Campaign of the ruling party Adalet ve Kalkinma Partisi, it has destroyed thousands of *gecekondus* and displaced the inhabitants of these structures from centrally located urban areas to the peripheries.[7] In Morocco, the Cities Without Slums (also known as Villes Sans Bidonvilles, VSB) program targeted 362,000 settlements and focused on displacing centrally located communities of the urban poor to the urban periphery.[8] In Syria, the Assad regime has targeted opposition areas for demolition based on classifying their property as informal. The regime has weaponized urban planning, and the concept of informal settlements has been integral to this process.[9]

Even in oil-rich Saudi Arabia, the region's largest economy, there are significant levels of urban informality and practices of displacement through this concept. In Jeddah, for instance, the most populous city in the west of Saudi Arabia with around 3.4 million people, around one-third of the population is considered to be living in informal settlements.[10] The Jeddah municipality has established enormous urban development projects, including a multibillion dollar project to "modernize" these "slums" or informal areas—developments that have threatened these populations with displacement rather than improve their urban living conditions.[11]

In this study, I seek to illuminate how and why informal urban settlements emerged as central to the politics of many governments in the Middle East. This study is structured into four parts. After outlining the concept of urban informality in the first section of the chapter, I then consider how the concept of "informal" settlements emerged. I show how, in the 1960s, in countries like Egypt and Turkey, government funding for housing was reduced in favor of factories constructed on the urban fringe, creating a housing crisis that was largely ignored until the 1970s. I then detail how, in the 1970s, the World Bank and United States Agency for International Development (USAID) pushed governments to address, through a "site and services" approach, what it identified as specifically "informal" housing. I argue that the Egyptian government—setting a broader regional trend—shifted from a policy of neglect in the 1960s, to concern in the 1970s, and, finally, to one of moral panic by the 1990s.

In the third part of the chapter, I focus on the Middle East in the 1990s, during which time there was an intensification in government attention toward urban informality. As I explain, this was in part because urban informality became associated with Islamist militant groups. This shift occurred at a time of great internal economic and political instability in the region. It was a period in which neoliberal policies intensified, and with it the commodification of land, with notable implications for the urbanization process which led to increased attention paid by governments toward eradicating urban informality. In the final section, I contend that the Arab uprisings beginning in 2010 represented a dramatic moment of empowerment for those groups associated with being from informal areas. Notably, I argue that the uprisings enabled the urban poor to highlight the informality of elite groups and to challenge the very formality of the state. This was a fleeting moment, however, and I contend that it was perhaps the powerful challenge these groups posed to the state and elites that has resulted in the fierce backlash against these communities in Egypt and across the region.

Informality

Informality as a concept in social science—and urban informality in particular—has always been a vague one. The concept of informality emerged in the 1960s and 1970s concentrating on informal labor in Africa, and studies of urban informality—overlapping with closely associated terms like slums and squatter settlements—concentrated on squatter settlements in Latin America. In the 1960s, Keith Hart's studies on employment practices in Ghana was foundational for the work on informality.[12] While Richard Harris has argued that the work on urban informality has multiple and complex origins,[13] scholars broadly credit the work of John Turner to be foundational for the idea of urban informality as a form of shelter and service provision.

Both scholars and policymakers have largely understood informality and urban informality to be confined to the Global South. The scholarship in recent years, however, has changed drastically, growing in volume and applied globally.[14] This scholarship has stressed that informality is not unique to impoverished areas or poor countries. Informality is global and predominantly urban condition. As the OHCHR report notes, "it is estimated that one quarter of the world's urban population lives in informal settlements. Informal settlements exist in nearly all regions and countries, including in highly developed countries."[15] Richard Harris in his extensive review of the contemporary scholarship on informality, has argued that this concept is a universal one and applies to all societies.[16]

Informality has a strong association with urban settings, and while it can apply equally to New York and Cairo, the degrees and types of informality can manifest differently, and it is always in flux.[17] The fluidity of (urban) informality can be attributed to the wide range of contexts and issues to which it is applied. McFarlaine and Waibel contend that formality and informality can be conceived as a territorial formation (e.g., the slum); categories of particular groups (e.g., informal labor); forms of organization (e.g., rule-based, structured, or unstructured); and modes of knowing the city (e.g., formal and informal knowledge and practices of the city).[18]

Governments in the Middle East and international organizations like the World Bank continue to view informality in a negative light, seeing it as a signifier of a lack of development and associating it with slower GDP growth, weaker governance, higher poverty, and greater inequality.[19] Meanwhile, among scholars and some policymakers, more nuanced views have formed in relation to the highly variegated types of informality that exist within and across countries of both the Global South and North, their urban character, and the complex relationships that exist between the informal and broader frameworks of social power—specifically, the state and the market. As Harris argues, stereotypes and conceptual barriers are coming down, with researchers recognizing the interrelation between formal and informal developments.[20]

This study is not concerned with contributing to the vast scholarship on what constitutes the concept of informality, specifically urban informality. I am not concerned with the precision of the concept or the exact urban morphologies it applies to in the particular contexts of Egypt or the region more broadly. Rather, I am focused on how this concept of urban informality has been weaponized across the Middle East and how it has been used in contemporary political practice in the region. It is my contention that the framework of urban informality in the Middle East is sometimes deployed not to improve the urban conditions of vulnerable communities, but to further their marginality through displacement and dispossession. This use of urban informality by governments as a tool of governmentality and discipline is also visible if we trace the very political manner in which urban informality entered the region.

Informalizing the Middle East

The postcolonial era in the Middle East in the 1950s resulted in an intensification of the processes of industrialization and urbanization. In countries like Egypt and Turkey, this meant the construction of many factories and industries unaccompanied by programs for the construction of worker housing. In Egypt, government expenditure on the housing sector decreased from 32 percent of fiscal spending in 1952 to 12 percent in 1962.[21] This budget prioritization was not based on the idea that housing did not matter, but that a country with limited resources should prioritize sectors that were deemed to be productive and that generated foreign reserves. In both Egypt and Turkey, the logic of the state was embedded in a broader macroeconomic perspective of "no housing before factories."[22] Housing was in short supply and agricultural areas around factories soon urbanized, as workers set about creating their own settlement solutions.

In the 1960s, because of the rapid urbanization that had occurred, governments throughout the region began to focus more systematically on questions of urban planning, in particular in relation to housing. As part of this process, central governments in the Middle East slowly began to concede to what were then recognized as "spontaneous" urban settlements; in some cases, the government responded to calls from the inhabitants of these settlements to install basic urban services.[23] However, in the cases of both Egypt and Turkey (and elsewhere), there were notable tensions between the central state and municipal government. The central state was often more reluctant to accept the existence of these self-built settlements that had been created beyond their reach and legal framework. Furthermore, the central state frustrated local governments by creating laws that municipal authorities could not enforce as they had to deal with the everyday reality of increasing numbers of rural migrants requiring urban settlement. The result was a standoff. Many Middle Eastern governments did not recognize the existence of informal settlements, but made concessions in these areas when it was deemed politically expedient to do so. Although spontaneous settlements had spread throughout the region, no government had a policy framework that explicitly addressed "informal settlements." This changed in the 1970s.

The 1973 oil crisis and the rise of the oil-rich Gulf states is a notable moment in the urbanization—and expansion of spontaneous settlements—of the region more broadly, and Egypt in particular. Around this time, President Sadat announced a major new policy that would become known as *infitah* (open-door policy), which would allow for greater foreign investment into Egypt, and would facilitate Egyptians to travel abroad more freely. Many Egyptians migrated to the Gulf for work and sent remittances back home. They often put this capital into the built environment and into areas outside of central government control, i.e. informal areas.

The Sadat era shifted government policy to a more concerted intervention by the state, elites, and Western organizations into the Egyptian built environment. Sadat's famous 1974 October Paper announced the construction of several new desert cities during this period. Government officials argued that these desert cities would release the pressure of urbanization in Cairo, Alexandria, and the Nile Valley, and they became the government's principal approach to address informal housing. Thus, the concern around informal housing would be dealt with indirectly.[24] The government transformed the General Authority for Physical Planning (GOPP) and granted it greater autonomy, legislative power, and its own budget with responsibility for planning the entire country.[25] The open-door policy also meant that many international companies sought space in downtown Cairo. Land prices continued to rise in the Sadat era, and a real estate industry began to emerge as a significant part of the country's economy. David Sims writes that the level of construction on the urban fringe "rose to fever pitch" by 1977, noting that "new buildings appeared and, equally common, vertical extensions were added to existing buildings."[26]

Infitah marked the dawn of the neoliberal period in the Middle East and the end of Arab socialism. This process of neoliberalization was sped up by the debt crisis in the 1980s that had a severe impact on the region, and resulted in a rapid commodification of land. Several scholars have framed this capital takeover of urban areas in the Middle East as a neoliberal turn,[27] with select cities around the region emerging as principle sites for capital accumulation. This resulted in greater external investment in the built environment and increased central government control of municipal urban areas in which it organized the built environment around the needs of the market. The urban poor in strategically located parts of urban centers throughout the region now found themselves the target of displacement initiatives, and urban informality became an important concept through which governments achieved this.

It is of note that urban informality as a policy framework entered the Middle East with the *infitah*, which resulted in the increased presence of international organizations within Egypt, in particular the World Bank and USAID. These organizations entered Egypt at a time of rapid urbanization. In the 1970s, based on its experience in Latin America, the World Bank viewed poverty alleviation and housing as central to its mandate. The World Bank pushed a global policy of "aided self-help," which sought to identify "informal" settlements and encourage governments to facilitate the legalization of these shelters and allow the urban poor to find their own housing solutions. Importantly, the World Bank required governments in the Global South to stop building subsidized public housing and to start formalizing and supporting what was identified as "informal" urban areas. Although by the 1970s, large swathes of Egypt, and in particular Cairo, had experienced rapid urbanization outside the formal logic of the central state, the government still did not recognize or have a policy to address "informal" housing.

Most of urban Egypt was literally off the map; these areas were not documented in official statistics and were not part of how the central government formalized policy.

The World Bank and USAID pushed an otherwise reluctant Egyptian central government to address what they identified as informal settlements through policies of legalization, building infrastructure, and "aided self-help"—or what the World Bank called "site and services." Hoda Tolba Sakr, a senior planner in the GOPP who worked for the Egyptian government on the first World Bank-sponsored studies on informal settlements, noted that the 1977 World Bank project on "Egypt Urban Development Project," and the 1978 USAID study on "Housing and Community Upgrading for Low Income Egyptians," were the first reports to alert the Egyptian central government of the significance of the informal sector in the country.[28] These were followed in 1982 by the famous Abt Associates study on "Informal Housing in Egypt," which was financed by USAID and undertaken with the General Organization for Housing, Building, and Planning Research. These organizations pushed the Egyptian government to formulate policies and devote resources to analyze the existence of "informal" housing and settlements and to harness this phenomenon to solve the country's housing problem. The World Bank and USAID attempted to get the Egyptian central government to legalize informal areas and to embrace a self-help policy.

The World Bank and USAID studies cited high levels of informality in Egypt, and the Abt Associates report stated that 84 percent of all housing in Cairo and 91 percent in Beni Suef between 1970 and 1981 was what it defined as informal.[29] While the latter study noted the diverse definitions of what could be considered informal in Egypt, the authors of the Abt report took a rigid legal definition. Informal housing was considered to be on land that was illegally subdivided, in contravention of Law 52 of 1940 and 1975. In using this definitional framework, the Abt study inevitably recorded high levels of informality because, as the report itself states, "this law has been ineffective since enactment."[30]

If the idea was for the World Bank and the USAID to shock the Egyptian central government into action over informal settlements, then its reports and projects were highly effective. However, they were not effective at convincing the government to take an "aided self-help" approach to informality. As David Sims argues, once the Egyptian government woke up to informal housing, its reaction was negative.[31] Throughout the 1970s and 1980s there was an intensification of informal urban development at the same time as there was a series of orders and decrees by the Egyptian government to make it increasingly difficult to build shelters on what was deemed precious agricultural land and other state-owned land.[32] Rather than heeding the World Bank and USAID suggestions to decriminalize the large swathes of informal housing that they had rigorously identified over a period of a decade, the Egyptian central government decided that it would tighten legislation, thus increasing the informality of these settlements. The government extended its policy of creating modern, planned desert cities as an alternative to informal planning.[33]

By the 1980s, governments across the Middle East began to address urban informality more concertedly. Increasingly, government policies formulated to address "urban informality" followed the path ploughed by the Egyptian government. The rising social tensions of the 1980s in the Middle East meant that there was a new urgency in which to identify urban informality by the 1990s. This determination was not based on a motivation by governments in the region to identify urban poverty and alleviate it. Rather, identifying urban informality became part of a strategy for identifying certain communities in central urban areas where land values could be raised, and relocating them to satellite cities in peripheral urban areas. Additionally, central governments viewed informal urban areas as a threat to their power.

The ʿashwaʾiyyat

In the 1990s, informal areas shifted from being a growing issue of policy concern for central governments to being considered a national security threat across the Middle East. A number of violent incidents involving Islamists, the intensification of the "war on terror," and the deepening of neoliberal policies all bolstered this framing. It was also around this period that the term *ʿashwaʾiyyat* (meaning haphazard or random) became popularized in Egypt to denote informal areas and their inhabitants, and it spread throughout the Arabic-speaking world. As Walter Armbrust argues, it came to symbolize a problem of urban overcrowding, poverty, drugs, and gangster culture; an image was built of *ʿashwaʾiyyat* "as a particularly virulent site of social pathologies."[34] The term *ʿashwaʾiyyat* applies not only to buildings or certain areas; it also refers to types of people and modes of conduct. In Egypt, the *ʿashwaʾiyyat* ostensibly denotes those who migrated from rural areas to the city. As Bayat and Denis argue, "the *ashwaiyyat* are perceived as 'abnormal' places where, in modern conventional wisdom, the 'non-modern' and thus 'non-urban' people, that is, the villagers, the traditionalists, the non-conformists and the unintegrated live."[35] But as the authors further noted almost twenty years ago, the growth of secondary cities and the urban fringe across the Egyptian "countryside" meant that the ʿashwaʾiyyat were no longer migrating from rural areas, but between urbanized ones.

The ʿashwaʾiyyat population and their associated areas came to prominence in Egypt following an earthquake in 1992—a year of social tensions marked by Islamic militant groups attacking the lucrative tourism industry. In Cairo, the earthquake resulted in the death of more than 500 people and injured thousands of others, many of whom the government deemed to be living in precarious structures in areas that were increasingly identified as ʿashwaʾiyyat. However, as Sims has detailed, this was not actually the case.[36] The response to the earthquake—or rather, the absence of a response—by the government caused much anger in the country, and contrasted with Islamic charities and groups that were viewed as acting far more effectively. At the time, James Napoli reported that "Islamic groups invited favorable comparison with the government, rushing in to help victims with blankets, food and medicine, while the immediate official response was tangled in red tape and confusion."[37] The government did not take kindly to the comparison and tore down tents that Islamic groups had distributed to victims. In the ʿashwaʾiyyat area of Boulaq, the inhabitants launched anti-government demonstrations because of the lack of effective relief.

Another notable incident involving Islamist groups soon followed the earthquake. In December 1992, the "siege of Imbaba"—a district in Cairo renowned as an ʿashwaʾiyyat area—involved 18,000 paramilitary police with armored cars and bulldozers, who seized the area to "cleanse" this poor community of the militant Islamist group, al-Gamaʿa al-Islamiyya. The government claimed that the group had turned the area into an Islamic "state within the state."[38] The "Imbaba siege" provoked the Mubarak regime to launch a plethora of initiatives around informal urbanism and the built environment more broadly. This included a national program to upgrade informal settlements and resulted in a greater presence of the central government in these areas. It also introduced a policy of urban upgrading, "site and services," supported by USAID and European NGOs that funded several basic urban services projects and constructed roads in this area.[39]

In the 1990s, a strong association in the minds of state officials and the broader public began to form between militant Islamist groups and the areas and peoples deemed to be ʿashwaʾiyyat. Asef Bayat has argued, however, that although deeply embedded within the Egyptian popular imagination, the idea that so-called 'ashwa'iyyat areas provide an urban ecology for militant Islamist groups is spurious.[40] He contends that while there is some truth that militant Islamists have sought shelter in 'ashwa'iyyat areas in their attempt to avoid state surveillance, and that the populations in these areas have sought assistance from Islamic charities and NGOs in the state's absence, it does not render the "urban disenfranchised anomic, alienated, extremist, nor the strategic ally and the social basis of militant Islamism."[41] Bayat insists that the influence of Islamists in 'ashwa'iyyat areas is often exaggerated, and that these groups often showed little interest in the political mobilization of the urban subaltern: "In Egypt, many among the poor had no direct interaction with Islamists and remained confused as to their intentions, while others, such as the residents of Imbaba's ashwaiyyat, remained apprehensive and yet appreciative of the services they provided."[42]

The association, however, has been that Islamic militant groups and the 'ashwa'iyyat would only grow stronger with broader geopolitical events, notably 9/11 and the intensification of the "war on terror." Governments placed a strong link between territories deemed to be outside government control—so-called "ungoverned" areas—and terrorism.[43] Informal areas, the absence of state-provided basic urban services and physical infrastructure, as well as the informal economy were taken to be key indicators of ungovernability.[44] Because of this association, the weaponization of urban informality to displace the urban poor was intensified across the region.

In Morocco, for instance, the 2003 Casablanca bombings were the deadliest terrorist attacks in the country's history, killing forty-five people. The suicide bombers came from Sidi Moumen, an urban periphery of Casablanca classified as an informal area. Following the bombings, the government viewed informal areas as environments conducive to fomenting rebellion and people within them as the primary agents of the attack. To this effect, Bogaert notes that "the slums became a primary political concern for the preservation of stability and the securitization of the city."[45] Much like in Egypt, the Moroccan government shifted from a reluctance to engage with informal areas of the urban poor to one of active management following the Casablanca attacks, prompting the launch of the VSB program in 2004.[46] The program emphasized informal areas as a threat and called for immediate action, targeting 362,000 households. Notably, this program has focused on the resettlement of inhabitants from the urban center to the periphery.

Governments in the region no longer tolerated a decentralized hands-off approach to areas it designated as informal. More recently, however, and in accordance with Bayat's earlier assertion noted above, the theory of a link between so-called "ungoverned spaces" and terrorism has been largely dismissed by counterterrorism experts, who argue for instance, that terrorist groups have flourished in areas where state control is strong and that so-called ungoverned spaces are not in fact ungoverned.[47] Despite this, the assumed link between terrorism, militant Islamism groups, and informal areas remains strong both within the Middle East and internationally in policy circles and among the broader public.

It is important to note that the broader shift to the idea that the *'ashwa'iyyat* were a national threat also arose with economic restructuring that intensified the rate of urbanization and the role of the market in Egyptian society. At the start of the 1990s, Mubarak's Egypt was suffering from a debt crisis, and was placed on an International Monetary Fund (IMF) stabilization plan. The IMF reform program instituted fiscal and monetary discipline, but, as Timothy Mitchell has detailed, this monetary control and fiscal discipline was accompanied by dramatic urban growth: "While government budgets were contracting, Cairo was exploding."[48]

The process that had begun with the *infitiah* had now deepened and accelerated. As part of this economic restructuring, both private developers and the state were engaged in huge urban developments—a web of investment-linked speculators, bankers, government entities, and military officials. Real estate emerged as the country's third-largest non-oil investment and was closely associated with the country's second-largest sector, tourism. Mitchell argues that "the state turned resources away from agriculture and industry and the underlying problems of training and employment. It now subsidized financiers instead of factories, cement kilns instead of bakeries, speculators instead of schools."[49] As Sims also notes, "huge tracts of subdivided land were sold at nominal, some would say give-away, prices to ... private developers."[50]

The Egyptian state turned towards financiers and real estate, and away from agriculture and industry, producing a dramatic intensification of the urbanization process—and an expansion in the number of areas characterized by the government, albeit informally and without irony, as *'ashwa'iyyat*. Officially, the Egyptian government reports that 44 percent of the country is considered to be urban, and that the urbanization growth rate is 2 percent.[51] This government-issued rate of urbanization has not changed since 1986.[52] In the era of Mubarak, the government claimed that no new informal settlement appeared. Perhaps unsurprisingly, most scholars and analysts do not deem Egypt's official rate of urbanization credible. Hegazy and Kaloop, for instance, in their

GIS study of the Egyptian governorate Daqahlia, which includes the secondary cities of Mansoura and Talkha, show that urbanization increased about 32 percent from 1985 to 2010.[53] They note a marked rise in the rate of urbanization from 2000 to 2010; the built-up area increased over five times while areas of agriculture decreased by 31 percent in this period.[54] They state that this rapid urbanization will continue and may increase a further 16 percent over the next decades.[55] This dramatic increase in urbanization is not specific to Egypt, but is occurring across the Middle East. There has been a remarkable intensification of the processes of urbanization throughout the region, which has been rooted in neoliberal policies.

Revolting ʿashwaʾiyyat

Following the Arab uprisings, the debates over urban informality intensified within the region. This period shows the extent to which conceptions, legal framings, and material and social practices of informality are linked to broader organizations of social power. It was in this period, albeit temporarily, that the tables of informality were turned. In the media and in popular discourse, elite developments—rather than the settlements of the urban poor—were now framed as being illegal and informal, with developers even (briefly) arrested for dubious land deals. Citizens were taking it upon themselves to connect to infrastructure that previously bypassed their communities.

In Egypt it was in areas that many in the country referred to as ʿashwaʾiyyat that the January 25 revolution was deemed to have begun. The journalist Jack Shenker has written that the original protest organizers publicized twenty different places around Cairo to congregate, plus one secret location in front of the Hayyis sweet shop in the ʿashwaʾiyyat neighborhood of Bulaq al-Dukror. He writes:

> By the early afternoon, at the end of el-zuhr prayers, over 300 had gathered at the Hayyis storefront and begun marching towards Tahrir; the crowd swelled as it moved, and by the time police had realized what was happening there were too many protesters to hold off, too much anger to baton-whip back into submission.[56]

This revolt of ʿashwaʾiyyat neighborhoods around Tahrir Square in downtown Cairo occurred in the context of ongoing battles between residents of this area and the government, specifically in Bulaq. The Vision 2050, which fed into Vision of Cairo 2050, envisaged a total redevelopment of downtown Cairo, and outlined plans for the vast displacement of the residents in Bulaq to desert cities.[57] These communities led the march to Tahrir Square. Documented by several scholars, there was also a notable broader empowerment of ʿashwaʾiyyat communities in their intervention into the urban fabric,[58] which included the ʿashwaʾiyyat undertaking their own "site and services" projects. Informal neighborhoods, for example, began to build their own highway entry points that otherwise bypassed their communities, and which linked the downtown area to the gated communities populating the desert.[59]

Based on a year-long residence with squatters in the gated Haram City in Cairo, the ethnographer Nicholas Simcik Arese details how a squatter community consolidation was empowered following the revolution to assert its presence. Arese also highlights how the term ʿashwaʾiyyat was appropriated, deployed, and instrumentalized by its very subjects.[60] Arese notes how the squatters in Haram City came from areas deemed to be ʿashwaʾiyyat in the inner city of Cairo, specifically Duweiqa, in which the inhabitants were also deemed to be lawless and without secure tenure—they supposedly illegally converted their land from agricultural to residential use. Arese states that the squatters, the ʿashwaʾiyyat, were also cognizant of the dubious legality of the gated communities and the "legal-geographical double standard" of those who accuse them of illegal occupation. Arese details how many of the middle-class homeowners who live in "compounds" have subdivided or added extra floors to their homes in clear violation of government building codes, and often use the labor of the ʿashwaʾiyyat, noting that "squatters are not only aware of this but also dependent on the few jobs that literally construct this double standard."[61] In his time with the ʿashwaʾiyyat community in Haram City, Arese details how the squatters gradually developed critiques over legality, and the very constitution of the legal:

> By linking bulk home construction to everyday market practices such as the sale of cars, sunglasses, or shoes, while reminding that homes are built on undervalued state land in the name of the deprived, squatters distinguish between property for productivity and profit, between use and exchange values. They also question whether ownership inherently includes absolute control over a property, whether mass-manufacturing homes for sale even qualifies as ownership, and, if so, whether it allows one to restrict uses to a degree that urgently needed homes remain empty.[62]

One of the most significant impacts of the 2011 revolution on urban housing was how the legal framework regarding the illegality of housing shifted from the poor to the gated communities of the middle and upper classes. Ananya Roy and Nezar AlSayyad have argued that informal housing and land markets are not just the domain of the poor, but are also important for the middle classes and the elite in both the Global North and South.[63] Following the 2011 revolution, the informality of many middle- and upper-class urban developments were briefly illuminated when twenty-seven businessmen, controlling 80 percent of land reclamation projects, and several ministers were indicted for illegal land deals. However, nearly all of these cases were dropped following the military coup in 2013.[64] Unlike the informal urban poor, the middle- and upper-class informal settlements were not only represented as formal by the state and media, but also enjoyed premium infrastructure and security of tenure.

The threat that those from informal areas posed to authoritarian regimes around the region was not confined to Egypt. In the case of Syria, there was also a strong correlation between protests and location within the urban periphery and informal settlements.[65] While data is poor in this context, some research has pointed to the fact that recently developed working-class urban neighborhoods in Aleppo and Damascus that were disconnected from basic urban services were at the forefront of the Syrian revolt. David Kilcullen and Nate Rosenblatt report that in the early stages of the conflict, 65 percent of deaths occurred in just seven neighborhoods in Damascus that had similar urban characteristics: they had all grown rapidly over the past decade, they aligned closely with the opposition and were even controlled by them, and they were all working-class areas.[66] Since the areas classified as informal correlated with those that had strong associations with the opposition, the Syrian regime immediately attempted to assert its control on such neighborhoods. A 2012 decree allowed the demolition and replacement of entire informal neighborhoods, and the regime intensified this process in 2018 with Law 10 that again targeted opposition areas through the rubric of informality.

Conclusion: Urban Informality as a Threat

As governments across the region have been challenged by bottom-up mobilizations, in particular over the past decade, urban informality has increasingly been seen as a threat. It is of note that the Sisi regime's engagement with informal populations has involved highly visible projections of order, launching major campaigns through the construction of prominent and highly visible state-subsidized public housing projects on the urban fringe. The Sisi regime has been most actively promoting these new projects (see Fig. 6.2), and framing informal settlements using combative language. As an Egyptian media site notes, "a major war" against the spread of informal settlements has been launched in Cairo and Alexandria with the construction of 9,864 housing units.[67] An order for houses to be painted certain colors is once again imposing a visual appearance of order rather than engaging with the complex urban ecologies that constitute contemporary Egypt. The announcement stated that "the painting of these façades must be uniform and not [the current] uncivilized view where there are many different buildings with [only] red-bricks as their façade. This appearance shows these areas to be un-civilized."[68]

The government approach across the region has been to consider urban informality as a threat and target it for removal, a tactic that has caused immense human suffering. Rather than providing improved shelter with better access to basic urban services, whether in Morocco, Saudi Arabia, Egypt, or Syria, the ways in which governments address informal areas have frequently resulted in residents being displaced from their communities and livelihoods. The regional government policy to view informality as a threat only pushes already vulnerable communities ever further into immiseration and increases the chance of revolt. Thus, the perceived threat from informal areas is potentially materialized through the very policy that is supposed to address it. The task of de-weaponizing the concept of urban informality is urgent.

Fig. 6.2: Social housing in Gamsa—Dakahlia.

There are signs of hope, however, with grassroots organizations across the region mobilizing to create plans and possibilities for the urban poor to receive the services they require. In Egypt, for example, 10 Tooba has developed a series of projects in Greater Cairo that stress bolstering local knowledge and capabilities through participatory planning approaches. Similarly, in Turkey, a range of civil society groups are working to "reclaim Istanbul" and promote community-driven planning processes in poor urban areas. The potential for more pragmatic and nuanced engagements with the complex urban ecologies of the Middle East is present, but the ability to meaningfully fulfil this presence continues to be absent.

7

VOLUNTARY ASSOCIATIONS AS SOCIAL MICROMOVEMENTS

THE CASE FOR GRADUAL SOCIOPOLITICAL CHANGE IN ALGERIA

Nejm Benessaiah

Introduction

Up until the massive 2019 protests and subsequent ouster of former President Bouteflika, the scholarly consensus was that Algerians had opted for political stability over radical democratic change, especially since the government implemented superficial reforms to quell any dissent during the Arab uprisings. The 2019 protests demonstrated that, while Algerians are now calling for wholesale transformation of the political system, they are still adamant that grassroots pressure remains non-violent. This study challenges the idea that political change can come only from formal political institutions such as parties, or indeed formally organized protests movements. I suggest instead that voluntary associations can and are acting as vehicles for gradual, inclusive sociopolitical change in an informal sense in contrast to formal politics. The idea of civil society as the great hope for democratic change in the Middle East has largely been sidelined by scholars and commentators who argue—somewhat cynically, though often true—that it aids the legitimacy of authoritarian regimes.[1] This view may have softened somewhat since 2011, when civic groups in Tunisia, for example, formed the Tunisian National Dialogue Quartet and aided the democratic transition by holding the interim government accountable, winning the Nobel Peace Prize in the process.[2]

Drawing on a case study in Ghardaïa, central Algeria, this study contests the negative view of civil society by arguing that voluntary associations may act as agents of change in general society, though not necessarily in political society—the latter being dominated by what Algerians refer to as *le pouvoir* (the power), the largely unaccountable military and secret service acting behind the scenes of the regime.[3] What is changing, I suggest, is the formation of a new political subjectivity as well as a social imaginary regarding how society can be organized and how the environment should be governed. This study adds to the literature on informal politics by providing a new perspective on the governance of natural resources—specifically, the changing political culture of an Algerian oasis region, with a focus on agricultural civic organizations.

How are nature and politics linked? The non-human environment becomes inherently political when commodified into resources for which demand is high and distribution is scarce. This is especially the case for biologically and economically important elements, such as water and oil, which exist in varying states of abundance in the Middle East and North Africa. Put another way, a view of politics that lacks a consideration of material and environmental resources is inept at best, especially given current conditions regarding climate change.[4] Political ecology is a field of practice that links various scholars from different fields working on the political dimensions of the material and discursive conflicts of the environment.[5] I do not explicitly use a political ecology framework here, but some of the overarching concepts are closely linked, such as the contestation of power for the purposes of social and environmental justice. This includes issues such as access to natural resources, environmental conflict, and environmental social movements, of which I am concerned with the latter.

Here, I am concerned with desert oases as socio-natural complexes, where water is the key element around which other layers are arranged, incorporating a range of biological, ecological, social, economic, and political relationships. Currently, although oases are politically and economically marginalized, they are still incorporated into the different levels of national, regional, and local administrations. The governance of oases is also multilayered; as peripheral geographic entities, many areas of social life that were historically governed at the local level continue to be managed in this manner—including conflict mediation over the contested resources of land and water, both of which at different times fall into either private or collective ownership categories.

Oases historically played a central role within geographical and political economic assemblages as nodes linking vast trade routes. Today, they play a smaller part on the global stage as peripheral areas where informal activities abound beneath the radar of the state—especially, according to Western imaginaries, as the abode of migrants, jihadists, and black market traffickers in weapons, drugs, and other contraband.[6] These sites continue to play an important role regionally as nodes around which different actors necessarily constellate, due to the relative abundance of flows of water, trade, and ideas. This is contrary to popular views of deserts as dead zones empty of human and non-human life,[7] and as ecological aberrations rather than complex ecosystems in their own right.[8] Today, within the milieu of elite control of most of Algeria's natural resources and their markets, combined with rising public *hogra* (discontent) and international development efforts aimed at increased political participation, voluntary associations are emerging alongside traditional tribal structures and local governments as sites of collective activity that may be termed "informally political."

Non-state governance at village level is well known in literature on Arab world. Collectives such *djemma* or *qabila* (village council) constitute a form of tribal politics based on kinship and political allegiances and logic, often conceived in terms such as solidarity and segmentarity. In many areas of the Middle East, these types of local governance continue in some form, while new voluntary associations are emerging that operate alongside, hybridize with, or gradually replace these traditional organizations,[9] which is the case in my area of study, the M'zab valley of Ghardaïa. In the M'zab, traditional governance, characterized by clan groups overseen by a religious authority called the 'azzāba, is being replaced by new groups that are organized according to different ethics and structures, from forms that are less hierarchical and more consensual. However, these changes are even more complex, as I explain below. This is significant in a region often characterized by conservative patriarchal modes of life. Even where cultural traditions and scriptures have emphasized egalitarianism, this has not been evident in practice; rather, what has been seen constitutes an egalitarianism among equals—that is, male household heads.[10] Today, however, voluntary associations in Algeria embody the potential for a different institutional ethos of political life, including women, and various classes and ethnicities.[11]

Before delving into the general and specific details of civil society in Algeria, it is important to clarify what I mean by informal politics and how this relates to the environment. Sociocultural anthropology deals with the informal side of politics, perhaps by default. Anthropologists study how norms of human behavior are reproduced, encoded, or resisted, through symbolic, discursive, and embodied mediation, replicating or challenging social phenomena and institutions from patriarchy to military organizations. We explore how influence may be gained through gift giving, which may be used as a tool to coerce; how, through their forceful rhetoric, charismatic leaders persuade and influence; and how governance can be built on informal rules or norms. I have elsewhere argued that *'urf* (customary law), which often governs environmental concerns such as land and water use, lies on both sides of the apparent formal/informal divide.[12] In reality, informality and the formal generally overlap, as do shari'a and state law. For example, political alliances may be based on formal contracts, but also on historical relationships. Informality may be seen as a gray area where legal boundaries may be transgressed, breaching the public–private domains in terms of accessing advantages and resources.[13] Obtaining the support of powerful patrons—often called *wasṭa* in the Arab world—is usually characterized as corrupt and unjust, yet necessary to get anything done (e.g., gaining employment). In contrast, in China this practice (known as *guanxi*) is linked to Confucian philosophy and is seen as necessary for strengthening social connections.[14] Informality regarding the environment can include, for example, paying bribes or favors to inspectors or engineers in order to access water infrastructure.[15]

This study takes a different view of informality. I argue that, while forbidden from formal political activity according to Article 40, voluntary associations in Algeria are inherently political due to their collective nature. Perhaps more importantly, I suggest that associational activity has wider implications for social and political change in Algeria, involving not sudden but gradual cultural change.[16] I characterize the agents of this change as social micromovements, which differ from ordinary social movements whose aim is for sudden society-wide changes. Social micromovements are instead focused on making changes at the local level through small, incremental adjustments to culturally acceptable forms of social organization. This type of theorization is important, especially at a time when the focus has been on sudden revolutionary change, resulting mostly in disappointment in achieving democratic change in the Middle East,[17] and chaos involving regime strengthening through disastrous foreign intervention or the force of counter social movements.[18] Furthermore, this then does not involve radical changes that may not be morally acceptable to the society in question.

At stake here are culturally embedded notions of patriarchy and elite power, in the light of emerging political subjectivation among peasant farmers, through their regional and transnational connections for a more socially just configuration of society. In other words, farmer associations are challenging local power structures not through direct confrontation, i.e. through formal political procedures, but informally and indirectly by building alternative organizations that are inclusive, representative, and accountable, and thus slowly changing the way that society thinks about the very basis of social organization. These farmers have repurposed the international development language of "participation" into their own cultural categories, thus experimenting with new forms of social organization.

Civil Society, Voluntary Associations, and Gradual Cultural Change

Social and political change is most often viewed in terms of exogenous shocks that originate outside of the system in question, such as colonialism, or in terms of sudden events, such as revolutions. Here, I consider some ways in which change may be conceived in a different register—that is, as gradual and incremental. First, I examine some of main trajectories of thought on civil society. After that I outline a model of gradual change that comes from within institutional systems. Then I contrast change that arises from external shocks to cumulative everyday change, with reference to Sahlins,[19] who argues for cultural forms of change through the dialectic relations between individual creativity and changing cultural categories, as I explicate below. This refers theoretically in new ways to the classic structure–agency debate in a way that attempts to combine the two in a dynamic fashion, one informing the other, encapsulated by the question: does the person make history or does history make the person? It is usually the events that stand out and are recorded, but change arising from the background fabric of history is often more complex, and this requires a closer focus, as I attempt to do with this ethnographic case.

In 1965, Kenneth Little argued that voluntary associations in West Africa "served as adaptive mechanisms of members of communities experiencing rapid change, with tribal institutions becoming replaced or supplemented by new organizational forms, such as tribal unions, friendly societies, and occupational and recreational associations."[20] Civil society may be thought of as "the totality of self-initiating and self-regulating volitional social formations, peacefully pursuing a common interest, advocating a common cause, or expressing a common passion."[21] This entails a position that is "independent of the state ... [and] occupies the space between the latter and the individual."[22]

During the 1990s, civil society was held as the great hope for democracy to take root in Algeria and the rest of the Middle East, following de Tocqueville's formulation of such groups as "schools for civic virtue."[23] This perception was maintained, even during the great violence of that decade.[24] Without any significant political transformation by the turn of the century, not to mention the cancellation of the first truly democratic elections by the military in 1992, the democratic potential of voluntary associations became increasingly questioned by scholars. For others, voluntary associations were categorized as too weak or too divided to make any meaningful change. One argument was that effective political transformation is stifled by the corrupt patronage networks that hold up authoritarian regimes.[25] During the Arab uprisings of 2011, Algerian voluntary associations were criticized for their lack of coherence and for their weak response. Then again, they were criticized by the regime for not having prevented enough trouble.[26] For example, if civil society is viewed as the intermediary between society and the state then it can be blamed by the government for not managing public discontent. As one Algerian MP put it, "The associative movement was not able to manage the riots that broke out in January [2011], it is not listening to citizens. It does not even exist, because the state has locked this field for many years under the pretext of the black decade."[27] In turn, the Algerian populace was very resistant to seeing yet more violence and instability, even though many were disgusted by state corruption and lack of basic services despite quite considerable oil wealth.

In his comprehensive analysis of Algerian associations, Liverani argues that rather than supporting a democratic transition, state strategy was to permit a limited form of civil society to perform the tasks of administering the social services that the state was failing to provide.[28] Thus, when social services continued to break down, civil society could be scapegoated. Leca contests Liverani's depiction of the Algerian government as a "weak state," explaining that while Algerians generally may not have faith in the government per se, governed solely by the National Liberation Front (FLN) party, they proudly believe in the state as a national representation of collective identity.[29]

In direct contrast, a handful of scholars have recently argued that in the absence of political parties and any true opposition, voluntary associations do create a space in which politics is enacted. Butcher challenges criticisms laid upon Algerian associations during the Arab Spring, pointing out that in reality a number of associations from different backgrounds, both Islamist and secular, which formed the National Coordination for Change and Democracy, achieved several significant goals.[30] This included the Algerian League of Human Rights, cultural organizations, student bodies, trade unions, and groups of activists and intellectuals. This platform called for political reform, and, in response, the government ended the state of emergency that had been in place since 1992. In fact, Algeria has a long history of religious and local community-based, collective decision-making and associational activism. The FLN itself, in its rise to power after the 1962 war of independence, was heavily reliant on associative connections during its early formation.[31] Later, however, the party, under the narrative of unification, refused to accept political plurality and conflict, and thus freedom of association became extremely limited. The associative sphere was reopened in 1988 following popular protests and riots, under the condition that voluntary associations were forbidden under Article 40 from engaging in formal politics and challenging the state. Since then, voluntary associations have exploded, with over 93,000 organizations currently covering activities such as sports, disability, unemployment, neighborhood groups, and farmer's collectives.

In the same vein, Northey demonstrates how cultural heritage associations challenge state narratives regarding the unitary ethnic and religious identity formed during its nation-building project as Arab and Islamic, which ignores groups such as the Amazigh, who played an essential role in the anticolonial war.[32] Northey argues that these associations function according to democratic principles that are inclusive and tolerant. Importantly, she argues that associations "do not necessarily need to directly oppose the government to contribute to political reform."[33] In other words, they create pressure upon government structures, constituting an informal political activity. While some civil society leaders go on to run for office in town councils, associations create a space for public engagement through the enactment of voluntary relations and tolerance of different opinions under the aegis of common goals, thereby creating the possibility of more inclusive social structures.

While voluntary associations in Algeria have a history of direct involvement in politics, today, due to prohibitions, they may not engage in overt political activities such as forming parties. Even though the Algerian government tried to prevent all associational activity, it was forced to concede to the wishes of the population, which occurred during an inflection point when its rentier economy was weak due to low oil prices.[34] Since then, the regime has conceded only minor reforms, rather than any significant changes.

The massive protests that unseated president Bouteflika in April 2019 were called off on March 20, 2020 due to the COVID-19 pandemic, after 57 straight weeks of demonstrations.[35] Protestors, who gathered every Tuesday and Friday called for a complete overhaul of the political system. This led to something of a stand-off between military Chief of Staff Ahmed Gaid Salah, widely seen as the most powerful figure in Algeria, and the protestors. In July 2019, opposition parties and activists, dubbed the National Forum for Dialogue, called for independent civilian rule. However, Salah denounced the call as a "false slogan" created by people who are "repugnant to the smooth running of the constitutional process."[36] The military, as the most historically powerful institution in Algeria, with an operating budget of $10 billion, is unlikely to cede power willingly. Moreover, it has a political calculus to make now that it has experienced the loss of its previously high popular approval, coming into the foreground of the political stage and thus becoming accountable. Either it installs a puppet leader, which is unlikely to be accepted by the populace; retreats to the background and keeps an eye on a new independently elected regime, who may attempt to gain control over the military and its budget, something never achieved before by government; or attempts to crack down on the protestors—which has already begun by proxy through the police security services. If the Algerian populace does not achieve wholesale transformation of the ruling elite, which I argue is unlikely, what other avenues are there for enacting change, other than protests and revolution? Below, I present the case for gradual change by means of voluntary associations that have the potential to transform everyday power relations in Algerian thought and practice.

Gradual Institutional Change

In contrast to scholarship that characterizes societal change in abrupt terms, Mahoney and Thelen propose a theory of gradual institutional change "grounded in a power-distributional view of institutions that emphasizes ongoing struggles within but also over prevailing institutional arrangements."[37] According to this view, stability and change are closely linked: institutional stability is a result not just of positive feedback loops but of sustained political mobilization. This vulnerable status is ongoing, not only during crisis events. Some examples of institutions that evolve over time, rather than those that emerge and collapse, include constitutions and property rights arrangements.

Similarly, in cultural terms, Das argues that societies are not reproduced by unthinking repetition and static tradition,[38] as posited by Badiou and Bourdieu,[39] but rather constitute sites of maintenance and care. Badiou denigrates the everyday as a site of change, which he claims consists of a passive acquiescence to the conditions of life. He argued that only an event, such as revolution in Algeria, can break allegiance to socially inherited obligations so as to become historically significant.[40] For Badiou then, change is generated by the transformational potential of a transcendent moment over the static force of the immanent, in turn making history. If, however, we take the everyday not as a given but as a site of contested forces—of groups struggling for resources and representation—then continuity of social ties is not a given.[41] This means that institutions exist at various degrees of vulnerability, more or less ripe for change rather than continuation. This presents an alternative to the normative discourse on the resilience of institutions that is common today.[42]

What is less clear is how change may arise from within, who or what these change agents are, and the variables that are affected.[43] Drawing on Mahoney and Thelen, I outline four modes of gradual institutional change: 1) displacement, where existing institutions or rules are replaced by others; 2) layering, where institutions change from the introduction of new rules alongside old ones; 3) drift, involving the dissonance created by the gap between the existing rules and changes in the world; and 4) conversion, where the ambiguity of existing rules are interpreted differently.[44] Displacement can be abrupt in the replacement of one system by another; this can include revolutions, but it can also lead to layering as a gradual process whereby new institutions directly compete with older ones, rather than adding to them. This has been in the case in Ghardaïa, as I illustrate below, with new associations emerging alongside village councils. Drift is when rules stay the same, but their impact changes according to changes in the environment. This can happen when actors choose to ignore a change in the world—for example, if parties choose not to respond to population shifts in electoral districts, with calculated inaction leading to a particular outcome. However, this can also be passive, such as when monarchies fail to change with the times and are replaced by republics or are entirely removed and made obsolete. There is some potential for this to occur in Algeria with the protest movement. Finally, conversion is when the rules remain the same, but are interpreted differently. The difference between rules and their implementation here is not one of neglect in the context of a different environment; instead, the gap is produced by actors actively exploiting ambiguities within the system.

To gauge change we must also pay attention to both the characteristics of the existing institutions and the political context. For example, does the political context support defenders of the status quo? And does the institution allow for actor discretion in the interpretation of rules? In situations where agents of change are faced with strong veto, displacement possibilities will be limited, as will active conversion. In this case, drift and layering present more optimal strategies to effect change, as these do not involve a direct challenge to existing structures. Regarding layering, those with veto powers may be able to prevent changes to existing institutions, but will be unable to block new ones.

When it comes to progress on theorizing cultural change, Marshall Sahlins' work has been of foremost importance. While many anthropologists have long abandoned the culture concept due to its connotations of bounded, unchanging societies in light of the effects of history, Sahlins has added to the disciplines of both history and anthropology by offering several important models of change that do not sacrifice strong models of culture (and which retain a strong flavor of structuralism). His most well-known contribution is based on a study of the effects of cultural contact by Captain Cook on the Hawaiian Islanders; the latter believing the former to be an incarnation of their god Lono, thus interpreting the event according to their cultural categories rather than experiencing it as a form of rupture.[45] This constituted a form of change that came from outside the system, however, and Sahlins' critics were left wondering how a strong cultural theory of change could be conceptualized from *within* a system, one that did not involve such radical cultural discontinuity. In response, Sahlins developed two models of endogenous change.[46] The first was named, after Bateson, complementary schismogenesis, where groups that start off sharing a cultural background gradually differentiate from each other, leading to cultural change. Sahlins defines this as "competition by contradictions, in which each side organizes itself as the inverse of the other."[47] In this identity politics, "it is the culturally shaped understandings people possess about themselves and others that leads them to modify their own culture in relation to a negative example."[48] Sewell differs from Sahlins by arguing that change can only arise from an extra-cultural source, where transformation originates from individuals who interpret cultural rules differently, or experience creativity in times of cultural breakdown.[49] Sahlins responds to state that "individual idiosyncrasies only gain a foothold on cultural process in situations that have themselves been *culturally* prepared for them to do so."[50] Therefore, it is not that culture has stopped functioning, but that cultural categories have become so explicit that actors are able to aim not only at achieving their private goals, but to modify the categories themselves. I return to these ideas in light of the ethnographic material that I present below, where I illustrate how received cultural traditions (e.g., religious hierarchies or the hegemony of the merchant elite) are seen among Algerian Mozabites not as God-given but socially constructed, and therefore malleable and contestable.

This chapter presents a form of gradual institutional change (related to the environment), through the efforts of voluntary associations as micro-social movements. I posit that these movements have structural effects, in terms of culture (ideas and values), and social and material organization (distribution), which are deeply intertwined. This theorization also departs from neo-Gramscian notions of counter-hegemony: what is sought by micro-social movements is not, in this case, an overthrow of the current status quo (local or state) by the subaltern, but a subtler, non-zero-sum shift, where peasants and their knowledge systems achieve greater recognition and legitimacy.

Tazdait Agricultural Association, Ghardaïa, Algeria

The desert city of Ghardaïa lies 400 miles south of Algiers, on the inner edge of the Sahara Desert. Its original inhabitants, the Mozabites, have lived there since the first millennium AD. They are ethnically Imazighen (Berbers; sing. Amazigh) who practice the Ibadi form of Islam. They are now outnumbered by Chamba Arabs, among others, and the total population is around 300,000 for all ethnic groups combined. The majority of Mozabites are merchants, from small shopkeepers to large factory owners, but many practice numerous other professions in a range of expert and manual fields. Peasant farmers, landless agriculturalists, and local agronomists are considered here.

Mozabites, along with other Imazighen, have historically experienced a difficult relationship with the Algerian state and in other North African nations, further complicated by their religious differences. Contested relations with overarching authorities, however, go back centuries, as Mozabites have negotiated various degrees of sovereignty from successive waves of rulers, including the Ottomans and the French. A tenet of Ibadi faith, known as *barā'a*,[51] holds that if the political authority of the day is held as illegitimate—on moral or political grounds—then members can withdraw their support. The M'zab eventually decided to support and nominally integrate with the Algerian nation-state after debate between conservative and progressive factions. This outcome was based largely on strategic and ideological grounds; the formation of the Algerian republic with an explicitly Islamic identity meant that the Mozabites could relate to this authority on grounds of common values. This point is important to this study as it provides the background to how Mozabites commonly relate to power. *Barā'a* can be translated as dissociation, while its opposite is *walaya* (association).[52] These notions can refer to both spiritual and political stances towards another individual or group.

Before describing some of the voluntary associations in the region, it is important to briefly outline how Mozabite society functioned in the past in order to understand how and which elements of society are changing. Mozabite society was traditionally organized according to theocratic and patriarchal principles. Once a part of the successful cosmopolitan Rustamid dynasty in North Africa (777–909 AD), upon being sacked by the Fatamids, the group finally settled in the M'zab valley, present day Ghardaïa, around 1011 AD. Despite a strongly egalitarian ethos, Mozabite society is highly hierarchical, with the smallest unit—the extended household—presided over by the family patriarch. Households are organized according to *'ashā'ir* (sing. *'ashīra*, meaning ten), similar to the concept of "clan." These are usually made up of more than ten households, represented by male heads, collectively named after a common ancestor. The *'ashīra* are responsible for assisting the common interest of the group, such as with marriages, funerals, redistribution of funds, and housing for the poor. Redistribution may be done through the *'ashīra* council, or directly by wealthy families to poorer ones. Women also have their own separate *'ashīra* meetings.

Beyond this, several *'ashā'ir* are grouped into *'arūsh* (sing. *'arsh*) or tribes. The *'arsh* as vestiges of tribal units rarely meet; instead, from each *'ashīra* certain wealthy, powerful male heads make up the *majlis ayyen* (council of notables). This group deals essentially with administrative issues at the town level, and today form a link in the chain of national governance between local and regional municipal councils. Previously, senior to them was the *halqa 'azzāba* ("the circle of saints")—the clerisy that previously held moral and disciplinary authority, who today retain only moral authority. Punishment for infractions used to be meted out by the *'azzāba* in the form of *tebria* (Tumzabt form of the Arabic *barā'a*)—temporary social ostracism or excommunication.

This overall political organization was accurately described as a theocracy. The loss of power of the ʿazzāba is largely due to the fact that upon national integration elite groups began to ignore any pronouncement of tebria and instead looked to the state legal system for justice.[53] Merchant elites have maintained a different form of hierarchy, displacing religion with capital as the paramount value and practice. However, today the effects of voluntary associations may be subtly countering this hegemony.

The Tazdait (date palm in Tamazight) association was formed primarily for the purpose of safeguarding the livelihoods of date palm climbers. Date palms are a cultural keystone species for many in North Africa,[54] such as the M'zab, where I undertook twelve months of ethnographic fieldwork during 2012–13. Date palms require significant intervention, involving hand pollination and thinning, in order to produce an effective yield. Local knowledge and expertise regarding the date palm and its cultivation is dwindling as new generations are drawn to the petrochemical sector and other vocations with perceived higher status, but also greater income, generating potential for both skilled and unskilled work. Tazdait was spawned during a five-year participatory management program for the genetic diversity of date palms in the Maghreb in 2005 by Bioversity International and funded by the United Nations Development Program Global Environmental Finance (UNDP-GEF) program. Farmers and date palm climbers—the latter also known as phoeniciculteurs—who participated in this initiative decided to continue it themselves, thus forming Tazdait. The primary role of Tazdait was to protect and valorize phoeniciculteur livelihoods and knowledge, and to protect date palms against the deadly disease bayoud, which has devastated much of Morocco's date industry. Tazdait has around eleven members made up of tree climbers and agronomists. However, as association leader, Belhadj Tirrichine, told me, Tazdait needed to act as an agent of change in Mozabite society, albeit not one aimed at upsetting the status quo—i.e., the overarching hegemony of the merchant class—but at gradually altering social organization to be more inclusive. This was due to the fact that Tirrichine was highly aware of local sensibilities and sought a more subtle shift in Mozabite thinking and organization rather than radical change that could upset the local conservative ethos.

Voluntary associations are organized very differently and cut across traditional clan-based structures, which are generally hierarchical and less inclusive. Positions such as president, secretary, treasurer, and so on are chosen through voting. I was present during one of these sessions in 2013, which took place in a ʿashīra house. The yearly finances were reported to the group members, after which a local research project on local medicinal plants was presented, and finally the elections were held. The affair was quite informal: a name would be suggested, and the members would vote yes or no, although in practice everyone agreed with the suggestions made. In practice, it was stated that there was a lack of young people represented in the election, and older members expressed worry about the renewal of the association. Therefore, young people were encouraged and cajoled into positions, such as vice treasurer and so on.

Tazdait receives funding from Biodiversity Exchange and Dissemination of Experiences (BEDE) based in Montpellier, France, and is audited regularly by a development professional to ensure proper use of funds. I attended one of these meetings. The development professional informed me that Tazdait was successful compared to other farming associations in Algeria due to several factors: they are proactive in searching for funding; they network with other regional or international groups and exchange ideas; they have a diverse membership comprising of individuals with different skills, such as research; and there is interaction with youth in the form of students.

Tazdait relates to other farming groups across the Maghreb, including Tunisia, Morocco, Mauritania, Chad, and Niger, under the umbrella organization Réseau Associatif de Développement Durable des Oasis (RADDO). The RADDO headquarters are located in the Association for the Protection of the Environment at Beni Isguen in Ghardaïa (APEB). It is an externally funded NGO that works to provide a network between different farmer groups across the Maghreb, working primarily on oasis issues. APEB is led by Salah Ba Ali, who also happened to sit on the *majlis ayyen*, thus providing a bridge between new and older local organizational structures. Some of the problems APEB are currently working on include adaptation to climate change, promotion of "responsible" tourism, integrated management of water resources, and the economic development of oases.

Arguably, the success of Tazdait stems from the fact that it has always created locally achievable goals, such as publishing an important book on local phoeniciculteur knowledge.[55] Also, through the support of BEDE, they have secured the assistance of Petzel, a company that makes mountain climbing harnesses, who agreed to work with Tazdait to design innovative harnesses for phoeniciculteurs, for whom falls constitute a real livelihood risk. Future Tazdait projects include developing further security for phoeniciculteurs, such as insurance, but also research and investment into animal traction for increasing crop production, creating a blacksmith's shop, and entering the fair-trade movement for local produce.

Another voluntary agricultural group in the M'zab is Faddān, an association of farmers that was also originally established to disseminate scientific information. According to a founding member of Faddān, the organization devolved from its original purpose of sharing knowledge to one that served a practical function—that of administrating a 450m-deep collective well. Such state-drilled wells have had beneficial effects, but not all outcomes have been positive. For one, many residents complain that the electricity from the communal pump is too expensive ($3DZD/m^3$). Payment of the bill is a collective responsibility, and therefore if one member fails to pay, the electricity is shut off with the result that none of the farmers have access to water until it is paid. It may be the case that certain farmers struggle to raise the monthly funds, but I was informed that in fact it was wealthier individuals, "hobby farmers" not reliant on agricultural income but with other revenue streams, who were more unlikely to pay the water bills. These individuals have less to lose if they fail to water their fields. Some farmers have individual wells to supplement the state well, but these are costly to drill and are not as deep. In Ntissa, there is no water catchment such as the ancient irrigation system in the oasis, therefore farmers are more reliant on the cooperative management of the deep well. When well water is cut off, farmers are forced to prioritize which crops to water, leaving other crops to wilt and die.

Associations organized solely on egalitarian, voluntary principles suffer certain problems that hierarchical ones do not, including coordination and enforcement.[56] For example, cooperation among farmers may be strained when individuals do not consult the others when performing actions that affect the collective. There are no formal coercion mechanisms due to the voluntary nature of associations, and so arguments and feuds may go on for some time, with serious matters requiring litigation through the intervention of the municipal council. Regarding making payments on time, there is little pressure that individuals can exert on one another, and because meetings are infrequent (about twice a year), some individuals prefer simply to go it alone to avoid the headache involved in having to negotiate with others.

Other associations, such the *djem'āt al ḥei* (the neighborhood associations), deal with problems such as adequate running water and electricity, and the upkeep of roads. Problems are made known to a *cartier* (president), who then informs the city council. Some oversight responsibilities overlap, and therefore conflict exists with other local institutions that have traditionally managed such problems, such as the *'ashīra*. As Bechir, a local town-planning student informed me, the neighborhood association:

... is different from the 'ashīra, because in the latter, everyone is part of a family group. The former group is comprised of different relations, of classmates and neighbors, non-blood relations. It is a relatively new thing, and it speaks to an Islamic sense of community. There is also the Protection for the Non-Material Patrimony in the M'zab Valley (OPVM). All men are expected to participate one night a week; it is a part of social duty and benefits. What is unique about APEB is that it is part run by the state and part local. That is, there is the agreement from the state, but it is run in a locally accepted, familiar way. Normally it takes time to trust something new, but here it is trusted because it is done in a locally accepted way, a friendly way. It is not done in a top-down manner, but with rules given by relatives, and therefore more acceptable to people.[57]

However, some confusion can arise between old and new institutions, as Nejib, a local farmer confided to me:

> There is no coordination, especially about who has responsibility over infra-structure issues. Thus, there may be conflict between 'ashīra and neighborhood associations, conflict between 'ashā'ir, and conflict between rich and poor neighborhoods, vis-a-vis respective projects. In the past, when the 'ashīra ordered someone to do something they used to do it. Now there are over fifty associations in Beni Isguen, there is no coordination, it is anarchy. They need the experience of running them over time, a new system.[58]

In his statement, Nejib highlighted a key distinction—that of authority—between the new and old institutions. Previously, traditional groups could give orders, or punish if orders were not followed, because local authority, whether based on religion, gender, age, or wealth, was respected. In the family, age—which involved the replacement of one generation by the next—was key, whereas relations between the genders was and still is immutable (although, of course, elder women exercised power over the younger women). Between families, the authority of the 'ashīra—made up of family heads—was observed, although the wealthy members held most influence. The 'azzāba held absolute authority over all matters, and, finally, L'oumna (the faithful), who oversaw water, building, date palms, and other communal matters, were in fact a kind of police force who derived their power to impose fines from the mosque.

Although voluntary associations are not supposed to use their clout to meddle in state policy—that is, to form unions or political parties—some of the associations were cautiously political. In fact, those I spoke to remarked that they did apply pressure—through their leaders—on the local council in order to improve roads and public services. I interviewed an association president, Mohamed Brik, from the nearby city of Laghouat about this issue. He related how he gathered a petition from twenty-five landowners and emailed it to the local council after a bridge was closed, forcing raw sewage into the river.

> The Ministry for Public Works built the new bridge over the river. They sealed it off, however, with large cans. The people on the other side had to drive down over the river. There was sewage running into the river. One day, I saw a kid hanging out of a car window, almost falling into the dirty water. I decided to write to the council with a petition of twenty-five landowners who lived on the other side of the river, and copied in other officials [on the email]. The official was away that day in Algiers, but his secretary called him and they decided in a rush to open the bridge the next day. When this worked, people asked me to intervene on other things, like being hassled by the gendarmes, but I refused, there must be a limit![59]

Brik related another case concerning a man who worked at the town hall and whose job it was to oversee building projects to prevent illegal and informal structures:

> He was killed during the violence of the 1990s, and it is not known if he was killed by Islamists or if someone he had fined took revenge. Now, there are environmental police at the town hall, but they do nothing. For example, when someone started building an illegal enterprise, a concrete silo on local farming land, they thought he was building a chicken coop. He started writing letters, and the gendarmes came and asked him for his permit, which he did not have. They moved him on, but the trouble was that, in the time they took to respond, he had already laid the foundations. We are the watchers, however, and I am not afraid to put my name on a document. The area is legally restricted to agricultural activities, thus there is a need for local monitoring ... So, activities in the area must be compatible, otherwise I will campaign against them.[60]

This story shows the importance of leadership in organizing campaigns to pressure the state. The state has attempted to extend its influence through other administrative means,[61] such as changing the regulations or making accounting rules more complex, to make it harder for certain troublesome groups. In September 2013, the state changed the rules again, requiring detailed accounts going back to the previous three years, along with other more stringent requirements.

These examples illustrate changes in the configuration of Mozabite society, with associations arguably emerging to fill the governance void left by the decline of the religious authority, the ʿazzāba. These voluntary groups appear to serve an adaptive function that is better suited to changes associated with modernity in contrast to the traditional institutions that served to maintain the status quo. Despite, or perhaps because of, their voluntary, inclusive nature, associations are not without problems, especially when it comes to dealing with individuals who have different interests, such as those who do not rely primarily on agriculture for their income. In the next section, by returning to the theory of gradual cultural change, I suggest that the very presence, and sometimes actions, of these associations constitute a form of informal politics, which in turn influences the way people think about social relations and issues of power.

Gradual Cultural Change and Informal Environmental Politics

It is clear that, despite restrictions, civil society is growing rapidly in Algeria. The timing of this emergence in the M'zab was concurrent with the relaxing of state laws around civil society at the end of the 1980s. Clan structures once managed disputes around land succession rules and physical infrastructures by reference to custom and scripture. The present proliferation of voluntary associations is taking over that role by referring to notions of justice and equality. I make this claim on the basis that, while tribal councils are good at maintaining the status quo, voluntary associations appear to be better at dealing with changing conditions in relation to the new expectations, values, and hopes that have come with the effects of globalization and a vision of a more just future. However, the new freedom of choice that has come with liberal modernity is seen by some Algerians as an attack on certain religious values, and is, therefore, a matter of debate. There are some problems related to collective governance and authority, for example, that voluntary associations have not yet resolved, such as how to enforce collective decisions, and even how to achieve common ground among groups with different identities, needs, and interests.

By locating the themes of this study in the realm of rural social movements, this chapter adds to the theory on social movements. However, it differs from other literature that places politics in either formal, civil structures, or informal, non-collective resistance movements, instead focusing on a gradual source of cultural change from below.[62] This is, therefore, not revolutionary change or simple reform, but change from the grassroots level—a "slow politics" akin to the slow food movement.[63] Here, the idea of change is motivated by a need for greater justice and dignity without overthrowing the local and national elite through direct contestation. As the local elite is part of the same minority ethnic group, the Mozabites, the goal is to become stronger without taking the power of the other. This is not then a zero-sum game, but is made with alliances from outside the M'zab valley, as well as from Algeria as a whole. This is a new gamble for Mozabite associations, as, historically, alliances have always been made within the boundaries of M'zab ethnicity and kinship.

Tilly and Wood, in their summation of aspects common to all social movements, list: 1) identity claims (e.g., we are Berber/Saharan farmers/environmentalists); 2) assertions for standings (e.g., the work of farmers is important for human and ecosystem health); and 3) program claims (e.g., legal recognition of environmental customary law).[64] Informal environmental politics fall under the first two categories, while the third would fall under formal politics. I suggest that voluntary associations constitute a micro form of social movement where change is created slowly and gradually rather than by radical shocks, and originates internally rather than from outside. How does this form of change fit with the aforementioned theories of Mahoney and Thelen, and Sahlins? And does this constitute individual agency or a more complex adjustment of cultural categories in relation to wider structural shifts?

To recap, Mahoney and Thelen provide a typology of four forms of gradual change: displacement, layering, drift, and conversion.[65] Their use of this typology should be clarified: according to the empirical material I have presented here, drift might first explain how traditional institutions such as the 'azzāba have become obsolete, as they have not adjusted to changes in the world. However, the concept of layering better explains the changes observed in Ghardaïa, as new associations have not displaced the old structures outright. According to Mahoney and Thelen's typology, however, layering comes from within institutions as new rules leave the old ones outmoded instead of directly challenging them (as in displacement). Yet again, the present constellation of social relations may not in fact represent a clear-cut, linear progression of the replacement of old groups by new ones, but instead may present an example of mixed modes of organization. This snapshot of life in Algeria arguably represents a hybrid form of local governance that mixes hierarchy and egalitarianism; exclusiveness and inclusivity; shari'a, Roman, and customary law; and neoliberal labor markets and mutual aid where labor is reciprocally shared. It is beyond the scope of this chapter to examine the question of whether these apparently contradictory forms are mutually exclusive or if they bleed into one another. Thus, layering presents the best theoretical framework for how gradual change is taking place today in Ghardaïa, where new institutions exist alongside older ones, gradually replacing them without confronting them directly.

Turning to questions of agency, does change come in extra-cultural terms from the creativity of individuals during moments of cultural breakdown? Robbins, using Sahlins' models of strong cultural change,[66] argues that in the case of Papua New Guinea society, individuals experienced humiliation due to the perceived technological advancement and material wealth of Westerners. In the M'zab, while individuals, especially youth, describe embarrassment regarding their culture in the light of experiencing others—whether through encounters experienced elsewhere in urban Algeria or Europe, or those portrayed by mass media—they still safeguard their cultural heritage and are proud of it. That UNESCO listed Ghardaïa as a World Heritage Site in 1982 has helped to bolster this sense of pride.[67] Yet, this does not prevent Mozabites from debating different ways of being an authentic Muslim, or a morally just member of society. Bourdieu, after visiting the M'zab, attributed this to a cultural periphery that was malleable, encompassing a cultural core of the local culture that cannot be corrupted or changed.[68] Whether this is the case is hard to prove, and a generation of social scientists has since attempted to characterize global cultural changes in terms of hybridization and creolization in arguing against the idea that the world is gradually moving toward cultural homogenization or "McDonaldization."[69]

Anthropologists have pointed out for some time that cultures are not discontinuous (bounded) in space and continuous in time (enduring), but instead have been continuous in space (intermixing) and discontinuous in time (changing).[70] Recently, scholars working on themes of globalization have utilized concepts such as syncretization and hybridization; however, critics argue that these terms explain very little as to how this process of hybridization actually happens and which elements are involved. The details of how culture actually changes are glossed over. Referring to the debates on cultural hybridization, Amselle points out that "'mestizo logics' details no logics at all, it just claims that things were mixed."[71] Some aspects of this may be clarified regarding Mozabite culture, however. In terms of principles, Mozabites are emphatic that certain details or rules of life that are mentioned in the Qur'an are settled; these can be isolated as core unchanging elements, at least for the less ambiguous writings. However, issues that arise in the world that are not established in the Qur'an are open to interpretation and can be characterized as both drift and conversion—where drift concerns a mismatch between institutions and the world, and conversion entails the reinterpretation of ambiguous rules. Central Mozabite cultural values include fidelity to one's religion, family, and society, as well as a strong work ethic. These constitute a particular constellation of values around relationality, specifically concerning correct moral relations between people, and between self and God. The encounter with "Western" liberal values, which arguably centers on the sovereignty or personal freedom and rights of the individual, corresponds with the period in which the merchant elite overtook the religious leadership in the M'zab.[72] Many Mozabites today complain about the rise of individualism and selfishness, especially among the wealthy, many of whom no longer engage in charitable works in society; among spoiled youth that no longer work; and among individuals engaging in conspicuous consumption by wearing nontraditional clothes or driving expensive cars—all of which are regarded as new characteristics of society.

But are voluntary associations a form of social organization alien to Mozabite culture? And are they being used to counter strains of selfish individualism? Regarding the former, probably not. It might be argued that civil society itself is a foreign concept that was first formally introduced to Algeria by the French. Furthermore, my interlocutors in the M'zab mentioned that they were inspired to continue the associations that had been initiated by the UNDP-GEF project. However, as a system of values, radical egalitarianism was a core principle of Amazigh culture that likely informed the choice of Ibadism as both a religious and political choice, as it supports the idea of ethnic inclusiveness (according to Ibadism, individuals from any ethnic groups could become Caliph, not only Arabs, during a time when Arabs were dominant over non-Arab Muslims).[73] In fact, Entelis argues that North African Amazigh had a tendency toward heretical forms of the invading religions, as they took up the Donatist form of Christianity previously (and later Arianism from the Vandals in the fifth century), probably as a form of political protest.

Representativeness is also present in Mozabite society, as Amazigh councils must include members from each family, or from the preceding level at the higher levels of governance. However, participation and inclusion of women, youth, and poorer classes, such as peasants, is arguably new compared with the hierarchy and patriarchy of the past. Women and men are not allowed to join the same voluntary associations, although women continue to participate in their own formal and informal associations, both traditional and new. This then supports a theory of hybridization, as individuals reflexively inspect their own cultural categories and add new elements to existing categories while discarding others. The evidence certainly does not present a case of cultural collapse, global homogenization, or McDonaldization.

Associational life in Algeria, which I suggest comprises a social micromovement, with its shared goals, clearly differs from Asef Bayat's social "nonmovements."[74] Bayat characterizes the latter as the collective endeavors of many non-collective actors embodying the shared practices of large numbers of ordinary people whose fragmented but similar activities trigger social change, even though these practices are rarely guided by an ideology or recognizable leaderships. The activity of associations in Algeria bears some relation to the quotidian informal politics in the associative sphere among farmers, agronomists, and environmentalists for conserving the environmental and cultural heritage in the desert oases of Ghardaïa by the Mozabites. Rather than mass movements, I theorize the action of voluntary associations as enacting gradual political change by changing cultural beliefs, thoughts, and practices. I term these groups as microsocial movements, as they take place at the micropolitical level within societies. By reforming relations along voluntary, inclusive lines, these organizations reformulate power relations away from traditional patriarchy. Despite being banned from challenging the state, the collective nature of these groups enables them to push for political action, especially regarding the demand for basic service provision and policy reform.

Conclusion

I have argued that voluntary associations are inherently political, albeit in an informal sense, due to their constituent nature as collectives, despite being banned from engaging in overt political activity by the Algerian state. Furthermore, voluntary associations appear to be restructuring hierarchical social relations toward more inclusive ones. While I claim, based on my observations and conversations, that this is taking place in the M'zab valley, I do not claim that this is taking place across the Middle East more generally. Other states hold a more pessimistic view of voluntary associations—such as in Morocco, where too often they consist of nothing more than hollow platforms for aspiring politicians.[75] The phenomenon of voluntary associations providing a space for democratic practice in Algeria is at least attested to by scholars such as Butcher and Northey; here, political activity can be either aspirational, in terms of inclusiveness, or actual, in terms of directly challenging the state.

I have chosen to term voluntary associations as microsocial movements to reflect that they may be more adept at dealing with change than conventional, formal political structures in the Beni Isguen, which may be more concerned with upholding the status quo. Indeed, Kerri presents a similar conception for voluntary associations.[76] To conclude, rather than a linear progression from traditional, hierarchical forms of governance to modern, democratic ones, the present composition reveals the continued existence of several mixed forms of political behavior: authoritarian (still to some degree the family, the *'ashīra*, the *'azzāba*, and the state); liberal market-driven, competitive behavior (the labor market, mercantile selling of goods, consumption of goods and services); and consensus-based egalitarian decision-making (associations). The existence of these mixed modes of governance could be seen as evidence of a society in transition, as newer forms gradually replace old ones. Instead of the eclipse of the "traditional" by a monolithic modernity, however, along with Pascon,[77] I would argue that this hybrid composition in fact constitutes a locally negotiated form of modernity itself.[78] The fact that Mozabite voluntary associations can challenge the hierarchy of the local elites, not by violence or even direct conflict, but by simply doing things differently—by organizing in inclusive, voluntary ways and achieving results—provides a compelling case for an informal politics of social change.

8

PERILOUS ADVENTURES

WOMEN AND CIVIL SOCIETY PARTICIPATION IN IRAN

Shahla Haeri[1]

The women's movement has been challenging Iran's male-dominated establishment for several years ... politicians now see educated and powerful women as a threat.[2]

Introduction

At the threshold of the fortieth anniversary of the establishment of the Islamic Republic in Iran, Parvaneh Salahshouri, a woman representative in the tenth Majlis (the Iranian parliament), articulated the pervasive social and political malaise in the country in her public address to the parliament:

[We] live in precarious sociopolitical times. Students, lawyers, teachers, workers, women, and environmental activists are either jailed or tagged (*setare dar*).[3] Disrespect of the law is rampant, distrust is common, and violence is widespread. Our environment is polluted and social dissatisfactions are endemic.... I thought of appealing to our religious leaders (*rohaniyun*), who used to stand by the people. But unfortunately, they are now more obsessed with a few strands of women's hair and with whether or not women should ride a bicycle, than with poverty, corruption, rampant embezzlement of the public treasury, and youths' rejection of religion (*din-gurizi*).[4]

Representative Salahshouri's unprecedented 2018 public speech provoked an immediate backlash from her hardline male colleagues in parliament, and by some powerful pro-government journalists—not for her diagnosis, but for articulating it. Her action, in short, is representative of women's perilous engagement with the state and civil society in Iran.[5] From the early days of the establishment of the Islamic Republic, educated urban Iranian women have actively engaged with the state and civil society in all spheres and domains, despite the many legal and political hurdles thrown in their paths by the state's "medieval" gender policies.[6] Their activism was not initiated by the drastic sociopolitical and structural changes of 1979, however. They had engaged with civil society well before the establishment of the Islamic Republic, but not as widely.

To paraphrase Ashraf Brujerdi—a high-ranking woman in President Khatami's administration, whom I interviewed several years ago in Tehran— one might wonder how Iranian women, be they from religious or secular backgrounds,[7] have been able to transcend political and legal restrictions to emerge as a pressure group that is hard to silence or ignore. How have women succeeded in demanding, and partially achieving, political authority and representation in governmental and NGOs? How have the relations between state and society, and between women and the Islamic Republic evolved since its establishment in 1979? From the hauntingly silent solo protests of Girls of Revolution Avenue against forced veiling in 2017; to the campaign to change the masculine face of parliament in 2016; to challenging the constitutionality of preventing women from running for president; to the popular One Million Signatures campaign against discriminatory laws;[8] to films that critically highlight aspects of gender relations in Iran;[9] and to women's literary productions, books, and magazines,[10] women have made their voices heard and have engaged the state, with varying success. Despite frequent setbacks, women have persisted in demanding entrance to sporting arenas for national and international matches, and continue to found and fund women-centered NGOs. Urban educated Iranian women have, despite hardship and serious challenges, actively and persistently engaged with and participated in civil society—individually and collectively. It is this category of Iranian women that is my concern in this study.

On its part, the state, while lauding the "high status of women in Islam," and promising veiled women a secured place in paradise, dismantled the

Family Protection Law (FPL) of 1967—a move that restored polygyny and has tacitly encouraged it.[11] Additionally, the state rolled back modest legal improvements in women's status granted through FPL, reinstated a restrictive and literal version of shari'a/Shi'a personal law, limited women's professional and career options, conditioned women's travel abroad to their father's or their husband's written permission, and mandated veiling in public. The Islamic Republic's forced veiling was a delayed response to the imposition of the Unveiling Act of 1936 by Reza Shah Pahlavi (1925–41). While the latter mandated the removal of veiling in the name of modernity, the former imposed it in the name of Islam. In both cases, a woman's body became the symbolic site of forced modernization or Islamization of Iranian society. In both cases, however, many women rose to challenge the state's attempt at criminalizing women's choice of public attire, whether to veil or not to veil.

The Islamic state's gender policies, however, have not all been negative or punitive, nor have different administrations pursued the same restrictive gender policies. Here lies the specificity of the Islamic Republic's brand of ideological patriarchy that sets it apart from other similarly restrictive Islamic societies, such as Saudi Arabia and the Taliban's Afghanistan. Iranian women, for example, have neither before nor after the revolution of 1979 faced restrictions on driving their own car. Nor did the Islamic Republic ban or restrict education for women. In fact, it expanded the previously initiated national literacy drive, and embarked on an education campaign to provide universal access for women.[12] Exceptional students—male and female—are sent to various international Olympiads, and women's literary achievements are honored with prizes and awards. The constitution of the Islamic Republic supports—however minimally—women's rights to elect, and be elected to local, statewide, and national institutions,[13] notwithstanding the Ayatollah Khomeini's earlier opposition to women's suffrage in 1963.

On the other hand, according to the Islamic Republic's civil law, a woman's legal status is systematically tethered to her father's authority and her husband's caprice; her legal rights are institutionally restricted, inferior, and conditional, which limit her social capital, restrict her professional options, and control her sociopolitical mobility. The tension between Iranian women's educational and professional advancements and the glaring injustice of their legal/political inequality, becomes tangible when viewed against the background of the medieval legal/political institutions on the one hand and the vitality of civil society on the other. Article 20 of the constitution of the Islamic Republic of Iran upholds equality of men and women, but subjects it to "the Islamic requirements." Exactly what those "Islamic requirements" are is left to the subjective interpretations of the ruling male elite and the changing sociopolitical climate of the country. Women, for example, have the right to vote and be elected to parliament—granted they pass through the ideological sift of the Guardian Council's "qualification" test—but are prevented from leaving the country without the permission of their husband or father, regardless of their educational, professional achievements, and class backgrounds.[14] The combination of such conflicting sociolegal injunctions has left many educated middle-class women—and some men—in double binds. Some of the alarming end results of an increasingly modern and sophisticated civil society facing medieval legal structure and restrictive political policies have been an increase in the median age at first marriage for both men and women, and higher rates of divorce.[15]

At issue here is neither blanket state censorship, nor its supports for, or opposition to, women's associations and creative productions. There are structural incongruities and clashes of sensibilities within and between state and society; these stem primarily from the state's worldview regarding the different "nature" of men and women that in their belief necessitates separation of the domains of gender and their activities, hence state justification for unequal rights and obligations. The result is increasing tension between the government and the people, and the widening gaps between them. The present political elite's ambivalent—if not necessarily antagonistic—attitude toward women and their collective demand for autonomy and political authority fluctuates between medieval rules and regulations and the expediencies of modern necessities and sensibilities. The state's treatment of women, hence, vacillates between acknowledging them as citizens and treating them as subjects.

Such structural rigidities and fluctuating policies also shift depending on the sociopolitical pragmatics on the ground, thus rendering the relationship between state and society unpredictable and precarious. As leaders rise and fall, and as governments change, people find their daily lives suspended in webs of political rivalries and power struggles beyond their expectations and control. The contentious relationship between state and society,[16] and the precarity of women's position and status is further exacerbated by the state's international relations and global geopolitical jousting.[17] Not only is the gap between state and society widening, the state itself is besieged by internal power struggles and charges of mismanagement, corruption, and nepotism.

Against this background, a widening gap exists between women's perception of their agency, individuality, and autonomy—i.e., what they expect as a citizen of a modern state—and what the theocratic state is willing to do to accommodate "gender parity," a concept alien to a political system that espouses gender "complementarity" at best. While the political/religious elite laud women's high status granted them by Islam, it dismisses their legitimate demands for gender equality as an import from the West, spinning it thus to mean alien and inauthentic—and, ultimately, un-Islamic. Neither the state nor women are monolithic, of course. Women come from all classes, positions, ethnicities, and educational and professional backgrounds. Likewise, the male political elite is far from uniform in its worldview regarding women's roles and status, or in terms of gender relations. Nonetheless, the political/religious elite by and large view a woman not as an autonomous individual, but in relational terms, i.e., as mother, wife, sister, or daughter—a second-class citizen needing male supervision at all times, and hence as something between "subject" and "citizen." It is within this in-between and liminal existence, between subject and citizen, that the state manifests its ambivalent attitude towards women, and adopts policies rooted in fractured perspectives regarding women's autonomy, legal status, and social standing.

Iranian Women's Legal Status

Islamic family law—perceived as divinely inspired and thus "immutable"—accords certain rights and *ahliyyat* (capabilities) to men and women from birth to death. Upon adulthood, Muslim men are recognized as full-fledged individuals and are conferred full rights, which include both capacities of execution and obligation.[18] For women, however, the capacity of execution and obligation—their adulthood and autonomy—are contingent, and depend on their age and marital status, i.e., virgin, married, divorced, or widowed. Even in maturity, where and when a woman can take autonomous action—for example, dispose of her property, take a job, or travel—are all subject to the legal requirements of obligation and obedience to her father or husband.[19] Married Iranian women, no matter how advanced in their education and profession, legally need their husband's permission to leave the country, though divorced and widowed women are freed from such restriction. Children born of marriage between Iranian women and non-Iranian men are not granted Iranian citizenship, but categorized as guest residents at best, and aliens at worst. This secondary—or alien—status, however, does not apply to the children of Iranian men married to non-Iranian women.[20] Depending on their stage of development—whether a child and underage, adult and unmarried or married—an Iranian women's physical maturity is not necessarily commensurate with her legal autonomy and independence, as it is with that of men's. In other words, depending on the stage of a woman's development and marital status, a woman's legal persona and social status are marred by legal inequalities, political restrictions, and sociocultural limitations.

Despite the legal restrictions and political precarities, Iranian society has changed drastically, and women have made huge advances in their education (some of which are due to the Islamic Republic), worldviews, and activities. They are keenly aware of their twisted legal citizenship status, lopsided gender hierarchy, and political under-representation. Middle-class, educated Iranian women's subjectivity and self-perception is, by and large, influenced by modern notions of individuality and autonomy—aspects of citizenship associated with a more democratic society.[21] They are also well aware of the conflicted and tortured national discourse on gender relationships, as was highlighted in the previous pages. Before discussing women's participation in civil society within the above context, I will briefly lay out arguments surrounding civil society discourse.

Civil Society

Civil society is "an idea which points to a complex of influential associations which may create themselves within the framework of liberal states. These associations are not creatures of the state but serve to comment on it and modify it. Civil society can exist only while the state tolerates its existence."[22] Although the modern discourse of civil society is a post-Enlightenment phenomenon imported from Western societies, a plethora of volunteer associations and guilds has existed in pre-modern Iran and has been written about extensively by Ahmad Ashraf.[23] During the last decade of the twentieth century, civil society discourse was trending—much like the discourse of "fundamentalism" a decade earlier—in academic circles. It appeared to hold the key to understanding the democratization processes of societies, particularly after the disintegration of the USSR, and the liberation and independence of many Eastern European countries. As the discourse of civil society gained worldwide prominence, Mehran Kamrava argues, it became "a global *cause célèbre*, seen by academics in the West and elsewhere as the new paradigm for analyzing the destiny of nations and understanding the nature of state-society relations everywhere."[24] The history of Iranian intellectual and scholarly discourse on civil society, in his view, is both recent and "in progress."[25] Acknowledging the cultural specificities of Iranian society, Kamrava discusses the views of four contemporary intellectuals—none of whom is a woman—and argues that even the sober assessments of civil society tended to discuss it in positive terms, and "in essence, the 'cure-all' political Islam of the 1970s appears to have been replaced by the civil society of the 1990s."[26] The general assumption was that citizen participation in civil society would lead to democracy promotion and would "help to hold states accountable, represent citizen interests, channel and mediate mass concerns, bolster an environment of pluralism and trust, and socialize members to the behavior required for successful democracies."[27] Amaney Jamal, however, challenges such generalized presuppositions regarding a cause-and-effect relationship between civil society participation and democracy. She argues that civil societies function within the parameters of the existing political and social structural limitations—whether democratic or autocratic. That is to say, civil societies may not necessarily lead to fostering citizens' rights, democratic government, and political toleration—it all depends on the cultural context:

> Despite their role in Western democracies, civic associations—regardless of whether they are church societies or sports clubs—reproduce elements of the political context in which they exist and structure themselves accordingly. Where associational contexts are dominated by patron-client tendencies, associations, too, become sites for the replication of those vertical ties.[28]

In Jamal's discussion, democratization through civil society does not take place automatically, no matter how much money international organizations pour into organizations in places such as Palestine or Pakistan, where such ideals are not pragmatically maintained by the political structure, nor are they fostered among the population from early on.[29]

Similarly, Kamrava argues that in an ideologically autocratic state such as Iran, the discourse of civil societies, more often than not, tends to reproduce the same autocratic structures and attitudes that already exist within the larger society, even when it espouses a more democratic outcome. In the same vein, while the Iranian state has deliberately fostered conditions antithetical to civil society, the family did so inadvertently, though in the twenty-first century, the pattern in the latter is changing rapidly.[30] The end result is the development of a greater sense of individuality and autonomy on the part of citizens, despite the "maximalist" attitude and politics of the state that privileges community over the individual—and, by extension, male over female. Kamrava attributes four characteristics to the development of the discourse of civil society in Iran, including: indigenization of the concept of civil society by Iranian intellectuals; theorization of rule of law, which implies a primary role for the state; the gravitational pull of Islam; and the importance of self-perception, which, in his view, is the intention of the lasting consequence of the discovery of civil society in Iran.[31] Pragmatically speaking, however, the arbitrary application of the rule of law continues to pose hurdles for various NGOs, particularly those founded and managed by women.

With the election of the reformist President Muhammad Khatami in 1997, space for the creation of a multitude of women's foundations and NGOs became a possibility.[32] Women and their organizations, however, continue to be impacted by the subsequent administrations' capricious and restrictive policies. Presently, women's NGOs operate with a greater or lesser degree of success, and most of them are concentrated in Tehran.[33] In several studies conducted on women's NGOs in different parts of the country, the general conclusions point to widespread desire, and subsequent recommendations, for achieving greater democratization of civil society—hence, recommendations for greater autonomy for women. These studies underscore the significance of NGOs as the conduits for raising women's social awareness and mobility. By joining an NGO and participating in its activities, they argue, many women feel empowered and become self-confident, which in turn increases their sense of themselves, including that of their ambiguous citizenship.[34] In the following section, I discuss briefly the history of Iranian women's participation in civil society, both individually and collectively.

Historical Background

The earliest systematic recorded information we have of Iranian women's engagement with civil society dates back to Iran's Constitutional Revolution of 1906–11. Despite the paucity of data, we know of some women's public activism and social participation at the time. As one of the early founders of school for girls,[35] Bibi Khanum Esterabadi leveled a scathing criticism in her book *Mayib al-Rejal* ("Men's Defects") against her fellow countrymen, particularly those of the privileged classes.[36] Braving the sociostructural and legal restrictions on women's collective activities, Iranian middle-class and educated women have periodically come together to make common cause to engage the structures of power—sometimes successfully, other times less so. From publishing newspapers and creating educational and literary organizations to challenging the blatantly discriminatory laws and patriarchal double standards, women—either individually or collectively—rose to challenge the unequal laws, patriarchal cultural values, and social structure, demanding changes to their status and those of their fellow sisters. Parvin Etesami (1907–41), a highly talented but reclusive poet at the turn of the twentieth century, summarized gender injustice in the following powerful verses:

به هیچ مبحث و دیباچه ای قضا ننوشت
برای مرد کمال و برای زن نقصان

Nowhere in the Preface has judgment been written
That man is perfect and woman deficient.[37]

When veiling was outlawed by Reza Shah in 1936, Parvin, as she is popularly known in Iran, took issue with the stereotypical equation of veiling with piety and morality:

چشم و دل را پرده میبایست اما از عفاف
چادر پوسیده، بنیاد مسلمانی نبود

Eyes and hearts need veiling (pardeh), but one of chastity
The flimsy veil (chadur) was not meant to be the foundation of Islam.[38]

Nonetheless, the constitutional revolution bypassed granting women legal rights, though the greater accessibility of education helped to usher in a more modern awareness and sensibility for many middle-class Iranian women and men.

Major political changes in women's status were introduced in 1963 through state-directed reforms, known as the White Revolution. Women were granted the right to vote and be elected to parliament—the same set of rights that ignited Ayatollah Khomeini's objection to the Shah, which eventually led to the revolution of 1979. Meaningful legal adjustments in family law, however, did not appear until 1967/1973—though soon the establishment of the Islamic Republic effectively scuttled the Family Protection Law and prevented its effective implementation. The point to be made here is that, although the adjustments in gender relations had the blessing of the state, the increasingly educated middle-class Iranian women were actively involved in demanding, safeguarding, and exercising their legal and civil rights. Furthermore, while in the first decade or so following the revolution of 1979 women supporters of the regime acted in lockstep with the religious/political elite, many gradually went through a rethinking of their identity and agency; one that, while maintaining their piety, was distanced ideologically from that of the unequal and rigidly prescribed gender hierarchy of the Islamic Republic.

The increasing ideological inconsistencies and structural incongruities in the rhetoric and policies of the Islamic state—be they legal/political, religious, or economic—in fact helped raise women's awareness regarding the discrepancy between their legal subordination and educational achievements. Many women were active in the public domain before the revolution, with or without a veil. But faced with forced veiling, they began to "own" veiling and moved to the public domain in ever increasing numbers, and not just in the major cities. Strange though it may seem, veiling initially allowed Iranian women greater mobility and visibility by legitimating their presence outside of the domestic domain, much to the surprise and chagrin of the clerics who might have expected veiling would, as in the past, keep women secluded and bound to the private domain.[39] This does not mean that all women accepted the forced veiling. In fact, many did not. But faced with an "immovable object," they found ways to get around it and go on with their objectives: to work and to participate in civil society.[40]

Emerging from the devastating eight years of the Iran–Iraq war, President Rafsanjani (1989–97) set out to open the country economically and politically to the outside world, and thus to allow greater freedom of activities for the public. Despite his efforts to move the state policies towards moderation, however, hardliners continued to have the upper hand and hold the levers of power, including that of the Guardian Council, which vetted and approved all political candidates to the state and national political office.[41] By 2018, and almost forty years into the establishment of the Islamic Republic, the Guardian Council's lopsided supervisory authority over Iranian national elections has become a significant source of public dissatisfaction.

The *himasi* ("epic") presidential victory of Mohammad Khatami in 1997 revealed the ideological rift within the Islamic Republic, while highlighting the popular demand for democratic reforms.[42] On that occasion, Vali Nasr wrote:

> For the first time in Iran's history, democracy was at the center of political debate in Iran ... The particular focus on democracy, which was now tied in with the reform movement, was essential for the continuity and democracy, and for the cultural maturity of the democratic movement.[43]

Likewise, Noushin Ahmadi-Khorasani, a well-known activist and editor of the quarterly *Jins-e Dovvom* ("Second Sex"),[44] and also a founder of the 2006 campaign to collect "One Million Signatures" to change discriminatory family laws, underlines the inclusiveness of the democracy movement in Iran at the time, which in her view consisted of "women's movements, students' movements, workers' movements, environmental pressure groups, religious reformist movements, ethnic and religious minorities, and (other) parties and guilds."[45] It is popularly believed that the overwhelming participation of women and youth in the presidential election of 1997 resulted in the landslide victory of President Khatami. They responded enthusiastically to Khatami's call for respect for the rule of law, individual autonomy and political tolerance, and collectively women and youth helped catapult him to the presidency over the handpicked candidate of the ruling establishment.

The aftershocks of Khatami's landslide victory, his popularity, and his stress on the rule of law and respect for individual dignity rattled the religious and political elite. But by the time the euphoria of the election died down, the Islamic Republic's political rift between state and society had become apparent. Two consequential yet opposing sociopolitical currents have since dominated the state–society relation in Iran: that of women's "movements" and their male allies, and that of hardliners who hold almost all the levers of power. Khatami's election spurred the blossoming of a wide range of social, artistic, and civic activities. Women's organizations and NGOs multiplied, as did women's publications and publishers. Iranian film and cinema captured international attention, and International Women's Day was celebrated by the government and nongovernmental agencies throughout Iran. Women from various backgrounds and professions found common ground and made their voices heard. The convergence of women's groups from different backgrounds and their efforts to build alliances was disrupted, however, under the presidency of Mahmoud Ahmadinejad (2005–13). Recovering from the shock of losing so decisively to Khatami, the hardliners swiftly moved to turn the political tide and strengthen their hold on power. They clamped down on civil society and did not hesitate to frustrate Khatami's policies of openness, national toleration, global friendship, and "dialogue among nations." Even though women and women's organizations came under attack during Mr. Ahmadinejad's administration, "the windows had been opened up, and women moved out of the dark corners (*pastu*) of their homes. They could no longer be pushed back," as a high-ranking woman activist told me in Tehran. It is within this history of politically turbulent and tumultuous state–society relations that I discuss women's NGOs and their individual and collective civil participation in Iran.

NGOs

NGOs have specific definitions and are generally associated with post-Enlightenment, Western industrial societies. What distinguishes modern NGOs from other comparable associations that have historically existed in many European and non-Western societies is the degree of NGOs' autonomy and independence from the state, and their ability to influence a functioning democracy. In that sense, although many guilds and volunteer associations existed in pre-modern Iran, they were not necessarily free from arbitrary interventions by the autocratic states.[46] The establishment of NGOs in their modern form and function is rather new in the Islamic Republic of Iran—with the exception of a few associations, such as the Center for Hemophilia (1964) and the Children's Book Council of Iran (1965). Known as *sazman-hay-e mardum nahad* (SAMAN) in Iran, NGOs are recognized under Article 26 of the Constitution of the Islamic Republic as autonomous and independent associations so long as they do not contravene "the basis of the Islamic Republic."[47] No one, the law further stipulates, can be forced to participate in or be denied association. The laws and regulations that affect the NGO sector, however, are numerous, unclear, and contradictory.[48] In practice, the state's attitude towards NGOs is, more often than not, subjective and ambivalent—particularly toward women's organizations, unless they are geared toward charitable religious objectives. Even then, such associations are not immune to the "maximalist" state's control and periodic arbitrary interventions.[49] Some NGOs, particularly those focusing on gender and sexual matters, such as AIDS or sexually transmitted diseases (STDs), are not only under the close scrutiny of the state, they also receive less assistance and contributions from the general public. Specifically, the political/religious elite takes a dim view of organizations that draw attention to women and not to the family as a whole, which is the focus of the stated and unstated policies of the government and the state. The NGOs are forbidden from getting any direct financial support from international organizations unless it is from a United Nations agency and unless it has the blessing of the state.[50] Consequently, no collaboration exists—or is allowed to exist—between international women's NGOs and their Iranian counterparts, unlike in other Muslim societies such as Pakistan or Afghanistan.

Under President Khatami's administration, funding was allocated to the Daftar-i umur-i mosharekat-i zanan (Office for Women's Participation, OWP) for the first time.[51] The OWP supported many NGO activities, including sponsoring conferences and research. Further, the State Welfare Organization recruited "NGOs and private sector organizations as contractors to deliver social services to disadvantaged populations."[52] At an NGO conference convened during the Khatami administration, as discussed by Sussan Tahmasbi, both NGO leaders and government officials participated and addressed "barriers to people's participation."[53] Sometimes, however, the state would take the initiatives away from NGOs by setting up its own organizations and associations. Unlike the NGOs, however, government-supported organizations were generously assisted with funding from the state, as well as donations from like-minded individuals and organizations.[54] Such lopsided competitions have led to marginalization and increasing dissatisfaction by independent NGOs, who find themselves increasingly sidelined.

Frequent changes in leadership and in governmental administrations further put women and their organizations in existential hardship and precarious positions. In the nature of the state–society relationship, neither the state nor the women organizers generally trust one another. Some better-known NGOs prefer to keep their autonomy and independence—minimal though it may be—away from the state's direct or indirect interference. This mutual distrust was particularly accentuated under President Ahmadinejad's administration, where the highly successful and rapidly expanding One Million Signatures campaign was forced to suspend its activities, with some of its activists and leaders arrested, jailed, or forced to leave the country. While the state's constitution allows for the creation and operation of these independent modern associations, in reality, many bureaucratic demands effectively block their proper civil functioning. In other words, although setting up NGOs should be relatively hassle-free, pragmatically securing official permission from the labyrinthine Iranian bureaucracy is daunting. Many women's NGOs are either ignored, linger in official and legal oblivion, or die of neglect.[55]

Women's NGOs in Iran

In this section, I briefly highlight five cases of women's organizations: three are from Tehran, one from northern Iran, and another from the Persian Gulf area. I conducted most of my research into these groups in Iran during the summer of 2018, and was assisted by Elham Rahmatabadi, a bright young PhD student. The activities of these organizations cover a range of social services, including education, public health (sexual and psychological), entrepreneurship, and job creation. Each organization started with specific ideas and objectives, and were motivated by the personal, educational, and professional experiences of its founder. One of these NGOs began before the 1979 revolution, and the rest were formed after. The founders are of different ages, coming from different parts of the country. They are mostly from educated and middle-class or upper-middle-class backgrounds. Their broader objectives, generally stated, are to make tangible differences in the sensibilities, worldviews, and ways of life of their fellow citizens, particularly women. Their stories reveal their active engagement with people of all backgrounds, the state, other institutions of power, and the larger civil society. These NGOs are primarily—but not exclusively—by women, of women, and for women. By bringing together vulnerable and disadvantaged women—as well as children and some men—the Iranian NGOs have contributed to the creation of layers of reality and social relations that have been unacknowledged, ignored, or downplayed by the ideologically infused state. The following are but a few examples.

Touran Mirhadi

Born to an Iranian father and a German mother, Touran Mirhadi traveled to Europe in 1947 at the age of nineteen, where she discovered the extent of the ruin and devastation left in the aftermath of the Second World War.[56] While attending college to study psychology and education, she volunteered at some local organizations whose objectives were to rebuild the war-ruined cities and rehabilitate their traumatized citizens. This turned out to be a lifetime experience, which she put to good use when she returned to Iran in 1952[57]—a tumultuous period in Mohammad Reza Shah's reign (1941–79). Her young husband, a politically left-leaning military man, was executed in 1954 for "anti-state" activities, leaving behind Touran and their newborn son. In 1956, she started up a coeducational kindergarten named Farhad, aiming to apply the knowledge and experiences she had gained in Europe. As a modern educator, her goal was to move away from the method of rote learning that was then the established paradigm in Iran's educational system, and to foster a democratic and autonomous sensibility in her students. The objective of her innovative approach to education was to allow students to discover their own potentials and to help them maximize their capabilities. She recognized the need to shape her students' perspectives of themselves and their society at an early age. By 1979, she had expanded her school to include primary and secondary levels. Shortly after the establishment of the Islamic Republic, however, it was confiscated and she was forced to retire. Mirhadi then turned her boundless energy to other educational endeavors, determined to continue with her goals.

In 1962 and 1963, Mirhadi and a group of like-minded women and men, including the man she had married in the meantime, registered Shuray-i Kitab-e Kudak (Children's Book Council of Iran), one of the few NGOs in

Iran at the time. Later in 1979, the Council was expanded to include Farhang Nameh Kudakan va No-Javanan (The Encyclopedia of Children and Young Adults). Both organizations are still going strong, funded primarily by interested individuals and dues-paying members. Touran Mihrhadi died in 2015 at the age of eighty-nine, leaving behind a rich and lasting legacy. The seventeenth volume of *The Encyclopedia of Children and Young Adults* was published shortly before her death. The current organizers are planning to publish twenty-five volumes in total.

Akram Movaghari

Moving to the north of Iran, to Gorgan, the capital of the Golestan province on the Caspian Sea, we meet Akram Movaghari, a woman in her mid-to-late thirties. Elham and I met her in Tehran and interviewed her in a café. She is the founder of the NGO Gandom (meaning "wheat") and the director of Pars Friendship Schools or Pars Research Institute for Development in the Golestan province.[58] This institute has two other branches in Yazd and Zahedan in central and western Iran, respectively.

Although independent, Pars Friendship Schools have the blessing of the state—specifically that of the Supreme Leader, Ayatollah Khamenei, who in 2014 instructed that no Afghan child should be deprived of education. Gandom and Pars Friendship Schools are among the few NGOs receiving some financial aid from the United Nations Children's Fund with the blessings of the state. The objective of the school is to provide a friendly and conducive environment for Afghan and Iranian children who, for one reason or another, have fallen behind or not been able to go to school. Since the schools opened in 2016, some 136 students have registered in the branch in Gorgan. This NGO occasionally arranges workshops for women and girls in various cities where it has a branch. The objective of these workshops is to empower refugee women and girls, and to enable them to improve and sustain their lives and those of their families. These workshops' topics include entrepreneurship classes on sewing, cloth production and market presentation, home economy, and financing.

Leila Arshad

Back in Tehran, I met with Leila Arshad and her coworker/friend, both social workers, and talked with them about their experiences with civil society, their social services, their participation, and their activism. Together, these two women founded Zanan-e Khane Khorshid (Women of the House of Sun; henceforth, The House) in 2007. Their objective has been to reach out to destitute women such as prostitutes and drug addicts, most of whom have been rejected by their families, are homeless, and often abandoned with their young children. Arshad is active on several fronts, keeping her organization in the public eye by contributing essays to newspapers, attending official meetings, participating in private and state-sponsored panel discussions and conferences, and granting public interviews.

Arshad and her team established an office in a run-down neighborhood in south Tehran known as *darvazeh ghar* (literally, "the gate to the cave"), where most of their clientele live. Elham arranged my meeting with Arshad, and we interviewed her in her office in The House. Arshad and her team have recruited volunteer doctors, nurses, and drivers to provide daily sustenance and healthcare, including medical, dental, and psychological services, for these women and children, and occasionally for their husbands.[59] While Arshad and her team enjoy the deep gratitude of the people they serve, they face begrudging tolerance by the political elite. Arshad is, however, an intrepid social worker. Periodically, The House's volunteer social workers, nurses, and drivers go around the neighborhood distributing clean needles, condoms, shampoo, towels, first aid kits, and the like. The House also arranges regular workshops and sessions to educate women on prevention and safeguarding themselves against STDs, HIV, and AIDS. Addiction is one of the biggest problems many women face, and The House has been proactive in helping them check into rehabilitation centers and finding places for them to stay. So far, they have treated over 900 addicted women who are often from poor backgrounds. It is not clear how they became addicts, but once they reach that stage, they are rejected by their families and have nowhere else to go. Facing cultural prejudices, addicted and homeless women are inevitably forced into prostitution. Getting women admitted to rehabilitation centers is not easy; these women often do not have proper identification and are usually refused admission. Even if The House succeeds in getting an addicted woman admitted, and even if she succeeds in kicking her habit, she may be automatically rejected for a job if a potential employer learns of her background, which forces her back into homelessness, prostitution, and addiction—and thus the vicious cycle continues. The problem with lacking official identification is not restricted to Iranian women; it involves some Afghan women refugees who share much of the suffering and abuse with their Iranian sisters, and then some. Many of them also end up as clients of The House.

The House's daily agenda is packed by planned and unexpected activities, tending to the needs of their women clientele and of those who drop in seeking help. More importantly, The House provides daily lunches for more than one hundred women and their children. As of August 2016, only five women's shelters or *khanehay-i amn* ("safe houses") for abused and fleeing women existed in Tehran; the number rose to twenty-two by 2017, thanks to pressure from women activists. Due to limited resources, each shelter/house has the capacity to maintain only five women.[60]

The House has volunteer workers and occasionally organizes fundraising. This NGO also gets some modest financial assistance from the state, but that help is often delayed—sometimes by more than a year—and by the time The House actually gets the funds, prices have gone up and the value of the fund has substantially decreased. Arshad's frustration with the government's persistent delays and inattentiveness prompted her to run for a city council seat in the mayor's office, for which she was elected. Asked by a reporter why she wanted a job in the government, she said it was out of frustration with the state's unwillingness to provide for the poor, addicted, and destitute women and their children. She thought that a seat in the mayor's office might put her in a better position to help her main constituencies. Fearing her straightforward approach to issues and her determination to bring these cases to the public's attention, however, she was persuaded—likely pushed—to give up her seat. Finally, in 2010, Arshad was invited to collaborate with the Sazman-i Behzisti (Welfare Department), with the objective of reaching out to the community of her constituency to help its needy citizens—but that arrangement has not been without its hassles.

Arshad and her coworkers are displeased with the cultural and institutional moral ambivalence toward their clientele, and the way the latter are treated as non-citizens—if not non-entities. These women, according to Arshad, are abused and rejected by their families, and disowned by their leaders. Lacking ID cards, political standing, or social capital, this particular category of women is treated shabbily, and the state neither takes responsibility for the care of the women and their children, nor provides for them systematically. Frustrated by the lack of compassion, Arshad once threatened to close down The House and leave, but she was persuaded to stay. While the authorities are not willing to do much for the destitute women, they conveniently delegate this responsibility to others.

Shahin Oliyaee Zand

Shahin Oliyaee Zand is a professor and a practicing clinician who holds a PhD in psychology from a university in the United States. Elham introduced us, and I met with her for an interview in her office in northern Tehran. Like Leila Arshad, Oliyaee Zand is an articulate and courageous woman. Against all odds and cultural prohibitions, she has sought to publicize the tabooed subject of child sexual abuse, whether committed by family members or strangers. She has published an educational graphic book for children on the subject (see Fig. 8.1),[61] with the intention of making children aware of their bodies and to alert families to signs of sexual abuse. Her genuine concerns over child abuse and violence against women led her to establish a center for the prevention of child sexual abuse—Markaz-i Pishgiri-i Azar Jinsi—the first center of its kind, she told me. When she applied to register the center, however, she was told to drop the word *jinsi* (sexual) from the organization's name. She adamantly refused to do so. Sexual topics, particularly those involving child abuse, are just beginning to emerge out of centuries of secrecy

Fig. 8.1: Shahin Oliyaee Zand's book on child sexual abuse titled, *I Like Everyone, But...*

and layers of cultural hypocrisy to become part of the national discourse, but it is still a topic treated gingerly. Oliyaee Zand has done extensive research on child abuse and has interviewed abused women, and some men, who have overcome their inhibitions enough to agree to talk with her about it. She arranges regular workshops and counselling sessions for battered women and abused children.

In 2012, Oliyaee Zand was approached by the Sazman-i Behzisti and asked to conduct a national research on prostitution. She was assigned a team and was told to submit the results within one year. Oliyaee Zand accepted the challenge but rejected the time limit. "I do not give in to compulsion [*zur*]," she told me. "You cannot put a time limit on such an important study."[62] In the course of this research, she became aware of the extent of child sexual abuse and its connection with prostitution.[63] She faulted "our society" for not believing in prevention, and consequently finds the community ill-equipped to deal with the sexual health crisis. Like Arshad, Oliyaee Zand spoke at length about the difficulties she has faced in relations with the political elite, the "moral guardians" who strongly discourage any public discussion of such topics. She said, "in this town you have to compromise all the time, and if you do not, you are bound to fail." On that matter, she said pensively, "psychology has failed in this country." She is, however, much appreciated by her students and her clientele.

Roghieh Zakeri

On the shores of the Persian Gulf in the south of Iran we visit the city of Minab. There we meet Roghieh Zakeri, a woman possibly in her mid-forties. I came to know of her through Mina Keshawarz, who shared with me a documentary she made about Roghieh called *Dar mian-i amvaj* ("Braving the Waves").[64] This documentary depicts Zakeri's perilous engagement with her city's opportunistic leaders and its labyrinthine bureaucracy. Zakeri, like the other women activists I have interviewed, is educated and is highly articulate. She married very young, but divorced her husband when he became a drug addict and abusive. Zakeri remarried and has four children from her second marriage, in addition to a child by her first husband. Her current husband is a farmer, and is supportive of her public activities.

Around late 2008, with the encouragement of the then *farmandar* (governor), Zakeri managed to rent a vacant lot from the city hall in order to organize a market for women vendors, who were scattered throughout the city. She called it Thursday Bazaar. She registered her NGO as the Anjoman-e Zanan-i Sahel-i Minab (Association of Women of Minab Seashore). Zakeri had the new open market covered with bamboo, under which women could sit, shaded from the burning sun. She would charge each vendor a small fee. Further, she had washroom facilities and a small prayer room built on the premises, as well as a small concrete office for herself. She would occasionally walk outside to inspect the situation to ensure that things were working out properly between the women vendors and their customers. The Thursday Bazaar was bustling, and all seemed to be working well.

When a new mayor came to office, everything changed. This is a perennial problem in Iran: the quick turnaround of bureaucrats and their rotation from one job to another renders life highly unpredictable and precarious for many workers. The new mayor quickly recognized that the land used by the vendors was prime real estate and decided to confiscate it. Zakeri was accused of having used the land without permission and was unceremoniously evicted. The mayor had the door to her office locked and told the women vendors to pay their rent to the city hall. Zakeri tried to negotiate with the mayor, but to no avail. She took her case to the local court. Although the vendors were supportive of her, they did not show up in court when she needed them. Zakeri sued the mayor in a court in Tehran and sought help from the Office of Women's Affairs. They promised to help, but nothing happened and no help was forthcoming. After frequent trips back and forth to the court in Tehran, and after talking with the judge—whom she said talked down to her—he ruled against her. In the meantime, the mayor eventually evicted all the women vendors, and destroyed her office, the little prayer room, and washroom facilities. A huge concrete building is now being erected in its place.

Iranian women activists, such as these few mentioned here, do not live in isolation. Many are actively engaged with other NGOs and the civil society in their immediate surroundings or in the community at large. In the process, they have become highly visible. Their struggle to help and empower their fellow citizens has inspired creative women artists—and some men—to document such endeavors and to publicize their civil society activities, as mentioned above. Such collaboration highlights the intersectionality of art, civil society, and politics—the subject of the next section.

Politics, Art, and Civil Society

At the threshold of the twenty-first century, and when least expected, forty-seven Iranian women nominated themselves for president in 2001. At the time, not many women from the Global South were expressing interest in or taking action to run for the office of president. Almost nothing was written about Iranian women activists in the US media and little was also known about them in the their own country—except for some short bios and sporadic articles in more progressive newspapers, including an article by the leading woman's monthly magazine *Zanan* ("Women").[65] None of the applicants, unsurprisingly, was approved by the Guardian Council. A gender-ambiguous term in Article 115 of the Constitution of the Islamic Republic of Iran provided the opportunity for women to challenge the official reading of the constitution. The term *rijal* is a borrowed term from Arabic, meaning "men;" lacking gender preposition in its Persian usage, the term means the "political elite." The women contended that gender should not be a barrier to the presidency because they are also a part of the political elite.

The first woman to advance such an astute argument was Azam Taleghani, a former representative of parliament and a daughter of Ayatollah Taleghani (d. 1979). She stood for presidential election in 1996 and has done so in every presidential cycle since[66]—and just as persistently, the Guardian Council has disqualified her every single time. I interviewed six of these women candidates in 2001, and directed a documentary on the subject titled, *Mrs. President: Women and Political Leadership in Iran.*[67] With brave eloquence, the women expressed indignation regarding gender inequality, political deprivation, and social injustice. They highlighted their disappointment with the state and the male political elite, and challenged their ambiguous in-between citizenship in their society. One of the women contenders informed me: "Presidency requires intelligence, wisdom, strategizing and consulting. It has nothing to do with the size of one's biceps, or physical strength. Both men and women are just as smart and intelligent. So, why can't women become the president of a country like the Islamic Republic of Iran?"[68] The women political candidates—and many more citizens—see no reason why women should not or could not be president of Iran, or at least be given a chance to compete. While women are allowed to file their application for the presidency, they have been systematically rejected by the Guardian Council.

On the occasion of International Women's Day in 2006, during the early days of President Ahmadinejad's administration, a small group of women gathered in a peaceful rally to voice their demands for political/legal equality and gender justice. The police interrupted their gathering and arrested some of them, but the women persisted and began to chant and march on. Simin Behbahani, one of Iran's most beloved modern poets (d. 2014), describes her participation in and observation of the women's interrupted demonstration as a vision she never forgot.

Women began to move!
They sang as they walked.
Demanding their rights,
They sang as police brutalized them.
O women,
You who are the essence of life,
The days of your slavery are numbered.[69]

A few months before the 2009 election, and in anticipation of the upcoming elections, women of different persuasions came together to brainstorm, make common cause, and decide on a united strategy. Organized and mobilized, women once again manifested their determination to have a say in the election. Led by Iran's world-renowned film director Rakhshan Banietemad, they requested interviews with the presidential contenders on camera. Of the four presidential candidates approved by the Guardian Council at the time, only the incumbent, Mr. Ahmadinejad, refused to be interviewed. The others agreed and, for the first time, appeared on camera accompanied by their wives—except for Mr. Karrubi. The result was a popular documentary directed by Banietemad called *Ma nimi az jami'yat-i Iranim* ("We Are Half of Iran's Population").

Likewise, during the 2015–16 presidential election, women activists embarked on a new strategy. Calling their campaign "Ta'ghir-i chihreh mardaneh majlis" ("To Change the Male Face of Parliament"), their goal was to increase the number of women's seats from the existing nine to at least fifty of the total of 290 seats in the parliament.[70] They actively sought to mobilize the educated and qualified women to register for the upcoming election, knowing that more seats at the political table would enable them to influence real structural and legal changes. By all appearances, women were successful in getting people to register: more than 1,200 women filed their applications for the election, but only 587 were deemed qualified by the Guardian Council. Specifically, the Guardian Council disqualified more than ninety percent of the reformist women who had ventured into this rough territory, and almost the same percentage of male reformist candidates were also disqualified. Such a widespread rejection of moderate and reformist candidates prompted many citizens to object to the lopsided political manipulation. President Hassan Rouhani expressed frustration, saying that an election without competition was meaningless.[71] Faced with widespread objections, including from some within the parliament, the Guardian Council requalified a few of the early candidates to give the electoral competition a semblance of fairness. The women's campaign managed to send eighteen representatives to the parliament, though one of them was later disqualified by the Guardian Council—against the parliamentary rules, and over the objections of some senior members of the parliament, (she had allegedly shaken hands with an unrelated male).[72] Parvaneh Salahshouri (mentioned earlier) was one of this new wave of elected women. Ultimately, however, while the women's campaign fell short of achieving its goal of fifty seats, it was able to double the number of independent women representatives, and, more importantly, their activism represented an exercise in democracy and highlighted the coalition's ability to encourage voter turnout.

In the realm of art, similar to that of politics, Iranian women have been highly engaged and productive, particularly in the areas of cinema, theater, and visual arts. But as in the other domains of public activities, women's artistic productions have not been free of arbitrary governmental interventions—sometimes supportive, other times opposing. Women activists, artists, and intellectuals often collaborate over areas of mutual interest to highlight pressing issues to women and to the public. Rakhshan Banietemad, mentioned above, is active in cinema, and has focused her creative attention more on modern women of all class backgrounds. Her films straddle drama and documentary, and much of her work highlights gender relations and the tensions Iranian urban women have to grapple with in the course of their lives.

Inspired by the life and legacy of Touran Mirhadi (mentioned above), Banietemad portrayed her life in a feature-length documentary *Touran*.[73] This film was completed in summer 2018, but was not given permission to be screened in regular cinemas. Banietemad and her colleagues initially screened *Touran* at private venues and galleries before launching it on the Internet, to much public praise. Before making *Touran*, however, Banietemad had directed and produced a documentary on the lives and activities of Leila Arshad and her coworkers, highlighting the invaluable services they provide for some destitute women (discussed earlier). Banietemad and her crew spent a few days with Arshad's team and the downtrodden women of The House. The result is her 2009 documentary, *Hayat khalvat-i khaneh khorshid* ("Angels of the House of Sun").[74]

The collaborations between women's NGOs and creative artists such as Mina Keshavarz and Rakhshan Banietemad are ongoing. With the financial support from the Entrepreneurship Development Foundation for Women and Youth NGO, Banietemad and a few of her artist friends launched the Karestan Documentary Film Series. In Banietemad's words:

> Together we could turn our common concerns into enduring works in the documentary cinema.... These documentary films are based on lives and works ... of [w]omen and men whose life stories can provide inspiration, beyond geographical and cultural boundaries, for anyone in the world. The diversity of these personalities due to gender, type of activity and various places of abode, provides a fascinating rainbow of Iranian society that perhaps has not been seen till now, not just in international societies but also in Iran. Praiseworthy people who, without any government connections, have managed to be influential in improving the conditions of their society.[75]

Thanks to the collective effort made under the Karestan's auspices, several documentaries and short films have been produced by young male and female directors. They have tackled artistic and social issues to much public attention and acclaim.[76]

Some Reflections

Iranian women have transformed the knowledge and experiences they have gained since 1979 into power—or, more contextually speaking, into the "power of *presence*" in their engagements with the state and civil society.[77] Women have systematically and persistently organized and mobilized—with varying degrees of success—to agitate for social justice, political representation, and legal equity. One of the most prominent examples is the One Million Signatures campaign to change the discriminatory laws. Basing their approach on the law's attribute of "universal application"[78]—for example, legally, all married women regardless of class, education, and profession have to secure their husband's permission to leave the country—a group of fifty women from all classes and religious and political backgrounds came together in June 2006 to draw up a "manifesto" for legal justice.[79] Wisely, they argued that legal equality and gender justice benefits not just women but the entire family. Their legal rationale and face-to-face methodology to inform the public gained rapid popularity in Tehran and in many other provinces of the country where the campaign sent representatives. Their popularity and effective legal reasoning, however, became their undoing. The government of President Ahmadinejad, fearing the emerging persuasive power of women's collective political agency, sought to stifle the movement. The organization was soon banned, and many of its leaders were hauled before the court and jailed, or left the country.[80]

Iranian women have excelled in every educational, scientific, and artistic field that has been open to them, despite many official or unofficial roadblocks littering their paths. Collectively, they have leveled challenges to the traditional male privileges and patriarchal authority that can no longer be denied or ignored, even though legally they are still considered the "second sex." In this postmodern world and in the second decade of the twenty-first century, many Iranian women are no longer willing to be treated sometimes as a subject and other times as a citizen. They actively engage with and participate in civil society, be it individually or collectively. They have founded NGOs and associations in order to raise the public's consciousness, to improve women's and men's health, and change the discriminatory laws. That women activists have not been always successful in realizing their demands has not discouraged them from trying nor driven them out of the political game. Though these challenges might have made skeptics of some and cynics of others, many women have not given up. While under no illusions, they are aware of the serious obstacles and challenges ahead of them. Systematically and persistently, they have tried to overcome numerous barriers and to alter the political landscape through educational achievements, political activism, and social participation. For these public causes, women have benefitted from the global digital revolution, and some have the support of men such as their fathers, brothers, and sons—and possibly one or two presidents of the country, God willing.

9

POST-2013 EGYPT

DECLINING FORMAL POLITICS
AND RESILIENT SOCIAL ACTIVISM

Amr Hamzawy

Introduction

Egypt's current authoritarian regime has cracked down on civil society and secular opposition parties, and has severely inhibited Islamist movements. The regime has empowered the security services to exercise outright repression, and, since 2013, has enacted numerous antidemocratic laws with little resistance from a submissive legislature. Meanwhile, the Egyptian media has propagated populist rhetoric that legitimizes the unchecked power of the regime and ridicules demands for democratic alternatives. In the face of this holistic repressive campaign, various pro-democracy politicians and opposition parties have grown demoralized and have lost hope. For them, the current Egyptian reality offers few opportunities to effect democratic change and to protect human rights. Thus, at first glance, it seems that the regime has succeeded in equating the post-2011 brief democratic opening with chaos and the worsening of social and economic conditions. Egypt's formal politics appears to be dominated by the regime and overshadowed by the double-sided image of an authoritarian regime and a powerless opposition—reflecting just how effective the crackdown on liberal, leftist, and Islamist parties has been.

However, this picture ignores another crucial narrative: the emergence of resilient and adaptable social activism. Since 2013, popular protests spearheaded by young activists, professional associations, student groups, and labor movements have been shaping Egypt's reality as much as individual initiatives tackling human rights abuses and police brutality. These actors are linked by their informal nature and their resilience to authoritarian tools and tactics. They hold the promise of restoring a degree of openness in the public space and of reviving pluralist politics despite the regime's stiff resistance. Since 2013, activists, students, and human rights groups have taken the helm of numerous advocacy initiatives. They often lack organizational capabilities and remain committed to a single cause related to human rights abuses, such as extrajudicial killings, forced disappearances, or torture in places of custody. In aiming to raise citizens' awareness and mobilize them to demand an end to human rights abuses, these initiatives have to navigate a social and political environment in which large segments of the population are either resigned and less interested in standing up for the victims of abuses or are simply fearful of being targeted themselves by an increasingly repressive regime. This represents a significant departure from the pre-2013 coup environment in which similar advocacy initiatives were able to mobilize citizens with less fear.

For example, before the 2011 revolution, the "We are all Khaled Said" Facebook page was instrumental in drawing public attention to the death of the young Alexandrian Khaled Said at the hands of the security services. It focused on two demands: ending torture and holding accountable the security officials implicated in acts of torture. The page administrators called for the popular protests on January 25, 2011, that culminated in the revolution.[1] In the spring of 2011, the Maspiro Youth Union was formed to demand justice and accountability for Egypt's Coptic Christians after the army and police forces killed dozens of them during a rally to protest increased sectarian violence and attacks on churches. The union's activism has sustained public awareness about the incident and challenged the official attempts to erase its memory. However, army and police officers implicated in the Maspiro killing have yet to be held accountable.[2]

Single-Cause Initiatives

In post-2013 Egypt, Freedom for the Brave represents the most significant example of a single-cause initiative.[3] A group of lawyers, activists, students, and journalists launched the initiative in 2014 to support victims of political detention and prisoners of conscience, and to improve conditions in prisons and other places of custody. The group formed primarily in response to the mass arrest of more than 1,000 citizens by the security services on the third anniversary of the 2011 revolution.[4] The press statement announcing the initiative referred to its members' determination to carry out "vigils and marches to demand the release of all political detainees and prisoners," including those victims affiliated with the Muslim Brotherhood and other Islamist movements, whose involvement in acts of violence or terrorism remains unsubstantiated.[5] Since 2014, Freedom for the Brave has spearheaded attempts to shed light on human rights abuses committed against activists, students, and members of the Muslim Brotherhood.

In particular, Freedom for the Brave has been a champion for the rights of victims of forced disappearances. The group has documented several cases of both forced disappearances and police detention without judicial investigations. The reports have been informed by direct contact with victims' families and information provided by human rights and legal assistance organizations.[6]

Freedom for the Brave has also been attempting to raise public awareness about the gravity of human rights abuses and the deteriorating conditions for prisoners and detainees. For example, in February 2014, the group launched a campaign called "Support Them," in which interested citizens were able to send telegrams to the general prosecutor and the National Council for Human Rights to inquire about the treatment and health status of prisoners and detainees and to demand that prisoners' complaints be investigated. In June 2016, the group also started a media campaign to draw attention to the negative psychological and physical repercussions of solitary confinement, which is a widely used punishment in Egyptian prisons.[7]

Freedom for the Brave has depended primarily on informal activism and social media networks to disseminate information about specific victims and to organize activities designed to demonstrate solidarity with them. Lawyers associated with the initiative have taken up several cases for imprisoned victims, have identified the litigation against them, and have argued in their defense in court. Additionally, these lawyers have documented human rights abuses in prisons, such as torture, solitary confinement, and denial of medical treatment. Although these efforts have neither led to the release of prisoners nor improved prison conditions, they have made the prisoners' stories accessible to the public and have revealed the details of the injustice they have faced.[8]

Freedom for the Brave has not been able to organize peaceful protests to draw attention to its cause. The regime's widescale repression and the draconian laws passed to criminalize freedom of expression and of association have made the cost of protesting immensely high.[9] Fearing the arrest of its activists and students, the group has refrained from calling for rallies or demonstrations. Individual group action, which lies at the core of Freedom for the Brave, is too limited and too fragile to take on the new authoritarian regime in streets and public spaces, but collective action stemming from professional associations, student movements, and labor activism is not.

Professional Associations

Some professional associations have also been pushing back against the new authoritarianism over issues related to their autonomy and general concerns about freedom of association. In particular, the Syndicate of Doctors and the Syndicate of Journalists have taken on larger roles in the resistance since 2015.[10] The elected boards of both syndicates have been instrumental in mobilizing the base—either by calling for emergency general assemblies or by other means—and in motivating members to peacefully oppose authoritarianism. The resulting activism has restored pluralist politics to professional associations, created new spaces for the informal resistance of authoritarian policies and practices, and significantly increased popular awareness about the details of daily repression in which the regime is implicated. The role of Egypt's professional associations today is reminiscent of the one they played in the 1980s and 1990s, in which they were at the forefront of challenging the authoritarian control over civil society and pushing for their autonomy by defending the right of members to elect the syndicates' boards without security interference.[11]

In 2015 and 2016, there was a profusion of incidents—documented on social networks and other media sites—in which police personnel attacked doctors, nurses, and other individuals administering medical care in public hospitals. One event involved the arrest, assault, and death of a veterinarian in a police station. In another incident, two policemen attacked medical doctors at the government-run Matariya Teaching Hospital.[12]

In the wake of the Matariya incident, doctors at the hospital organized a full strike and closed the facility pending legal action. The two doctors who were attacked filed a legal complaint in a police station, accusing nine security agents of physical assault.[13] The elected board of the syndicate issued a public statement to detail the incident and the reasons for the strike. The board also filed a complaint with the general prosecutor, demanding that the security agents implicated in the incident be held accountable. In response, the general prosecutor ordered the arrest of the security agents, but they were released a few hours later. The board perceived this action as a manifestation of the regime's arrogance and disregard for the legitimate demands of the syndicate.[14] Consequently, nearly 10,000 doctors congregated at an emergency session of the General Assembly on February 12, 2016.[15] Leading the protest and articulating the demands were two charismatic figures of the board: the president, Dr. Mohamed Khairy Abdel Dayem, and the vice president, Dr. Mona Mina.

Under the board's directive, the doctors unanimously approved a package of decisions and demands to pass on to regime officials. The syndicate called on the regime to recognize the right of doctors to refrain from work if medical staff or facilities came under attack. The doctors also demanded that the general prosecutor act quickly to investigate police personnel implicated in the attacks. The syndicate also lobbied both the legislature and regime to immediately pass legislation clearly criminalizing attacks on medical staff and facilities, pushing for harsher punishments for such crimes. Further, the syndicate asserted its right to hold protest vigils on February 20, 2016—known as vigils of dignity—for doctors who were victims of attacks.[16] The vigils were held in numerous public and private hospitals, and were also supported by many pro-democracy groups, NGOs, and individual activists.[17] The syndicates of journalists, teachers, engineers, and public transportation workers all expressed their solidarity with and support for the doctors' protests. The protestors garnered sympathetic attention from the general populace and placed their demands at the center of debates about rights and freedoms.

Caught off-balance by the scale of the protests and the evolving public interest in the matter, then Prime Minister Sherif Ismail announced that the regime was committed to accountability and intended to punish those involved in the attacks on doctors and hospitals.[18] He confirmed his readiness to meet with the elected board of the doctors' syndicate and respond to its demands.[19] These official statements were followed by the commencement of criminal investigations and subsequent trials against police personnel involved in the Matariya hospital incident. The unprecedented popular rally around the syndicate's board caused the regime to reign in the security services by instigating criminal proceedings and promising no further attacks on medical staff and facilities.[20] The board celebrated this as a step toward rule of law—a guarantee of rights and freedoms in a society marred by repression and human rights abuses, and a milestone in the effort to end the impunity of the unruly security services.[21]

The regime's initial retreat, however, only disguised its long-term strategy to inhibit the doctors' protests and to intimidate the syndicate's elected board. Since 2016, the regime has used its judicial, executive, and media tools to contain the syndicate's activities. The administrative court system, which governs the syndicate's affairs, issued a ruling annulling the decisions of the emergency General Assembly, and the regime blocked the legal amendments that would have introduced harsher punishments for attacks on medical staff and facilities.[22] The regime-controlled public and private media launched a campaign aimed at discrediting the syndicate's elected board, especially Abdel Dayem and Mina.[23] The regime's intimidation of Mina went further: the general prosecutor interrogated her about statements she had made regarding the regime's health policies, describing them as being based on wrong information, inflammatory, and threatening to Egypt's national security.

Still, the regime's initial retreat in the face of the doctors' protests demonstrated that collective action aimed at defending rights and freedoms could, to a degree, restrict the regime's repressive behavior and limit the security services' transgressions. The campaigns to discredit the syndicate's elected board have failed to undermine popular sympathy for its actions, and, after interrogating Mina, the general prosecutor decided not to pursue charges against her.[24]

Between 2013 and 2016, Egypt became one of the world's worst jailers and abusers of journalists,[25] currently only second to China in terms of number of journalists serving jail time.[26] The elected board of the Syndicate of Egyptian Journalists repeatedly demanded between 2013 and 2016 the release of its imprisoned members, described the prosecution of journalists as an authoritarian policy aimed at undermining the free flow of information and freedom of expression, and exposed the systematic interference of the security services in the affairs of the syndicate to discredit the board and to spread disaccord between it and its members. In response, the authoritarian regime ignored the demands of the syndicate's board and pursued a confrontational course.

In the spring of 2016, the syndicate's headquarters in downtown Cairo was the site of major protests against the maritime border agreement between

Egypt and Saudi Arabia. Thousands of journalists, students, and young activists, along with public figures, gathered at the syndicate on April 15, 2016, to peacefully demand Egypt's withdrawal from the agreement—which recognized Saudi Arabia's sovereign right to the islands of Tiran and Sanafir.[27] They denounced the agreement as the sale of Egyptian land to the wealthy oil kingdom.[28] The April 15 gathering was larger than the doctors' emergency General Assembly meeting. In fact, it was the largest assembly of citizens in any public site since the dispersal of the Muslim Brotherhood's sit-ins on August 14, 2013, and it garnered broad popular support.[29]

While thousands of people peacefully protested and rallied in front of the syndicate,[30] the security services arrested 110 demonstrators, including journalists.[31] Further protests were held on April 25, 2016, but the security services surrounded the syndicate and closed roads leading to it, preventing the demonstrations. During the dispersal of the protests, they arrested hundreds of citizens, including journalists.[32] Stepping up their repression, the security services demanded that the general prosecutor issue two arrest warrants for Amr Badr and Mahmud el-Saqqa, two journalists at the January News Gate, who were accused of violating the law and endangering national security by inciting violent demonstrations and gatherings.[33] A few days after the warrants were issued, on April 30, 2016, Badr and el-Saqqa started an open-ended sit-in at their syndicate's headquarters. The security services responded by raiding the two journalists' homes, prompting Badr and el-Saqqa to ask the syndicate's elected board to express solidarity with them and publicly state that they were being targeted by the security services for political purposes. Although the board refrained from issuing a collective statement, some of its members spoke out in defense of the two journalists.[34] On May 1, 2016, the security services stormed the syndicate and arrested Badr and el-Saqqa—an unprecedented incident in the syndicate's long and often rocky relationship with Egypt's various authoritarian regimes.[35] Never before had the syndicate's headquarters been stormed.[36] During their interrogation in the general prosecutor's office, Badr and el-Saqqa were served with additional charges, including "attempting to change the constitution of the country and to undermine its republican system as well as its current regime," "violating the stipulations of the constitution and existing laws," and "preventing state authorities and public institutions from carrying out their work"—violations that could land them with prison sentences, if not death sentences.[37]

Many journalists perceived these actions as an attack on their independence. Yehia al-Qalash, president of the syndicate's board in 2016, expressed strong dissatisfaction with the actions of the security services. He called on Egypt's president to take the necessary steps to resolve the crisis and restore the dignity of journalists.[38] Other board members also raised their voices in protest. The most prominent of these journalists included Gamal Abdel Rahim, the syndicate's secretary general;[39] Khaled el-Balshy, chairman of the syndicate's freedoms committee;[40] and Mahmud Kamel, secretary of the syndicate's cultural committee.[41] They sharply criticized the security services' provocative actions and attempts to surveil and control the syndicate. They also called for the release of Badr and el-Saqqa and demanded an apology from the minister of interior, who had ordered the raid on the syndicate.

On May 4, 2016, an emergency session of the General Assembly convened to address the security services' raid and to articulate collective demands. Similar to the Syndicate of Doctors, thousands of journalists attended and rallied around the cause of defending their independence. The list of demands included the resignation of the minister of interior, an apology from Egypt's president for the raid, the passage of legislation that eliminates existing jail sentences for so-called publishing crimes, and the release of all journalists imprisoned or detained under this pretext.[42] Pro-regime journalists largely boycotted the assembly.

In contrast to the relatively subdued way it initially handled the demands of protesting doctors, the authoritarian regime dealt with the protests of journalists with a full arsenal of repressive tools and tactics. The security services meddled in the syndicate's internal affairs to create a rift between the elected board and pro-regime journalists. On May 8, 2016, for example, a group of journalists known to have close connections to the security services organized a so-called journalistic family meeting at the state-owned and state-run *Al-Ahram* newspaper.[43] They issued a statement accusing the syndicate's board of placing itself above "state authorities and public institutions," practicing "politics," and acting "as a political party that monopolizes the syndicate as a platform for its objectives." These pro-regime journalists tried to split the embattled board from the inside by highlighting that five board members attended the family meeting because they resented the board's actions and its manipulation of the General Assembly.[44]

On May 28, 2016, the authorities summoned the board's president, vice president, and secretary general for questioning and interrogation by the general prosecutor, and accused them of aiding the escape of journalists Badr and el-Saqqa and publishing false news related to the details of their arrests.[45] After the investigation, the general prosecutor referred the board's members to a criminal court.[46] The court sentenced them to two years in prison, but the sentence was appealed.[47]

In 2016, the regime continued to escalate its campaign against the Syndicate of Journalists by ignoring the board's well-founded demands for the repeal of jail sentences handed down for publishing crimes. It also continued to use pro-regime journalists to sustain internal conflicts within the syndicate and to undermine the board's authority, leading to the election of a new, loyal board. Moreover, journalists continue to be imprisoned. For example, on October 26, 2016, the general prosecutor issued arrest warrants for sixty-three journalists associated with news websites and media production companies allegedly affiliated with the Muslim Brotherhood.[48] However, the bold position taken by the syndicate between 2013 and 2016 added a significant space of activism and resistance in Egyptian politics. More than in the case of the Syndicate of Doctors, the Syndicate of Journalists combined activism in defense of its members' rights in the face of repression with a broad challenge to the regime's authoritarian policies and practices.

Student Activism on University Campuses

Despite its repressive tactics, the regime has also failed to totally vanquish student activism. Between 2013 and 2016, students continued to hold protests and mobilize against pro-regime candidates in student union elections.[49] The crackdown was harsh. The regime used laws, regulations, procedures, and security tools to subdue student dissidents. The regime also employed private security companies to patrol public university campuses and pushed university administrations to enforce harsh penalties against noncompliant students. The general prosecutor transferred hundreds of student dissidents to criminal courts, and even more remained in police detention.

In the wake of the 2013 coup, students affiliated with and sympathetic to the Muslim Brotherhood demonstrated in public universities to demand the return of the deposed president, Mohamed Morsi. Unsurprisingly, their demonstrations led to altercations with the new regime and its security services. The security forces responded to a few instances of student verbal and physical violence with excessive displays of force and the mass imprisonment of students.[50] In the first semester of the 2013–14 academic year, there were 1,677 student protests at public universities across Egypt, with the largest numbers occurring at Al-Azhar University, whose campuses—Cairo University, Ain Shams University, and Alexandria University—are scattered across several provinces of the country.[51]

In the face of increasing regime-sponsored violence, several student groups gradually began to call for the wholesale rejection of the constitutional, legal, and political measures adopted by the regime. Students' demands gradually shifted away from emphasizing the return of Morsi to denouncing Egypt's authoritarian regime for its crackdown on the Muslim Brotherhood, liberal and leftist parties opposed to them, and independent NGOs. Students began to mobilize informally around the condemnation of human rights abuses and advocacy for students who experienced repression. Between 2013 and 2016, student groups protested the ban of the Muslim Brotherhood and its branding as a terrorist entity. They condemned the mass killing of Muslim Brotherhood members and supporters during the violent dispersal of sit-ins on August 14, 2013. Students also took bold stances regarding the security services' implication in human rights abuses on university campuses and elsewhere. They demanded trials for police personnel involved in student murders and forced disappearances, and insisted on the immediate release of students imprisoned and detained for political purposes. Some student protests decried the provision in the 2014 constitution that referred civilians to military courts and the passage of undemocratic laws, such as the protest and terrorism laws.[52]

In addition, efforts to restrain the role of the security services on campuses moved up on the student agenda. Between 2013 and 2016, students held vigils to oppose the September 2013 decision of Egypt's Supreme Council of Universities that made administrative security units operating on campuses responsible for "maintaining security and preventing riots, violence, and bullying." They also protested the legal right given to security units to issue arrest warrants and initiate litigation against students.[53] The Council's decision essentially overruled a 2010 court ruling that banned the presence of any security units or forces on university campuses.[54] Despite student protests and doubts about the legality of the decision, the security services sustained their presence on campuses.[55]

Faced with the rise of student activism, Egypt's authoritarian regime has engineered a far-reaching set of tools to repress the student movement. In 2014, the interim president, Adly Mansour, amended the Organization of Universities Act to give presidents of public universities the authority to dismiss, without litigation, students charged by university administrations with subverting the educational process, endangering university facilities, targeting academic and administrative staff members, or inciting violence on campuses.[56] Mansour's amended law still allows dismissed students to appeal to academic disciplinary boards and even allows the appeal of dismissal decisions before the high administrative court.[57] But since the amendment was made, university administrations have demonstrated a higher propensity to take punitive action against students involved in protests. For example, in the 2013–14 academic year, 1,052 students were referred to university disciplinary boards for investigation and more than 600 students were dismissed.[58] Dozens more were prevented from completing exams.[59]

The judiciary has been supporting the repression of student activism by issuing harsh sentences, such as imprisonment and exorbitant fines for students arrested in protests and charged with endangering university facilities, rioting, attacking staff members, inciting verbal violence, and possessing weapons. The charges are typically based solely on statements by the security services.[60] This campaign of repression continued in the 2014–15 academic year and resulted in a decrease in the number of student protests. During the first semester, student groups organized 572 protests—the largest numbers of which occurred, once again, at the universities of Al-Azhar, Cairo, Ain Shams, and Alexandria.[61] Students participating in the protests included members of the Muslim Brotherhood as well as liberal- and leftist-inspired student groups, which gradually began to oppose the regime's repressive tactics. These latter groups drew their members from parties such as the Egypt Strong, Bread and Freedom, Constitution, and Movement of Revolutionary Socialists parties.[62]

Frequent clashes on campuses between students and administrative security units, and between students and private security units, facilitated a dramatic increase in the overall number of security forces operating in university spaces. Violent dispersals of peaceful vigils became the norm, and often resulted in mass arrests and even the killing of some students.[63] The regime continued to employ its other repressive tools to crush student activism, such as dismissal from universities, arrests, and court proceedings resulting in harsh sentences.[64]

In the 2015–16 academic year, the political scene at Egyptian universities changed drastically. Vibrant student activism, which had characterized the two preceding years, seemed to largely disappear, revealing the efficiency of the regime's authoritarian tools.[65] The few student protests to occur during this period consisted of vigils and demonstrations designed to show solidarity with imprisoned and detained students, but they did not go unpunished by university administrations and the security services: thirty-two students were arrested during the first semester and fifty-two during the second.[66] The arrests were made by either the administrative security units, private security forces, or police forces, whose visible presence on campuses continued.

University administrations punished ninety-seven students by either dismissing them, preventing them from taking exams, or referring them to disciplinary investigations.[67]

Despite the decline in student activism, two significant incidents in the 2015–16 academic year demonstrated that student groups were not completely quashed. First, in late 2015, the regime, through the Ministry of Higher Education, attempted to exert control over student union elections in public universities but was relatively unsuccessful. In October 2015, the Ministry of Higher Education instructed university administrations to exclude certain students from running in the elections. The effort targeted those allegedly affiliated or sympathizing with the Muslim Brotherhood, with those who led or participated in anti-regime protests facing disciplinary punishment. On October 8, the ministry issued a decree to enter these changes into law.[68] The decree stipulated that union candidates should not be affiliated with organizations or entities that are criminalized under the law or declared terrorist. It also stipulated that candidates' university records should be free of any disciplinary punishment.[69]

In November 2015, student union elections were held in public universities across the country, and three main student platforms participated. The Voice of Egypt's Students Coalition, with strong ties to university administrations and, through them, to the security services, pushed for the depoliticization of universities. Mostly liberal and leftist students aspired to oppose the new authoritarianism and reinvigorate student activism, and groups of independent students rejected ties to both the regime and opposition; they portrayed student unions as being responsible for representing the rights and interests of the student body. The Muslim Brotherhood, meanwhile, was banned from fielding candidates and decided not to participate in the vote.[70]

Liberal, leftist, and independent students won most of the unions' seats, much to the chagrin of pro-regime candidates.[71] Ties to university administrations, the security services, and promotion campaigns managed by the Ministry of Higher Education had failed to ensure the success of the Voice of Egypt's Students Coalition.[72] Two independent members of the student unions were elected to head the executive office of the General Union of Egyptian Students, an umbrella union: Abdallah Anwar, who was a student in the Faculty of Mass Communication at Cairo University was elected president;[73] and Amr al-Helew, who was a student in the Faculty of Engineering at Tanta University, was elected vice president.[74] Both were known for their commitment to students' rights and interests, their advocacy efforts for students who faced regime-sponsored repression, and their rejection of the regime's and security interventions in public universities.[75]

These unanticipated election results demonstrated that student opposition to the regime remained strong and that its assault on student activism neither took politics out of university campuses nor silenced student groups. These were the only elections in which pro-regime candidates lost. Further, the security services had failed to control the process, as it had done during the presidential elections in 2014, the parliamentary elections in 2015, and the elections of professional association boards.

However, following the student union elections, the Ministry of Higher Education refused to ratify the results and therefore denied the elected union the legal basis for its existence.[76] In December 2015, the ministry dissolved the executive office of the General Union of Egyptian Students, citing a "procedural error."[77] These steps underscored the regime's dedication to keeping public universities under its tight control. The regime continued to pursue student groups that resisted its clampdown and that mobilized against security interventions in universities.

The second incident in the 2015–16 academic year occurred in April 2016, when students joined other activist groups in holding vigils and demonstrations to protest the signing of the maritime border agreement between Egypt and Saudi Arabia. The protests highlighted that universities remain, to a degree, a site of opposition to the authoritarian regime and its policies. Protests against the agreement originated in universities and later spilled into the broader public sphere. Student groups and unaffiliated students organized massive protests between April 15 and April 25 in several public universities across Egypt, in tandem with the broader mobilization centered around the Syndicate of Journalists.[78] As they did with the syndicate's protests, the security services used excessive force to crush the student protests and arrested scores of students, who later faced court proceedings.[79]

This response aside, students' active participation in the April 2016 protests was the last sign that their interest in public affairs and political matters had not been quelled and, more broadly, that the regime's clampdown had not achieved the complete depoliticization of public universities. In different ways, student activism between 2013 and 2016 revived the activism of earlier periods on university campuses. Egyptian students were part of the global student movement against authoritarian politics in the second half of the 1960s. Further, in the 1970s, they spearheaded the local democratic movement, articulating its demands for citizens' rights and freedoms and for enshrining modern conceptions of regime accountability in Egyptian politics.[80] Throughout the long rule of former president Hosni Mubarak (1981–2011), universities—besides being the prime space for ideological contestation between secular and Islamist groups—continually challenged the regime's undemocratic policies and practices, and university students were plugged into political activism beyond the walls of their campuses.[81] However, student activism has diminished greatly since 2016.

Labor Activism

Despite security surveillance, forced dismissals of labor activists, and referrals of labor activists and protesters to military trials, labor activism remained at the forefront of societal resistance to authoritarian policies and practices between 2013 and 2016. Unionized workers in public and private industrial facilities, as well as civil servants in the state bureaucracy and local government, continued to demonstrate and organize strikes to articulate their economic and social demands, and to defend a worker's right to freedoms of expression and association.[82] Protests by labor activists even impacted key service sectors, such as public transportation and healthcare.

Between 2013 and 2016, labor activism primarily focused on Egypt's growing economic and social crises and the ongoing deterioration of living conditions for a majority of Egyptians.[83] Workers and civil servants used different tactics to make their voices heard: formal complaints, gatherings and rallies, protest vigils, media campaigns, sit-ins, work strikes, and hunger strikes, of which work strikes and protest vigils were the most widely used tactics.[84] While the total number of protests declined from 1,655 in 2014 to 933 in 2015, the frequency increased in 2016.[85] Economic and social demands were at the center of the majority of protests in all three time periods: 49 percent in 2014, 27 percent in 2015, and 27 percent between January and April 2016. These protests called for the payment of workers in public and private facilities who have had their salaries withheld, wage increases to balance the rising inflation rate, improvements in working conditions and safety benchmarks, and safeguards for the rights of temporary workers and civil servants. Other protests called for ending punitive measures (especially dismissals and arbitrary transfers), improving transparency and accountability standards, and introducing systemic anticorruption measures in the workplace, increasing efficiency and productivity standards, and recognizing the right to enjoy freedoms of expression and association without fear of intimidation or repression.[86]

In response, the regime used various administrative, security, legislative, and judicial tools to reject most of the protesters' demands, to punish the protest leaders, and to reign in their informal networks. While the Ministry of Manpower settled some formal complaints and requests filed by workers and civil servants between 2013 and 2016, most cases were referred to labor courts in the absence of acceptable settlements with public and private employers. In the first quarter of 2016, the ministry settled 1,392 of 5,322 individual complaints and 303 of 1,561 collective complaints, referring the rest to courts. This equates to low rates of settlement for individual and collective complaints (26 percent and 19 percent, respectively).[87] Furthermore, in line with common regime practices in Egypt, the ministry resorted to providing temporary financial assistance and other short-term benefits to appease some workers and civil servants during times of frequent labor protests.[88]

Between 2013 and 2016, authorities arrested dozens of workers and civil servants for demonstrating, and enabled the arbitrary transfers and dismissals of dozens of others involved in protests in both public and private facilities.[89] The regime co-opted the General Union of Egyptian Workers, which helped the regime attack labor activists and suppress their protests. In 2015, the security-controlled leadership of the union asked the president to issue a decree that criminalizes all work strikes for a year.[90] Several union leaders also announced their intent to form so-called committees of workers to resist sit-ins and strikes and to participate in counter-protest activities aimed at safeguarding the stability and security of the nation.[91]

No presidential decree criminalizing strikes was issued, and so the union's leadership reinforced its anti-labor-activism position in 2016. Union leaders continued to ignore the well-founded economic and social grievances of workers and civil servants.[92] Of particular note, the union backed the regime's decision and various court rulings[93]—and later the Labor Unions' Act—that banned the formation of independent labor and trade unions and ordered the dissolution of existing independent unions.[94] All of these unions had helped organize labor activism since 2011.[95]

Since 2015, the new authoritarian regime has been undermining labor activism, using the same legislative and judicial tools it has used against professional associations and student movements. In 2015, the regime built on the legislative prerogatives of the president to pass a new Civil Service Law, which significantly changed the employment conditions of civil servants. The law, approved in 2016 by parliament after the insertion of a few minor amendments, made civil servants' jobs easier to terminate and undermined their right to regular wage increases.[96] It affected more than 5 million Egyptians within the state bureaucracy and local regime. The judiciary, like parliament, has enabled the regime to surveil, repress, and punish protesting workers and civil servants. Reportedly, criminal courts have handed down various prison sentences for labor activists, and administrative courts have issued rulings that allow workers and civil servants who participate in protests to be forcibly retired.[97]

The regime has also used the security services to disperse vigils, demonstrations, sit-ins, and work strikes, and they have occasionally resorted to excessive force, using live ammunition and rubber bullets. Instead of holding the security forces accountable, the general prosecutor has issued arrest warrants for protesters and referred them to criminal trials with ambiguous charges that include violent bullying, blocking public roads, disrupting public and private transportation, refraining from work, demonstrating without formal authorization, preventing public and private facilities from carrying out their work, and disrupting public security.[98] For example, in September 2014, a workers' vigil that was protesting management practices in the government-owned Alexandria Spinning and Weaving Company and demanding the payment of late salaries ended in clashes with the security services. Fourteen workers were arrested, and some of them were injured due to the excessive use of force by the police.[99] Similar protests have continued to happen elsewhere in government-owned companies across the country, either inspired by economic and social demands or in response to termination of workers' contracts and their subsequent dismissal.[100]

Additionally, on May 24, 2016, the general prosecutor referred twenty-six arrested Alexandria Shipyard workers to military trials; the charges included refraining from work and protesting without formal authorization. This measure was the regime's response to a series of peaceful protests and vigils at which workers demanded wage increases, job security, workplace safety, and the improvement of efficiency and productivity.[101] The Alexandria Shipyard workers demanded independent arbitration between them and the company's management to reach a settlement, but the army-controlled management rejected this demand. Since the company has been classified as an industrial facility of the Ministry of Defense since 2007, the management used the military police to quell the protests and arrest the labor activists who were later referred to military trials.[102] This was a clear violation of constitutionally enshrined rights and freedoms that include the right of civilians to be tried in civilian courts.[103]

The regime's continued targeting of protesting workers and civil servants has impacted labor activism negatively. The banning of independent unions, referrals of protesters to civilian and military courts, and state-sponsored violence have dissuaded labor protests to an extent, and the regime's renewed co-optation of the General Union of Egyptian Workers has partially silenced the economic and social demands of labor activists. However, labor activism has not been quelled completely.

Spontaneous Eruptions of Popular Anger

Popular anger about specific regime policies and practices frequently erupted between 2013 and 2016. Groups of citizens took to the streets to protest the accumulating human rights abuses committed by the security services. These protests were different in that demonstrators were not part of discrete initiatives that had a lasting presence. Rather, the demonstrators engaged in informal activism in response to various incidents of abuse. However, the frequency of these protests has decreased since 2016.

Between 2013 and 2016, police brutality against citizens has been the major catalyst of popular anger. As of early 2017, extrajudicial killings and torture in places of police custody topped the list of causes pushing citizens—living as far apart as the capital Cairo and small southern city of Luxor—into the public sphere.[104] As the new authoritarian regime tightened its control over traditional forms of media, both publicly and privately owned, social media networks played a more central role in raising citizens' awareness of police brutality.[105]

In November 2015, hundreds of angry Luxor residents gathered to condemn the killing of a fellow resident, Talaat Shabib, inside the city's police station.[106] Police personnel arrested Shabib on charges of possessing narcotic substances, and took him to the police station where he was tortured and, ultimately, killed. The police officers and agents involved attempted to cover up their crime by moving the victim's body to the Luxor Governmental Hospital and claiming he had suffered a fatal heart attack. However, popular anger and social network activism in solidarity with the victim and his family forced the security services to yield. The Ministry of Interior announced the arrest of several policemen on charges of torture and murder and referred them to the general prosecutor, who then referred nine of them to a criminal trial.[107] One officer was sentenced to seven years in prison, five policemen were sentenced to three years in prison, and seven others were acquitted. The Ministry of Interior was also compelled to financially compensate the victim's wife and his sons in the form of 1.5 million Egyptian pounds.[108]

Other protests have been similarly successful. In February 2016, hundreds of residents of the Cairene neighborhood al-Darb al-Ahmar besieged the Cairo Security Directorate after the death of a local driver during an altercation with a policeman.[109] The driver's parents and supporters gathered and chanted slogans denouncing human rights abuses and demanding the murderer be brought to justice.[110] Meanwhile, social media networks and various news sites picked up on the incident and broke through the official barriers of denial and silence regarding the victim, the offender, and the responsibility of the Ministry of Interior.[111] Again, in response to popular anger and heightened public awareness of police brutality, the interior minister apologized to the victim's parents by publicly kissing the head of the victim's father.[112] The offender was arrested, and the general prosecutor referred him to a criminal trial.[113] He was sentenced to twenty-five years in prison.[114]

The newfound leverage that groups of angry citizens developed against the security services between 2013 and 2016 has at least raised the political and social cost of human rights abuses. Nevertheless, the cases detailed above still represent the exception rather than the rule, as demonstrated by hundreds of documented cases of extrajudicial killings, torture, and forced disappearances that remain unaccounted for.[115] Despite some arrests of police personnel for extrajudicial killings and torture, and their subsequent referral to criminal trials under massive public pressure, human rights abuses perpetuated by the security services have not subsided since 2013. Glaring problems of impunity also persist.[116] Moreover, citizens' dissatisfaction with the regime's economic and social policies has not led to similar eruptions.[117] This has been the case since 2016, even though the living conditions of most Egyptians have deteriorated. After years of political turmoil following the 2011 revolution, the poor and middle-class segments of the population have not regained their voices in the public space.

Despite the protests against incidents of police brutality, the few cases of sweeping popular support for doctors protesting police transgressions, and some activist journalists and students demanding the annulment of the maritime border agreement between Egypt and Saudi Arabia,[118] it seems that fear tactics and repressive tools have proved effective in instilling silence.

Concluding Remarks: Resilience Amid the Crackdown

Since 2013, four forms of anti-authoritarian informal platforms have shaped social activism in Egypt: 1) single-cause initiatives opposing human rights abuses and advocating for the rights and freedoms of the victims, 2) professional associations defending freedoms of expression and association, 3) student groups who challenge the systematic interference of the security services in their affairs and the permanent presence of security forces on campuses, and 4) the labor movement that was galvanized by deteriorating economic and social conditions and by the regime's repression of labor activists. In addition, spontaneous eruptions of popular anger in response to human rights abuses have become politically significant.

Egypt's new authoritarian regime—as part of closing the public space and cracking down on formal politics—has tried to manage these forms of social activism through repression, undemocratic legal frameworks, and aggressive judicial tools. It has intensified its efforts to intimidate professional associations, student groups, and labor activists; it has also expanded its targets to include young human rights advocates and citizens who have publicly stood against police brutality. Nothing has highlighted this fact better than the large number of young activists and students detained and arrested, as well as the systematic referral of protesting workers to military trials.

However, the new authoritarian regime has found it difficult to quash such a robust and resilient activism scene. At times, the regime has made concessions to the demands of professional associations and demonstrating workers. Angry citizens protesting police brutality have pushed the security services to apologize for their transgressions and to accept putting police personnel on trial. On a few occasions, student groups have mobilized successfully to challenge the security services' tight grip on university campuses and to subvert authoritarian tactics and tools of control.

Facing the COVID-19 pandemic since 2020, the Egyptian regime has continued to use its authoritarian arsenal to crack down on formal politics and repress activists in informal spheres. However, the regime has also expanded the role and prerogatives of the cabinet of ministers as opposed to the presidency and restored to the government a degree of balance between civilian ministries led by technocrats and those led by the military and security forces. On the one hand, the presidency, which has led government responses to national crises and spearheaded coordination between military–security agencies and civilian bodies within the government, is largely withdrawn in relation to the global pandemic. On the other hand, the military seems to be accepting that its role in the COVID-19 crisis management is defined and led by the prime minister and embedded within the cabinet of ministers.

This represents a departure from the long-standing pattern of autonomous roles performed by the military in times of national crises. The Egyptian armed forces are used to interfering directly to manage shortages in key societal sectors such as bread distribution and the availability of children's milk formula. Egyptians have also grown used to army-led quick fixes to shortages in essential medical supplies such as infant and childhood vaccines. Using its factories and productions lines, the army has staged its role in crisis management as autonomous and supra-governmental in nature. The self-image projected in this context has been of the mighty military establishment on which Egyptians can count when the government fails to deliver. In times of the global pandemic, however, the army is accepting of its role as being solely defined within the cabinet. For example, the prime minister has called on the army to help in the efforts to disinfect public buildings, increase capacities in public hospitals, and to join in the acceleration of face mask production both in military and private-sector factories.

But changes in regime responses are by no means limited to the roles of the presidency and the army; the cabinet of ministers, for instance, has seen a more substantial shift in its role. The prime minister, Mustapha Madbuli, has been leading government responses to the pandemic, assigning responsibilities to different ministers, enabling governorates to act autonomously in containing the pandemic, and announcing the phases and steps of government-led efforts to contain the pandemic and mitigate its economic and social damage.[119] The political significance of the leadership role of the prime minister in the COVID-19 crisis should not distract from a further significant shift in the division of labor and influence within the cabinet. Technocrats leading civilian ministries such as health and population, supplies, education, and finance have shouldered key tasks in shaping the government response and have steered it daily. The voices of these technocrats, along with that of the leading technocrat—the prime minister—have grown dominant in crisis management. They have also shaped the official rhetoric. Conversely, military and security voices, which are traditionally dominant within the cabinet in times of national crises, have taken a back seat. Similar to the army, which has come to accept the embeddedness of its role within the cabinet, the Ministry of the Interior and national security agencies, have been conducting themselves as government institutions to which tasks are assigned by the prime minister and key civilian ministers.[120] However, these shifts within the executive branch of government have not led to any significant changes with regard to the regime's sustained crackdown on formal politics and its repressive handling of informal activism.

10

CONCLUSION

THE FUTURE OF INFORMAL POLITICS IN THE MIDDLE EAST

Suzi Mirgani

Even though political informality is deeply ingrained into the daily life of communities across the Middle East, its compound relationships to formal political institutions remain understudied. The collection of chapters in this volume sheds new light on the complex and changing relationships between formal and informal political institutions and actors of the Middle East. Specifically, each chapter serves to highlight the nuanced, fluid, and evolving interactions between formal and informal political structures as well as how those people operating within them negotiate with each other on a daily basis. Formal and informal boundaries of political life are never mutually exclusive, but converge and diverge over different moments in time, over different social and political events, and over different geographies of the Middle East.

The chapters in this volume add to the literature on the politics of the Middle East by providing examples and analyses of the many subtle and unwritten ways in which formal and informal political actors and institutions interact in the regional context. By employing a range of theoretical and methodological approaches, these studies identify and analyze formal and informal political engagements in a selection of countries, including Yemen, Iran, Turkey, Kuwait, Qatar, Egypt, and Algeria, and in a variety of contexts, ranging from tribal alliances, gender politics, informal urban settlements, agricultural collectives, social activists, and religious organizations. Through multidisciplinary lenses, this book weaves together an assortment of countries, organizations, and issues from across the Middle East to reveal the many overlaps and disconnects between civil society and formal political institutions.

The book has been structured into two parts, each comparing and contrasting the ways in which formal and informal politics shape, regulate, negotiate, or negate each other, whether unintentionally or by design. The first part of this collection contains studies demonstrating how formal and informal political processes are engaged in a symbiotic, sometimes even harmonious, manner in the countries of the Middle East. These interactions often occur in liminal space, gray areas, and the margins of borders defining the distinctions between formal and informal institutions. These interactions are often reflective of historical state–society bargains cast before constitutional or legal splits between state structures and civil society—tacit sociopolitical agreements and relationships that predate the formation of the modern nation state. Ancient tribal and kinship bonds continue to be directly involved in a mutual negotiation regarding the administration of political institutions in many modern Middle Eastern states. These relationships often form a mutual and symbiotic symphony—at times in concert, at times a cacophony.

Chapters by Charles Schmitz, Michelangelo Guida, Clemens Chay, and Paulino Cozzi examine the historical and deeply rooted state–society relationships and the ways in which they interact. These contributors examine, respectively, tribes in Yemen and their continued influence on national politics; village leaders' power of political mobilization in rural Turkey; the *dīwāniyya* in Kuwait, where the lines between formal and informal politics are blurred; and, finally, the Shiʿa community in Qatar that has maintained a discreet yet persistent existence through negotiated interactions within the Sunni state. These chapters examine institutions that are politically powerful despite their informal organization. Networks of tribes, rural leaders, and kinship and family ties are sometimes either directly integrated into state structures or bear considerable influence upon state institutions.

The second half of this collection serves to highlight some of the dichotomies in the relationships between formal state structures and organized or ad hoc collectives. These studies examine a broad range of politically aware groups of people who struggle for survival or for recognition by formal state institutions. Many of these organizations have been excluded from the sphere of official politics, and so their demands are often directed at the lack of effective mechanisms for participation. Ironically, these communities collect and organize precisely because they have been denied access to formal institutions, and so construct their own politically charged charters that challenge the state. Chapters by Deen Sharp, Nejm Benessaiah, Shahla Haeri, and Amr Hamzawy discuss civil society groups and activists who operate on the margins of official political institutions, most often contentiously, as they call upon the state and make demands. These contributors examine, respectively, the predicaments of informal settlements of Egypt and elsewhere in the Middle East; rural voluntary agricultural associations in Algeria; the political demands of women in Iran; and, finally, tenacious political activists in Egypt determined to continue their revolutionary struggles against the failures of authoritarian governance and what they perceive to be a bleak future.

Of all the catastrophic scenarios forecast for the future of the Middle East, no academic, policymaker, or analyst could have foretold how much would change within the space of a few months, beginning in early 2020. At the time of writing in the autumn of 2020, as the world has been crippled by the novel coronavirus pandemic, countries across the Middle East are bracing for an unprecedented and unpredictable fallout. A region that continues to bear the brunt of many wars, conflicts, and authoritarian oppressions has been held hostage to an invisible virus rampaging through its nations, indiscriminately affecting and infecting all parts of their populations. Already dire socioeconomic situations in many of these countries have been exacerbated by the closure of workspaces and educational facilities, the concomitant rise in redundancies and unemployment, increased social and political frictions, decimation of markets, and a further plummeting of economies. As official livelihood structures crumble under the weight of increasingly impoverished and unsupported populations, the informality of life will only intensify across the Middle East, as it will elsewhere in the world. While informal networks of working, living, and socializing are crucial for the survival of disadvantaged communities across the Middle East, these have taken a direct hit from nationwide and government-mandated closures and restrictions and increased digital surveillance. These measures, combined with public fears and safety concerns, have largely kept Middle Eastern populations at home and off the streets. It is only a matter of time before these predicaments become intolerable for the many already trying to endure in precarious environments, compelling collective anger and resentment to once again spill out into the open.

NOTES

1. AN OVERVIEW OF INFORMAL POLITICS IN THE MIDDLE EAST

1. For a comprehensive overview of enduring authoritarianism in the Arab states, see Mehran Kamrava, *Inside the Arab State* (New York, NY: Oxford University Press, 2018), 11; Adham Saouli, *The Arab State: Dilemmas of Late Formation* (New York, NY: Routledge, 2012); and *After the Arab Uprisings: Between Democratization, Counter-Revolution and State Failure*, ed. Raymond Hinnebusch (London and New York: Routledge, 2016).

2. Laura Guazzone and Daniela Pioppi, "Interpreting Change in the Arab World," in *The Arab State and Neo-Liberal Globalization*, eds. Laura Guazzone and Daniela Pioppi (Reading: Garnet Publishing, 2009), 1–15; Raymond Hinnebusch, "Globalization, Democratization, and the Arab Uprising: The International factor in MENA's Failed Democratization," in *After the Arab Uprisings*, 131–53.

3. James A. Bill and Robert Springborg, *Politics in the Middle East*, 5th ed. (New York, NY: Addison-Wesley Educational Publishers, 2000), 114.

4. Asef Bayat, "Activism and Social Development in the Middle East," *International Journal of Middle East Studies* 34, no. 1 (2002): 5.

5. For an updated overview of the many civil society organizations in the Middle East and North Africa, see *The Power of Civil Society in the Middle East and North Africa: Peace-building, Change, and Development*, eds. Ibrahim Natil, Chiara Pierobon, and Lilian Tauber (London and New York: Routledge, 2019).

6. Bayat, "Activism and Social Development in the Middle East," 24.

7. Ibid., 1.

8. Ibid.

9. Guy Standing, *The Precariat: The New Dangerous Class* (London: Bloomsbury, 2011).

10. Linda Herrera, "It's Time to Talk about Youth in the Middle East as *The Precariat*," *Middle East–Topics & Arguments* 9 (December 2017): 36.

213

11. Ibid., 35.

12. Bayat, "Activism and Social Development in the Middle East," 2.

13. Guazzone and Pioppi, "Interpreting Change in the Arab World," 12.

14. Bayat, "Activism and Social Development in the Middle East," 3.

15. Suzi Mirgani, *Target Markets: International Capitalism Meets Global Terrorism in the Mall* (Bielefeld: Transcript Press, 2017), 121.

16. Bayat, "Activism and Social Development in the Middle East," 2.

17. Firat Oruc, "Introduction: Communities in the Playing Field of Pluralism," in *Sites of Pluralism*, 5.

18. For an overview of the Bahrain uprisings, see *Bahrain's Uprising: Resistance and Repression in the Gulf*, eds. Ala'a Shehabi and Marc Owen Jones (London: Zed Books, 2015).

19. Amal Khalaf, "The Many Afterlives of Lulu," in *Uncommon Grounds: New Media and Critical Practices in North Africa and the Middle East*, ed. Anthony Downey (London: I.B. Tauris, 2014), 272.

20. Bayat, "Activism and Social Development in the Middle East," 2.

21. Ibid., 8.

22. Ibid., 3.

23. Ibid., 19.

24. For a comprehensive overview of Iranian cinema, see four volumes of Hamid Naficy, *A Social History of Iranian Cinema* (Durham, NC: Duke University Press, 2011).

25. Nael Shama, "To Shoot or to Defect? Military Responses to the Arab Uprisings," *CIRS Occasional Paper* no. 22 (Doha, Qatar: Center for International and Regional Studies, Georgetown University in Qatar, 2019), 6.

26. Ibid., 3.

27. Bayat, "Activism and Social Development in the Middle East," 7.

28. Kristin Diwan, "Breaking Taboos: Youth Activism in the Gulf States," Atlantic Council Issue Brief, March 2014, 2–3, www.atlanticcouncil.org/images/publications/Breaking_Taboos.pdf.

29. Ibid.

30. Samia Nakhoul and Ghaida Ghantous, "State of Collapse: Can Lebanon's Troubled Leadership save the Country?" Reuters, August 14, 2020, www.reuters.com/article/us-bc-lebanon-security-blast-prospects-i/state-of-collapse-can-lebanons-troubled-leadership-save-the-country-idUSKCN25A2GG.

31. Bayat, "Activism and Social Development in the Middle East," 10.

2. WEIGHING THE TRIBAL FACTOR IN YEMEN'S INFORMAL POLITICS

1. April Longley Alley, "The Rules of the Game: Unpacking Patronage Politics in Yemen," *Middle East Journal* 64, no. 3 (2010): 385–409.

2. Isa Blumi, *Chaos in Yemen: Societal Collapse and the New Authoritarianism* (New York, NY: Routledge, 2011).

3. Sarah Phillips, *Yemen and the Politics of Permanent Crisis* (New York, NY: Routledge for the International Institute for Strategic Studies, 2011).

4. Victoria Clark, *Yemen: Dancing on the Heads of Snakes* (New Haven, CT: Yale University Press, 2010).

5. Ervand Abrahamian, *A History of Modern Iran* (Cambridge: Cambridge University Press, 2018), 34.

6. See Benessaiah's chapter in this volume.

7. Alley, "The Rules of the Game."

8. ʿAdel Al-Sharjabi et al., *al-Qaṣer wa al-Dīwān* ["The Palace and the *Diwan*"] (Sanaa: al-Murṣid al-Yemeni lil-Huquq al-Insan), 119, www.alyemeny.com/library/AlYemeny9167.pdf; Muḥammad Muḥsin Al-Zaheri, *al-Mujtamaʿ wa al-Dawla fi al-Yaman* ["Society and State in Yemen"] (al-Qāhira: Madbuli, 2004), 160.

9. Al-Zaheri suggests that the personalized rule of Yemen is a factor in the continuance of tribal society. See Al-Zaheri, *Al-Mujtamaʿ wa al-Dawla fi al-Yaman*; see also Al-Sharjabi, et al., *al-Qaṣer wa al-Dīwān*, and Alley, "The Rules of the Game."

10. As a broad generalization, tribal social order is strong in the far north of the western highlands (see map in Fig. 2.1); there are many tribes and two large tribal confederacies, and tribesmen are sought for their martial abilities for non-tribal conflicts involving states or political movements. In the highlands and lowlands of the south, tribes are more like community support groups. They play a role in the local community but not beyond the tribe's territory, with some significant exceptions.

11. Another feature of tribal society is that it is marked by a stark gender hierarchy—men dominate formal politics, carry weapons, and provide protection, and women are considered weak and in need of protection. Though women may exert substantial influence in tribal society, their influence is through the household and not directly in political decision-making. See Shelagh Weir, *A Tribal Order: Politics and Law in the Mountains of Yemen*, 1st ed. (Austin, TX: University of Texas Press, 2007), 37.

12. Al-Zaheri, *Al-Mujtamaʿ wa al-Dawla fi al-Yaman*, 202.

13. Ibid.

14. ʿAdel Al-Aḥmadi, "Qabaʾil Hizam Sanaa: sad bashari limaslaha tahaluf al-inqilab" ["The Tribes of the Sanaa Belt: A Human Wall for the Coup Alliance"], *al-ʿArabi al-Jadid*, December 2, 2016, http://bit.ly/2STxAJh.

15. Weir, *A Tribal Order*, 4.

16. Paul Dresch, *Tribes, Government, and History in Yemen* (Oxford: Clarendon Press, 1989), 346.

17. Al-Zaheri, *al-Mujtamaʿ wa al-Dawla fi al-Yaman*, 225.

18. Al-Sharjabi et al., *al-Qāṣr wa al-Dīwān*.

19. Robert D. Burrowes, *The Yemen Arab Republic: The Politics of Development 1962–1986* (Boulder, CO: Westview, 1986), 51; In Yemen, militias and irregulars are fighters that do not belong to regular military units and do not have a formal command structure, but that participate in warfare alongside regular military units. Irregulars or militias are often led by a shaykh who will gather fighters from among the tribe and negotiate payment for the fighters from whoever enlists the support of the militia, perhaps the state, a political party, or a foreign actor such as Saudi Arabia.

20. Marieke Brandt, "The Irregulars of the Saada War: Colonel Shaykhs and Tribal Militias in Yemen's Huthi Conflict," in *Why Yemen Matters*, ed. Helen Lackner (London: Saqi, 2010), 106.

21. Paul Dresch, "Tribal Relations and Political History in Upper Yemen," in *Contemporary Yemen: Politics and Historical Background*, ed. B. R. Pridham (Kent: Croom Helm Ltd, 1984), 168.

22. Muḥammad Muḥsin Al-Zaheri, *Al-Dur al-Siyasi lil-Qabila fi al-Yaman* ["The Political Role of the Tribe in Yemen"] (al-Qahira: Madbuli, 1996), 121.

23. Dresch, *Tribes, Government, and History in Yemen*, 245.

24. The People's Republic of South Yemen was the first name of south Yemen after independence in 1967. It became the People's Democratic Republic of Yemen in 1970, when the socialists wanted to claim all of Yemen, not just the southern portion.

25. Al-Sharjabi et al., *Al-Qaṣer wa al-Dīwān*.

26. Brandt, "The Irregulars of the Saada War: Colonel Shaykhs and Tribal Militias in Yemen's Huthi Conflict;" Weir, *A Tribal Order*, 6.

27. Al-Sharjabi et al., *Al-Qaṣer wa al-Dīwān*, 125.

28. This was the motivation for avoiding commerce prior to the revolution because, as Adam Smith argued, commerce creates dependency; Tomas Gerholm, "Market, Mosque and Mafraj: Social Inequality in a Yemeni Town" (PhD diss., University of Stockholm, 1977).

29. Al-Ẓaheri, *Al-Dur al-Siyasi lil-Qabila fi al-Yaman*, 108.

30. Weir, *A Tribal Order*, 194.

31. Ibid.; Martha Mundy, *Domestic Government: Kinship, Community, and Polity in North Yemen* (London: I.B. Tauris, 1995).

32. Weir, *A Tribal Order*, 134.

33. Surveys consistently show that Yemenis trust the local tribe more than the state to provide security and justice. Al-Sharjabi et al., *al-Qaṣer wa al-Dīwān*; Samīr Al-'Abdali, *al-Thaqafa al-Dimuqratiyya fi al-Hayat al-Siyasiyya li-Qabā'l al-Yaman* ["Democratic Culture in the Political Life of Yemen's Tribes"] (Beirut: Merkaz Dirāsāt al-Waḥda al-'Arabiyya, 2007).

34. Gerholm, "Market, Mosque and Mafraj," 116.

35. Ibid.

36. Dresch, *Tribes, Government, and History in Yemen*, 134.
37. Gerholm, "Market, Mosque and Mafraj," 118.
38. Peer Gatter, *Politics of Qat: The Role of a Drug in Ruling Yemen* (Wiesbaden: Ludwig Reichert Verlag, 2012).
39. Marieke Brandt, *Tribes and Politics in Yemen: A History of the Houthi Conflict* (Oxford: Oxford University Press, 2017), 19.
40. Ḥamza ʿAli Luqman, *Tarikh al-Qabaʾil al-Yamaniyya* ["History of Yemeni Tribes"] (Sanaa: Dar al-Kilma, 1985).
41. Dresch, *Tribes, Government, and History in Yemen*, 83.
42. Ibid., 85.
43. Brandt, *Tribes and Politics in Yemen*, 19.
44. Tribal society is built upon a gender hierarchy that prevents women from playing leading political roles. See Weir, *A Tribal Order*, 37; Al-Zaheri argues that the fact that Yemen's rulers include a number of women demonstrates that the central state is not tribal because tribal society would never allow a woman to govern: Al-Zaheri, *al-Mujtamaʿ wa al-Dawla fi al-Yaman*, 193.
45. Weir, *A Tribal Order*, 145.
46. Dresch, "Tribal Relations and Political History in Upper Yemen," 159.
47. Ibid., 163.
48. Ibid.
49. Ibid., 169.
50. Weir, *A Tribal Order*, 121.
51. Brandt, *Tribes and Politics in Yemen*, 57.
52. Al-Sharjabi et al., *Al-Qaṣer wa al-Dīwān*, 50.
53. Sultan Naji, *al-Tarikh al-ʿAskari lil-Yaman: 1839–1962* ["The Military History of Yemen: 1839–1962"] (Beirut: Dar al-ʿOuda, 1985), 226.
54. Gabriele Vom Bruck, *Islam, Memory, and Morality in Yemen: Ruling Families in Transition* (New York, NY: Palgrave Macmillan, 2005).
55. Brandt, *Tribes and Politics in Yemen*, 40.
56. Al-Zaheri, *Al-Dur al-Siyasi lil-Qabila fi al-Yaman*, 94.
57. Ibid., 139.
58. Al-Sharjabi et al., *al-Qaṣer wa al-Dīwān*, 34.
59. Dresch, *Tribes, Government, and History in Yemen*, 250.
60. Al-Sharjabi et al., *al-Qaṣer wa al-Dīwān*, 35.
61. Burrowes, *The Yemen Arab Republic*, 51.
62. Al-Sharjabi argues that the conservative faction was led by the Muslim Brotherhood whereas the faction for social change was led by the Movement of Arab Nationalists: Al-Sharjabi et al., *al-Qaṣer wa al-Dīwān*, 35.
63. Ibid., 129.
64. Ibid., 126.
65. Brandt, *Tribes and Politics in Yemen*, 57.

66. Ibid., 36.

67. Weir, *A Tribal Order*, 125.

68. Brandt, *Tribes and Politics in Yemen*, 60.

69. Alley, "The Rules of the Game: Unpacking Patronage Politics in Yemen," 396.

70. Paul Dresch, *A History of Modern Yemen* (Cambridge: University of Cambridge Press, 2000), 202.

71. Alley, "The Rules of the Game: Unpacking Patronage Politics in Yemen," 398.

72. 'Adn al-Ghad, "Ba'idan 'an Ta'iz.. Hamoud al-Mekhlafi 'al-'Aniq' Yaftah Jabha Jadida min Turkiyya," *'Adn al-Ghad*, August 9, 2016, http://old.adengd.net/news/215953/#.XUajAPIzaUk.

73. Brandt, *Tribes and Politics in Yemen*, 36.

74. Al-Zaheri, *Al-Dur al-Siyasi lil-Qabila fi al-Yaman*.

75. Paul Dresch, "The Significance of the Course Events Take in Segmentary Systems," *American Ethnologist* 13, no. 2 (1986): 314.

76. Weir, *A Tribal Order*, 212.

77. Naji, *al-Tarikh al-'Askari lil-Yaman: 1839–1962*, 232; and Dresch, *Tribes, Government, and History in Yemen*.

78. Al-Zaheri, *al-Mujtama' wa al-Dawla fi al-Yaman*, 166.

79. Al-Zaheri, *Al-Dur al-Siyasi lil-Qabila fi al-Yaman*, 121.

80. Naji, *al-Tarikh al-'Askari lil-Yaman: 1839–1962*, 256.

81. Dresch, "Tribal Relations and Political History in Upper Yemen," 168.

82. Dresch, *Tribes, Government, and History in Yemen*, 253.

83. Brandt, "The Irregulars of the Saada War: Colonel Shaykhs and Tribal Militias in Yemen's Huthi Conflict," 107.

84. The joke in Sanaa was that when Ali was teaching his son, Ahmad, how to run Yemen, he released mice from a cage and asked Ahmad to retrieve them. Ahmad preceded to swat at the mice to get them back in the cage, whereupon Ali Abdallah picked up another cage of mice and spun the cage around so fast that the mice became terribly dizzy. Upon releasing them, Ali Abdallah easily retrieved them in their bewildered state.

85. Dresch, *Tribes, Government, and History in Yemen*, 331.

86. Yahya Sāleh Muhsin, *Kharitat al-Fasad fi al-Yaman* ["The Map of Corruption in Yemen"] (Sanaa: Mursid al-Yamani li-Huquq al-'Insan, 2010), 132–7.

87. Al-Sharjabi et al., *al-Qaser wa al-Dīwān*, 123.

88. Serge D. Elie, "State-Community Relations in Yemen: Soqotra's Historical Formation as a Sub-National Polity," *History & Anthropology* 20, no. 4 (2009): 363–93. In the south of Yemen, in the territory that became the People's Democratic Republic of Yemen under the Yemeni Socialist Party, the balance between the tribal and religious leaders and those promoting social change tipped in the other direction, towards social change. The PDRY had deliberate policies to wipe out the vestiges of tribalism. Geographic regions were numbered to break the link between tribal names and geographic places, and tribal leaders were exiled.

However, twenty years of socialism did not erase tribalism in the south. As the last president of the PDRY remarked, "the Shaykhs have gone, the Sultans have gone, feudalism has gone, but their mentality and culture remain." Norman Cigar, "Islam and the State in South Yemen: The Uneasy Coexistence," *Middle Eastern Studies* 26, no. 2 (1990): 194.

89. "Today, the political landscape as well as the military and security forces, is divided between the two rival factions of one sectarian tribal group. One is the family of former president Saleh, his son and nephews. The other is based around Ali Mohsen al-Aḥmar, the commander of the First Armoured Division, and Hamid al-Aḥmar and his brother Sadeq, the heads of Yemen's biggest tribal confederation." Elham Manea, "The Perils Of Yemen's Cunning State," Norwegian Peacebuilding Resource Centre *NOREF Report*, September 2012, 2, https://reliefweb.int/sites/reliefweb.int/files/resources/110b9b8888fdfa61f083c2a9dda05407.pdf.

90. Weir, *A Tribal Order*, 134.

91. Al-Zaheri, *al-Mujtamaʿ wa al-Dawla fi al-Yaman*; and Al-Sharjabi et al., *al-Qaṣer wa al-Dīwān*, 119.

92. The most famous is the arrival of Yahya al-Hadi ila al-Haqq, the first Zaydi imam, who was invited by feuding northern tribes to mediate and thereby founded the Zaydi Imamate in Yemen in 893; Al-Zaheri, *al-Mujtamaʿ wa al-Dawla fi al-Yaman*, 194.

93. Dresch, *A History of Modern Yemen*, 212.

94. Brandt, *Tribes and Politics in Yemen*, 54.

95. Ibid., 70.

96. Ibid., 73.

97. Al-Sharjabi et al., *al-Qaṣer wa al-Dīwān*.

3. *ÇAY* POLITICS: INFORMAL POLITICS IN TURKEY AND VOTE MOBILIZATION IN ISTANBUL AND ŞANLIURFA

1. On the use of *şeref/sharaf* as a factor of tribal identity, please refer to Dresch, *Tribes, Government, and History in Yemen*.

2. This study is a revised and expanded version of my study on "Friendship, Kinship and Interest: Informal Politics in Turkey and the Example of Vote Mobilization in Istanbul and Şanlıurfa," *Alternatives: Turkish Journal of International Relations* 12, no. 4 (2013): 65–76. I would like to thank Zahra Babar, Mehran Kamrava, Suzi Mirgani, Chaïmaa Benkermi, and Charles Schmitz for their very helpful comments and suggestions. They, of course, bear no responsibility for the final version.

3. F. Michael Wuthrich, "Changing Media, Party Campaign Strategies and the Politics of Turkish Elections in Comparative Perspective," in *Party Politics in Turkey: A Comparative Perspective*, eds. Sabri Sayarı, Pelin Ayan Musil, and Özhan Demirkol (Abingdon and New York: Routledge, 2018), 45–60.

4. Roxane Farmanfarmaian, Ali Sonay, and Murat Akser, "The Turkish Media Structure in Judicial and Political Context: An Illustration of Values and Status Negotiation," *Middle East Critique* 27, no. 2 (2018): 111–25.

5. Nic Newman et al., *Reuters Institute Digital News Report 2018* (Reuters Institute for the Study of Journalism and University of Oxford, 2018), 109.

6. Servet Yanatma, *Reuters Institute Digital News Report 2017: Turkey Supplementary Report* (Reuters Institute for the Study of Journalism and University of Oxford, 2017).

7. Ibid., 30–1.

8. Dale F. Eickelman, *The Middle East and Central Asia: An Anthropological Approach* (New Jersey, NJ: Prentice Hall, 1998), 124–6.

9. A good example is represented by the Hamidiye regiments established by Abdülhamid II, who decided to co-opt the chiefs of the nomadic Kurdish tribes by creating regiments financed by the government and manned by the tribes. This policy provided security to the state, and military power to tribal leaders. See Janet Klein, *The Margins of Empire: Kurdish Militias in the Ottoman Tribal Zone* (Stanford, CA: Stanford University Press, 2011).

10. Alan Duben, "The Significance of Family and Kinship in Urban Turkey," in *Sex Roles, Family and Community in Turkey*, ed. Çiğdem Kağıtçıbaşı (Bloomington, IN: Indiana University Turkish Studies, 1982).

11. Dale F Eickelman, *Moroccan Islam: Tradition and Society in a Pilgrimage Center* (Austin, TX: University of Texas Press, 1981), 96.

12. Benoit Fliche, "The Hemşehrilik and the Village: The Stakes of an Association of Former Villagers in Ankara," *European Journal of Turkish Studies. Social Sciences on Contemporary Turkey*, no. 2 (2005).

13. Ayşe Güneş-Ayata, "Gecekondulara Kimlik Sorunu, Dayanışma Örüntüleri Ve Hemşehrilik" ["The Identity Problem, Solidarity Networks and Townsmenship in the Gecekondu"], *Toplum ve Bilim* 51, no. 52 (1990): 89–101. Similar conclusions were reached by Harald Schüler, *Türkiye'de Sosyal Demokrasi: Particilik, Hemşehrilik, Alevilik* ["Social Democracy in Turkey: Partisanship, Townsmenship, and Alevism"], trans. Yılmaz Tonbul (Istanbul: İletişim, 1999), 191–6.

14. Derived from the Arabic word for adolescent—*fatà*—*futuwwa* refers to organized groups of youth and artisans. The term first emerged in the ninth century in relation to a code of honor who devoted themselves to manly, noble virtues. They existed in the Middle East, Central Asia, and North Africa, and as *ahîlik* (brotherhoods) in Turkish-speaking areas, where they sometimes appeared as paramilitary fighters and had connections with *lonca* (guilds). Ziya Kazıcı, "Ahîlik" ["Brotherhoods"], in *TDV İslâm Ansiklopedisi* (Ankara: Türk Diyanet Vakfı, 1996–2014).

15. Duben, "The Significance of Family and Kinship in Urban Turkey," 86; Şerif Mardin, "Power, Civil Society and Culture in the Ottoman Empire," *Comparative*

Studies in Society and History 11, no. 3 (1969); Serif Mardin, "Some Notes on Normative Conflicts in Turkey," in *The Limits of Social Cohesion*, ed. Peter L. Berger (New York, NY: Routledge, 2018).

16. Ş. İlgü Özler, "Politics of the Gecekondu in Turkey: The Political Choices of Urban Squatters in National Elections," *Turkish Studies* 1, no. 2 (2000).

17. On Turkish transcendental state and it evolutions, see Metin Heper, *The State Tradition in Turkey* (Beverly: Prometheus Books, 1985). See also Ömer Çaha, *Aşkın Devletten Sivil Topluma* ["From Transcendent States to Civil Society"] (Istanbul: Gendaş Kültür, 2000).

18. All electoral results mentioned in this study were taken from the Turkish Statistical Institute TÜİK, "Basic Statistics," http://tuik.gov.tr/Start.do; and Supreme Election Council YSK, "Election Results," 2019, https://sonuc.ysk.gov.tr.

19. "Turkish Opposition Leader Quits over 'Sex Tape,'" BBC News, May 10, 2010, http://news.bbc.co.uk/2/hi/europe/8672672.stm.

20. The fieldwork and part of the survey that is quoted in this section were financed by TÜBİTAK (project #108K587). The results of our research were published as Ömer Çaha and Michelangelo Guida, *Türkiye'de Seçim Kampanyaları* ["Electoral Campaigns in Turkey"] (Ankara: Orion, 2011).

21. On the *Kulturkampf* (culture struggle) that polarizes Turkish voters, see Ersin Kalaycıoğlu, "Kulturkampf in Turkey: The Constitutional Referendum of 12 September 2010," *South European Society and Politics* 17, no. 1 (2011): 1–22.

22. Çaha and Guida, *Türkiye'de Seçim Kampanyaları.*

23. Ibid., 116–7.

24. Ibid.

25. Selected answers: ibid., 138–9.

26. Jenny B. White, *Islamist Mobilization in Turkey: A Study in Vernacular Politics* (Seattle, WA: University of Washington Press, 2002), 261.

27. Ibid., 6.

28. Soner Yalçın, *Hangi Erbakan* ["Which Erbakan?"] (Ankara: Başak, 1994), 106–8.

29. Marcel Mauss, "Essai sur le don forme et raison de l'échange dans les sociétés archaïques," *L'Année sociologique* 1 (1923): 30–186.

30. White, *Islamist Mobilization in Turkey*, 7.

31. Ibid., 22.

32. On this, see *Secularism and Muslim Democracy in Turkey*, ed. Hakan M. Yavuz (New York, NY: Cambridge University Press, 2009), 118–20.

33. On the relevance of the center-periphery divide, see Şerif Mardin, "Center Periphery Relation a Key to Turkish Politics?," *Daedalus* 102, no. 1 (1973): 169–90; Michael F. Wuthrich, "An Essential Center–Periphery Electoral Cleavage and the Turkish Party System," *International Journal of Middle East Studies* 45, no. 4 (2013): 751–73.

34. Ömer Demir, Mustafa Acar, and Metin Toprak, "Anatolian Tigers or Islamic Capital: Prospects and Challenges," *Middle Eastern Studies* 40, no. 6 (2004): 166–88.

35. TÜİK retrieved February 9, 2011, http://tuik.gov.tr/Start.do.

36. Ruşen Çakır and Fehmi Çalmuk, *Recep Tayyip Erdoğan: Bir Dönüşüm Öyküsü* ["Recep Tayyip Erdoğan: A Story of a Transformation"] (Istanbul: Metis, 2001), 49.

37. Wuthrich, "Changing Media, Party Campaign Strategies and the Politics of Turkish Elections," 45–60.

38. According to the electoral law, every ballot box has the capacity for nearly 300 votes.

39. AK Parti İstanbul İl Seçim İşleri Başkanlığı, *Sandık Esaslı Çalışma Programı* ["Working Programme for the Ballot Box"] (Istanbul, 2009). This is a manual distributed by AK Parti Istanbul branch to its volunteers. All translation from Turkish in this study are mine.

40. Interview with Sinan Aktaş (vice president of AK Parti, Üsküdar branch and Election Committee president), Üsküdar, April 14, 2009.

41. AK Parti İstanbul İl Seçim İşleri Başkanlığı, *Sandık Esaslı Çalışma Programı*.

42. Aktaş, Interview. Üsküdar, April 14, 2009.

43. Michelangelo Guida and Tülin Tuna, "Centre-Periphery Divide as a Key to Understand Electoral Choices in Istanbul," *European Journal of Economic and Political Studies* 2, no. 2 (2009): 129–43.

44. *Dünden Bugüne Sosyo-Ekonomik Yönleriyle Üsküdar* ["Üsküdar with its Socioeconomic Aspects from Past to Present"], ed. Sedat Murat (Istanbul: İşaret, 2006), 10.

45. Michelangelo Guida, "The Political Geography of Üsküdar," in *Uluslararası Üsküdar Sempozyumu Vi*, ed. Coşkun Yılmaz (Istanbul: Üsküdar Belediyesi, 2008), 338.

46. Forty-eight percent of CHP voters in 2007 declared to be born in Istanbul whereas only 26 percent of AK Parti voters declared to be from Istanbul. For more info, see ibid.

47. Joseph S. Szyliowicz, "The Political Dynamics of Rural Turkey," *Middle East Journal* 16, no. 4 (1962): 432.

48. Hacı Ömer Cevheri was elected in the ranks of DP in the ninth term (1950–54) of the Turkish parliament. His son, Necmettin Cevheri, was elected in the thirteenth (1965–69), fourteenth (1969–73), fifteenth (1973–77), sixteenth (1977–80), nineteenth (1991–95), twentieth (1995–99), and twenty-first (1999–2002) terms in the ranks of AP and later DYP. His nephew, Sabahattin Cevheri, was elected in the twenty-second (2002–07) and twenty-third (2007–11) terms in the ranks of AK Parti. He led the local football team, and, in the local elections of 2019, he ran as candidate mayor of *Şanlıurfa Büyükşehir Belediyesi* (Şanlıurfa

Greater Municipality) with SP, obtaining 36 percent of the votes. Mehmet Ali Cevheri was elected in the same party in the twenty-sixth (2015–17) and twenty-seventh (2017–present) terms.

49. Ali Fuat Bucak was mayor of Urfa between 1905 and 1906 and later elected in the fourth term of the Ottoman Parliament (1912) and second term of the Turkish National Parliament (1923–27); Mustafa Remzi Bucak was elected in the ninth term of the Turkish National Parliament (1950–54) in the ranks of DP from Diyarbakır; Mehmet Celal Bucak was elected twice in the fifteenth (1973–77) and sixteenth (1977–80) terms in the ranks of the AP; Sedat Edip Bucak was elected three times in the nineteenth (1991–95), twentieth (1995–99), and twenty-first (1999–2002) terms in the ranks of DYP; Eyyüp Cenap Gülpınar was elected in the eighteenth (1987–91), nineteenth (1991–99), twentieth (1995–99), twenty-first (1999–2002), and twenty-third (2007–11) terms, initially in the ranks of ANAP and later of AK Parti. His son Mehmet Kasım followed his path and was elected in the twenty-fourth (2011–15), twenty-fifth (2015), twenty-sixth (2015–17), and twenty-seventh (2017–present) terms in the same party.

50. TÜİK, "Basic Statistics."

51. Ministry of Industry and Technology, "What's GAP?," Southeastern Anatolia Project Regional Development Administration, 2015, www.gap.gov.tr/en.

52. Lâle Yalçın-Heckmann, "Kurdish Tribal Organisation and Local Political Processes," in *Turkish State, Turkish Society*, eds. Andrew Finkel and Nükhet Sırman (London: Routledge, 1990).

53. Ayşe Kudat, "Patron-Client Relations: The State of the Art and Research in Eastern Turkey," in *Political Participation in Turkey*, ed. Engin Deniz Akarlı and Gabriel Ben-Dor (Istanbul: Boğaziçi University, 1975).

54. Esra Çeviker Gürakar, *Kayırma Ekonomisi: Akp Döneminde Kamu İhaleleri* ["Favoritism Economy: Public Procurement in the Akp Period"] (Istanbul: İletişim, 2018).

55. Mehmet Yıldırım, "Ceket Değil, Fakıbaba Kazandı" ["Not Jacket, Fakıbaba Wins"], *Sabah*, March 30, 2009, http://arsiv.sabah.com.tr/2009/03/30/haber,F EDE1D50A3F34CB5A30D54BC03D5A255.html. However, Fakıbaba was soon coopted by AK Parti and was elected as MP in 2013 as the party's candidate. He then served as Minister of Food, Agriculture, and Livestock.

56. T. Taş, "Siverek: Aşiretler Konağı" ["Siverek: Tribes' Mansion"], *Atlas* 125 (2003): 104.

57. "Bağımsız Aday Fatih Bucak: Bucak Ailesinde Paralel Yapı Var," ["Independent Candidate Fatih Bucak: There Is a Parallel Structure in Bucak Family"], MyNet, March 30, 2015, www.mynet.com/bagimsiz-aday-fatih-bucak-bucak-ailesinde-paralel-yapi-var-110101771641.

58. "Ak Parti Bu Zaferi Nasıl Elde Etti?" ["How Did the AK Party Achieve This Victory?"], *Haberler*, November 4, 2015, www.haberler.com/ak-parti-bu-zaferi-nasil-elde-etti-7844072-haberi.

59. "Siverek'in En Karabalık Aşireti; Kırvar" ["Siverek's Most Black Tribal; Soot"], urFAnatik, February 22, 2018, www.urfanatik.com/sanliurfa/siverekin-en-karab-alik-asireti-kirvar-h78608.html.

60. Michael Meeker, *A Nation of Empire: The Ottoman Legacy of Turkish Modernity* (Berkeley, CA: University of California Press, 2002), 395.

4. DISSECTING THE SPATIAL RELEVANCE OF THE *DIWĀNIYYA* IN KUWAIT: AN INQUIRY INTO ITS "PUBLICNESS"

1. Literature on this sociological debate dates back to the works by: Friedrich Engels, *The Condition of the Working Class in England* (Oxford: Oxford University Press, 1993); Ferdinand Tönnies, *Gemeinschaft und Gesellschaft* ["Community and Society"], trans. Charles P. Loomis (New York, NY: Dover, 2002); Georg Simmel, "The Metropolis and Mental Life," in *The Sociology of Georg Simmel*, trans. Kurt H. Wolff (Glencoe, IL: Free Press, 1950), 409–24.

2. Fran Tonkiss, *Space, the City and Social Theory* (Cambridge: Polity Press, 2005), 8.

3. Yasser Elsheshtawy, "The Great Divide: Struggling and Emerging Cities in the Arab World," in *The Evolving Arab City: Tradition, Modernity and Development*, ed. Yasser Elsheshtawy (Abingdon: Routledge, 2008), 2.

4. Lewis Mumford, "Architectural Reader," in *The City Reader*, ed. Richard T. LeGates and Frederic Stout (London: Routledge, 2007), 86–7.

5. The following reference provides a concise account of the Gulf's political history: Rosemarie Said Zahlan, *The Making of the Modern Gulf States* (Reading: Ithaca Press, 1998).

6. Nelida Fuccaro, *Histories of City and State in the Persian Gulf: Manama since 1800* (Cambridge: Cambridge University Press, 2009), 160–1.

7. Farah al-Nakib, "Public Space and Public Protest in Kuwait, 1938–2012," *City* 18, no. 6 (2014): 725–7.

8. Barclay Raunkiaer, *Through Wahhabiland on Camelback*, trans. Gerald de Gaury (London: Routledge, 1969), 40–7; Stanley Mylrea, "Kuwait Before Oil: Memoirs of Dr. C. Stanley G. Mylrea," Oxford MEC Archives GB165–0214, 1951, 38.

9. Tonkiss, *Space*, 67.

10. Henri Lefebvre, *The Production of Space*, trans. Donald Nicholson-Smith (Oxford: Blackwell, 1991), 381–2.

11. Yasser Elsheshtawy, *Dubai: Behind an Urban Spectacle* (London: Routledge, 2010), 135. Elsheshtawy, who introduced the notion of architectural "spectacles," similarly argued that these spatial forms are power symbols. This creates a sense of alienation between the population and the material object or the built environment. It also cancels out any form of historical identification with the city. For instance, Abu Dhabi's Emirates Palace Hotel and Dubai's Burj Al Arab Hotel are both situated in residential areas, but do not reflect the areas' social characteristics.

12. Hala al-Dosari, "Silencing Dissent in Saudi Arabia," Carnegie Endowment for International Peace, November 7, 2017, http://carnegieendowment.org/sada/74653.

13. The UAE reportedly has one of the highest rates of political prisoners per capita in the world. See Joe Odell, "How the UAE Justifies its Clampdown on Dissenting Voices," *Middle East Eye*, December 21, 2017, www.middleeasteye.net/opinion/how-uae-justifies-its-clampdown-dissenting-voices.

14. Women's activists previously used Irada Square in May 2005 before a parliamentary vote on a women's suffrage bill. See Farah al-Nakib, *Kuwait Transformed: A History of Oil and Urban Life* (Stanford, CA: Stanford University Press, 2016), 211.

15. Frederik Richter and Michael Georgy, "Bahrain Protesters Swarm Square, Police Flee," Reuters, February 19, 2011, www.reuters.com/article/us-bahrain-square/bahrain-protesters-emboldened-after-retaking-square-idUS-TRE71I32920110219.

16. Amal Khalaf, "Square the Circle: Bahrain's Pearl Roundabout," *Middle East Critique* 22, no. 3 (2013): 270.

17. Al-Nakib, "Public Space," 731.

18. Henri Lefebvre, *Writings on Cities*, trans. Eleonore Kofman and Elizabeth Lebas (Oxford: Blackwell Publishing, 1996), 142.

19. Mumford, "Architectural Record," 87.

20. Tonkiss, *Space*, 59–60.

21. Hannah Arendt, *Crises of the Republic* (New York, NY: Harcourt Brace Jovanovich, 1972), 151.

22. Ghassan Salamé, "Small is Pluralistic: Democracy as an Instrument of Civil Peace," in *Democracy without Democrats? The Renewal of Politics in the Muslim World*, ed. Ghassan Salamé (New York, NY: I.B. Tauris, 1994), 86–7.

23. Mary Ann Tétreault, *Stories of Democracy* (New York, NY: Columbia University Press, 2000), 4.

24. The term "exceptionalism" was used by Herb in his book to explain how Kuwait deviates from the typically authoritarian regimes found in the rest of the Gulf states, cultivating its own political freedom within its vibrant parliamentarism. See Michael Herb, *The Wages of Oil: Parliaments and Economic Development in Kuwait and the UAE* (Ithaca, NY: Cornell University Press, 2014), 60–106. Owing to this particular historical and political trajectory, the Kuwaiti *dīwāniyya* may be similar to the *majlis* found in the rest of the Gulf, but only in form rather than substance.

25. Michael Herb, "The Origins of Kuwait's National Assembly," *LSE Kuwait Programme Paper Series* 39, 2016, 15–9, http://eprints.lse.ac.uk/65693.

26. Al-Nakib, *Kuwait Transformed*; Al-Nakib, "Public Space." See also Farah Al-Nakib, "Kuwait's Modern Spectacle: Oil Wealth and the Making of a New Capital City,

1950–90," *Comparative Studies of South Asia, Africa and the Middle East* 33, no. 1 (2013): 7–25.

27. The word "*diwaniyya*" has many orthographic variations in English such as "*diwan-iya*," "*diwania*," "*dewaniyeh*." In Kuwait, the plural of "*diwawin*" is commonly heard. For consistency, this chapter will employ "*dīwāniyya*" (sing.) and "*dīwāniyyas*" (plr.) throughout.

28. Fahad Ahmad Bishara and Patricia Risso, "The Gulf, the Indian Ocean and the Arab World," in *The Emergence of the Gulf States*, ed. J. E. Peterson (London: Bloomsbury, 2016), 175–6.

29. Saif Marzooq al-Shamlan, *Pearling in the Arabian Gulf* (London: Arabian Publishing, 2001), 57.

30. Stuart Knox, "Bushire Enclosing Notes of Political Agent's Tour in March 1906 of Southern Kuwait," in *Records of Kuwait 1899–1961: Internal Affairs 1*, ed. Alan Rush (Slough: Archive Editions, 1989), 29–30.

31. Ali al-Shamlan, interviewed by author, Kuwait City, May 5, 2013.

32. Al-Nakib, *Kuwait Transformed*, 36 and 43.

33. Clemens Chay, "The *Dīwāniyya* Tradition in Modern Kuwait: An Interlinked Space and Practice," *Journal of Arabian Studies* 6, no. 1 (2016): 19.

34. Abdullah Alhajeri, "The Development of Political Interaction in Kuwait through the 'Diwānīyas' from their Beginning until the Year 1999," *Journal of Islamic Law and Culture* 12, no. 1 (2010): 19.

35. Mary Ann Tétreault, "Advice and Dissent in Kuwait," *Middle East Report* 226 (2003): 38.

36. Mary Ann Tétreault, "Civil Society in Kuwait: Protected Spaces and Women's Rights," *Middle East Journal* 47, no. 2 (1993): 279.

37. Simon Smith, *Kuwait, 1950–1965: Britain, the Al-Sabah, and Oil* (New York, NY: Oxford University Press, 1999), 70–1; Jill Crystal, *Oil and Politics in the Gulf: Rulers and Merchants in Kuwait and Qatar* (Cambridge: Cambridge University Press, 1990), 82.

38. Ahmad al-Khatib, *Al-Duktur Ahmad al-Khatib yatadhakkar: al-Kuwayt min al-Imara ila al-Dawla* ["Memoirs of Dr Ahmad al-Khatib: Kuwait From Emirate to State"], ed. Ghanim Alnajjar (Casablanca: al-Markaz al-Thaqafi al-Arabi, 2007), 225; see also CAP Southwell, "Kuwait Oil Company to LAC Fry, Foreign Office, 21 February 1955," in *Records of Kuwait 1899–1961: Volume 3*, ed. Alan Rush (Slough: Archive Editions, 1989), 153–9.

39. Nawaf Bushaibah, interviewed by author, London, March 6, 2016.

40. IBRD, *The Economic Development of Kuwait* (Baltimore, MD: Johns Hopkins University Press, 1965), 23.

41. Lefebvre, *Writings*, 126–7.

42. Stephen Gardiner and Ian Cook, *Kuwait: The Making of a City* (Harlow: Longman, 1983), 21–2.

43. Al-Nakib, *Kuwait Transformed*, 122–3.

44. Ibid., 134–43. The only former townspeople who did not move from the old town to the new neighborhoods were members of the ruling family.

45. Ghanim Alnajjar, "Decision-Making Process in Kuwait: The Land Acquisition Policy as a Case Study" (PhD diss., University of Exeter, 1984), 121–4.

46. Michael Field, *The Merchants: The Big Business Families of Arabia* (London: John Murray Ltd, 1984), 118–20.

47. Al-Nakib, *Kuwait Transformed*, 137.

48. This is not an exhaustive list of the prominent family *dīwāniyyas* in Kuwait. Some families have split into key branches, each having a designated *dīwāniyya*.

49. Saskia Sassen, "The Global City: Introducing a Concept," *The Brown Journal of World Affairs* 11, no. 2 (2005): 38; Elsheshtawy, *Dubai*, 135.

50. Farah al-Nakib, interviewed by author, Salmiya, June 2, 2014; Ali al-Shamlan, interviewed by author, Kuwait City, June 1, 2014.

51. Abdulrahman al-Ghunaim, interviewed by author, Kuwait City, October 7, 2017.

52. Abdallah Qabazard, interviewed by author, Kuwait City, September 27, 2017.

53. "Affordability" here should be qualified. As mentioned earlier, *dīwāniyyas* were, in the pre-oil era, usually owned by affluent merchant families. However, with the advent of oil wealth and its redistribution, most Kuwaiti families are now able to afford *dīwāniyyas* not only as extended families, but also for nuclear families (within an extended family). Thus, *dīwāniyyas* are also indicators of how rich Kuwaiti families are, whether vis-à-vis the foreign population residing in the country, or relative to other Kuwaiti families in the societal pyramid.

54. Muhammad Khalid al-Jassar, "Constancy and Change in the Built Environment: The Case of Kuwait," *International Association for the Study of Traditional Environments* 208 (2008): 78–9.

55. In 2014, a Forbes article lists Kuwait as the country with the highest per capita use on Twitter. See Victor Lipman, "Top Twitter Trends: What Countries are Most Active? Who's Most Popular?" Forbes, May 24, 2014, www.forbes.com/sites/victorlipman/2014/05/24/top-twitter-trends-what-countries-are-most-active-whos-most-popular/#d9b896666521; Mohammad Sabah Al-Salem Al-Sabah, "Kuwait: Bridging the Gaps ... A Nation's Destiny," Lectures, October 6, 2011, http://drmalsabah.com/index.php/lectures/kuwait-bridging-the-gaps-a-nation-s-destiny.

56. Ibid.

57. Al-Nakib, "Public Space," 732.

58. Hamad Albloshi and Faisal Alfahad, "The Orange Movement of Kuwait: Civic Pressure Transforms a Political System," in *Civilian Jihad: Nonviolent Struggle, Democratization, and Governance in the Middle East*, ed. Maria J. Stephan (New York, NY: Palgrave Macmillan, 2009), 227.

59. Mary Ann Tétreault, "Bottom-Up Democratization in Kuwait," in *Political Change*

in the Arab Gulf States, eds. Mary Ann Tétreault, Gwenn Okruhlik, and Andrzej Kapiszewski (Boulder, CO: Lynne Rienner Publishers, 2011), 83.

60. Lefebvre, *The Production of Space*, 386.

61. Ameen Behbehani, interviewed by author, Ardiya, October 1, 2017.

62. Ahmed Hagagy, "Kuwaiti Gets 5 Years for Insulting Ruler," Reuters, February 3, 2013, https://uk.reuters.com/article/uk-kuwait-twitter/kuwaiti-gets-5-years-for-insulting-ruler-idUKBRE91207E20130203.

63. Daniel Brumberg, "The Trap of Liberalized Autocracy," *Journal of Democracy* 13, no. 4 (2002): 58.

64. Kristin Smith Diwan, "Kuwait's Balancing Act," *Foreign Policy*, October 23, 2012, https://foreignpolicy.com/2012/10/23/kuwaits-balancing-act.

65. When the parliament was unconstitutionally dissolved in 1986, opposition leaders held meetings in their *dīwāniyyas* on successive Monday nights in December 1989. This also involved several hundred thousand citizens who turned up at these *dīwāniyyas* and their surroundings, culminating in an overt public expression for the restoration of the parliament.

66. Tétreault, *Stories of Democracy*, 35; Yousef al-Mubaraki, *Hin Isti'ad al-Sha'b al-Kuwayyty Dusturahu: Waqa'i' wa Watha'iq Diwawin al-Ithnayn 1990–1986* ["When the Kuwaiti People Regained their Constitution: Events and Documents of al-Ithnayn *dīwāniyyas 1990–1986*"] (Kuwait: Kuwait National Bookshop, 2008), 35.

67. A translated version of the Kuwaiti Constitution can be found on the WIPO Lex database, which provides legal information on treaties, laws, and regulations of various countries: The Government of Kuwait, "Article 38 and 44," Kuwaiti Constitution 1962, www.wipo.int/edocs/lexdocs/laws/en/kw/kw004en.pdf.

68. Hasan Qayed Saeed-Subaihi, "Politics and the Press in Kuwait: A Study of Agenda-Setting" (PhD diss., University of Leicester, 1989), 122.

69. Seyla Benhabib, "Models of Public Space: Hannah Arendt, the Liberal Tradition, and Jurgen Habermas," in *Habermas and the Public Sphere*, ed. Craig Calhoun (Cambridge, MA: MIT Press, 1992), 78; Arendt, *Crises*, 143.

70. Hannah Arendt, *The Human Condition* (Chicago, IL: Chicago University Press, 1958), 177.

71. Maurizio Passerin d'Entreves, "Hannah Arendt," *Stanford Encyclopedia of Philosophy*, July 27, 2006, https://plato.stanford.edu/entries/arendt.

72. Arendt, *The Human Condition*, 199.

73. D. Logan, "Logan to Secretary of State for Foreign Affairs, 26 July 1954," in *Records of Kuwait 1899–1961: Internal Affairs 3*, ed. Alan Rush (Slough: Archive Editions, 1989), 128–30.

74. Arendt, *Crises*, 151.

75. Benhabib, "Models of Public Space," 78.

76. Tétreault, *Stories of Democracy*, 70.

77. Ahmed Hagagy, "Kuwaiti Politician Jailed for Insulting Emir," Reuters, April 16, 2013, www.reuters.com/article/us-kuwait-sentence/kuwaiti-politician-jailed-for-insulting-emir-idUSBRE93E11120130415.

78. Abubakar Ibrahim and Ahmed al-Naqeeb, "Opposition Diwaniya Plots Parliamentary Positions—Amir Renames Premier to Form Cabinet," *Arab Times*, December 1, 2016, www.arabtimesonline.com/news/opposition-diwaniya-plots-parliamentary-positions-amir-renames-premier-form-cabinet.

79. Haya al-Mughni, *Women in Kuwait: The Politics of Gender* (London: Saqi, 1993), 13.

80. The *dīwāniyya* space is situated within her father's house in Mishref, and she regularly holds her sessions on Monday evenings, inviting both male and female guests.

81. Ghadeer Aseeri, interviewed by author, Salmiya, Kuwait, April 4, 2017.

82. Lindsey Stephenson, "Women and the Malleability of the Kuwaiti *Dīwāniyya*," *Journal of Arabian Studies* 1, no. 2 (2011): 198.

83. Véronique Bertrand-Galli, interviewed by author, Kuwait City, May 16, 2018.

84. Jürgen Habermas, *The Structural Transformation of the Public Sphere: An Inquiry into a Category of the Bourgeois Society*, trans. Thomas Burger (Cambridge: MIT Press, 1991), 27.

85. Pierre Bourdieu, "The Forms of Capital," in *Handbook of Theory and Research for the Sociology of Education*, ed. John Richardson (Westport, CN: Greenwood Press, 1986), 250.

86. These merchant families are usually identified as those that migrated to Kuwait with the ruling Al-Sabah family, and share a common ancestral heritage as descendants of the Anizah tribe. These noble families are Al-Ghanim, Al-Shamlan, Al-Saleh, Al-Qatami, Al-Roumi, Al-Bader and others. See also Mostafa Ahmed Sagher, "The Impact of Economic Activities on the Social and Political Structures of Kuwait, 1896–1946" (PhD diss., University of Durham, 2004), 57–8; Michael Casey, *The History of Kuwait* (Westport, CN: Greenwood Press, 2007), 21.

87. Manfred Halpern, *The Politics of Social Change in the Middle East and North Africa* (Princeton, NJ: Princeton University Press, 1963), 56.

88. Tétreault, "Bottom-up Democratization," 76–7.

89. Nathaniel Howell, "The Merchant Families Lose Ground to the Al-Sabah," WikiLeaks, August 1, 1989, https://wikileaks.org/plusd/cables/89KUWAIT 3922_a.html.

90. Edward Gnehm, "Kuwait's Sunni Merchants: Unhappy Opposition Aristocrats," WikiLeaks, July 19, 1992, https://wikileaks.org/plusd/cables/92KUWAIT4025_a.html.

91. Shaykh Husayn Khalaf Khaz'al, *Tarikh al-Kuwayt al-siyasi* ["Kuwait's Political History"] (Beirut: Matba'at Dar al-Kutub, 1962), 43.

92. Abdallah Aborgobh, interviewed by author, Mubarak Al-Kabeer, October 6, 2017. The emir of the Aborgobh clan, Sheikh Mutlaq Aburgobh, presides over tribal matters in his *dīwāniyya* situated at the frontal street of Hadiya area.

93. Al-Nakib, *Kuwait Transformed*, 140.

94. Apart from maritime trade, tribal politics were the "high politics" of Kuwait's pre-oil epoch; striking military or political deals with tribal leaders was the exclusive prerogative of the ruling sheikhs. As Kuwait progressed towards a modern state, the sheikhs with familial ties to tribes used their connections to naturalize tribesmen and to acquire political support, resulting in tension between the townspeople (including the mercantile elite) and people of Bedouin/tribal origin. For a more comprehensive explanation, see Chapter 2 of Claire Beaugrand, "The Transnational Foundations of the Kuwaiti Emirate," in *Stateless in the Gulf: Migration, Nationality, and Society in Kuwait* (London: I.B. Tauris, 2018), 43–74.

95. Nicholas Gavrielides, "Tribal Democracy: The Anatomy of Parliamentary Elections in Kuwait," in *Elections in the Middle East: Implications of Recent Trends*, ed. Linda L. Layne (Boulder, CO: Westview Press, 1987), 166–70; Tétreault, *Stories of Democracy*, 108–11.

96. Ahmad Alowaish, interviewed by author, Kuwait City, Kuwait, September 14, 2016.

97. R. P. Barston, *Modern Diplomacy* (New York, NY: Routledge, 2014), 1–2.

98. Matthew Lodge, interviewed by author, Kuwait City, Kuwait, September 25, 2016.

99. Iver Neumann, "To Be a Diplomat," *International Studies Perspectives* 6, no. 1 (2005): 72.

100. Charles Fee, interviewed by author, Salmiya, September 21, 2017.

101. Tatang Budie Utama Razak, personal interview with author, Daiya, Kuwait, April 11, 2017.

102. Bayly Winder, "The Diwaniyya in the Digital Age," *The Arab Gulf States Institute in Washington*, January 22, 2016, https://agsiw.org/the-diwaniyya-in-the-digital-age.

103. Alexandra Gomes, Asseel al-Ragam, and Sharifa Alshalfan, "Reflections on COVID-19 and Public Space Use in Kuwait: The Potential of a New 'Normal'," *LSE Blog*, May 6, 2020, https://blogs.lse.ac.uk/mec/2020/05/06/reflections-on-covid-19-and-public-space-use-in-kuwait-the-potential-of-a-new-normal.

5. SHI'A-STATE RELATIONS IN QATAR: THE NEGOTIATION OF COEXISTENCE

1. Bender and Klassen examine religious pluralism as a prescriptive discourse whose main deficit is to think of religions as visible and clear-cut manifestations, and in doing so miss the contingent and dynamic elements of their practices; see *After Pluralism*, eds. Courtney Bender and Pamela Klassen (New York, NY: Columbia University Press, 2010), 12 & 15. This is especially problematic in nation-building processes—and the respective constitutionalism they entail—insofar as religious

identities are treated as fixed categories. Such an assumption fuels the ideal of cultural uniformity pursued in the efforts to create a national identity, but neglects the interactions between religious subjects and their correspondent resignifications. In this vein, Bender and Klassen bring forward the idea of hybridity and multiplicity, and invite the observer to take the many possible overlapping identities into consideration.

2. Nancy T. Ammerman, "The Challenges of Pluralism: Locating Religion in a World of Diversity," *Social Compass* 57, no. 2 (2010): 154.

3. Saba Mahmood, "Religious Freedom, the Minority Question, and Geopolitics in the Middle East," *Comparative Studies in Society and History* 54, no. 2 (2012): 418–46.

4. Bender and Klassen, *After Pluralism*.

5. The term was first used in Nader Hashemi and Danny Postel, *Sectarianization: Mapping the New Politics in the Middle East* (New York, NY: Oxford University Press, 2017).

6. Toby Matthiesen, *Sectarian Gulf: Bahrain, Saudi Arabia, and the Arab Spring that Wasn't* (Stanford, CA: Stanford University Press, 2013); and Frederic M. Wehrey, *Sectarian Politics in the Gulf: From the Iraq War to the Arab Uprisings* (New York, NY: Columbia University Press, 2013).

7. Justin Gengler, "Political Segmentation and Diversification in the Rentier Arab Gulf," Gulf Research Center Cambridge, July 1–5, 2013, www.personal.umich.edu/~jgengler/docs/Political%20Segmentation%20and%20Diversification%20in%20the%20Rentier%20Arab%20Gulf,%20v2.pdf.

8. Adam Gaiser, "A Narrative Identity Approach to Islamic Sectarianism," in *Sectarianization: Mapping the New Politics of the Middle East*, eds. Nader Hashemi and Danny Postel (New York, NY: Oxford University Press, 2017), 61–75.

9. Given the sensitivity of this research, and in order to protect the identity of the participants, the names of all my interviewees (except for the religious figures) are pseudonyms. An agreement of anonymity was established from the beginning. However, the information regarding age, occupation, nationality, and lifestyle, is accurate.

10. Jill Crystal, *Oil and Politics in the Gulf* (Cambridge: Cambridge University Press, 1995).

11. The term *'ajam* was first used by Arab conquerors of non-Arab lands (especially Persia) to refer to those who could not speak Arabic clearly and adequately (mainly Persians), and was thus seen as a pejorative label for the conquered people. As the Encyclopaedia Iranica states: "In origin, the verb *'ajama* simply means 'to speak indistinctly, to mumble;' hence *'Ajam* or *'Ojm* are 'the indistinct speakers,' sc. the non-Arabs. The Arabic lexica state at the outset that *'ajama* is the antonym of *'araba* 'to speak clearly,' so that *'ojma* becomes the opposite of *fosha*, 'chaste, correct, Arabic language.'" After the tenth century, the term became simply a geo-

graphical and ethnic designation. (Note: The quote uses the same transliteration system as the source: C. Bosworth, "'Ajam," Encyclopædia Iranica, December 15, 1984, www.iranicaonline.org/articles/ajam.

12. Graham E. Fuller and Rend Rahim Francke, *Arab Shi'a: The Forgotten Muslims* (New York, NY: St. Martin's Press, 1999), 17–18.

13. Justin Gengler, "Royal Factionalism, the Khawalid, and the Securitization of 'the Shi'a Problem' in Bahrain," *Journal of Arabian Studies* 3, no. 1 (2013): 54.

14. As of 2010, the C.I.A. World Factbook (Qatar chapter) reported that of the total population, Muslims made up 67.7 percent, Christians 13.8 percent, Hindus 13.8 percent, Buddhists 3.1 percent, and other religions make up barely 2 percent of the total population. Central Intelligence Agency, "Middle East: Qatar," The World Factbook, 2010, www.cia.gov/library/publications/resources/the-world-factbook/geos/qa.html.

15. Founded in October 2009; Ministry of Development Planning and Statistics, "The Population Policy of the State of Qatar 2017–2022," Permanent Population Committee, 2018, www.mdps.gov.qa/en/statistics/Statistical%20Releases/Population/Population/2017/population_policy_2017_E N.pdf.

16. The new axes of the population policy are: 1) Population and labor force; 2) Urban growth, housing, and environment; 3) Education, training and youth; 4) Public health and reproductive health; 5) Women and children; and 6) The elderly and persons with disabilities, see ibid.

17. Ibid.

18. Matthiesen, *Sectarian Gulf*; Gengler, "Political Segmentation and Diversification;" and *Sectarian Politics in the Persian Gulf*, ed. Lawrence G. Potter (New York, NY: Oxford University Press, 2014).

19. When asked about the percentage of Shi'a in Qatar, most interviewees suggested that they were between 10 and 15 percent of the total population, though a few would say 8 to 10 percent, and a smaller number mentioned a range of 15 to 20 percent.

20. Pew Forum researchers have relied on three primary sources to generate Sunni–Shia estimates: analyses by more than twenty demographers and social scientists at universities and research centers around the world who acted as consultants on this project; ethnographic analyses published in the World Religion Database (WRD); and a review of other published or frequently used estimates. See, "Mapping the Global Muslim Population: Sunni and Shia Populations," Pew Research Center, October 7, 2009, www.pewforum.org/2009/10/07/mapping-the-global-muslim-population/#sunni-and-shia-populations.

21. Martin Walker, "The Revenge of the Shia," *The Wilson Quarterly* 30, no. 4 (2006): 16–20; and Mehran Kamrava, *Qatar: Small State, Big Politics* (Ithaca, NY: Cornell University Press, 2013), 73.

22. The difference between the terms "expat" and "migrant" has been the result of

everyday use, and is directly associated with class, labor sector, and inclusion/exclusion dynamics. In that sense, an expat is often skilled, professional, and enjoys a generous income that allows him/her to access most spaces and services; whereas a migrant has a lower salary, and works in the industrial sector or basic services sector (cleaners, drivers, waiters, construction workers, maids, technicians, cooks, etc.).

23. Qatari Nationals are those residents of Qatar who have been resident in the country since before 1930, and who have maintained regular legal residence in the country until the enforcement date of this law. The residence of the ascendants shall be complementary to the residence of the descendants. "Law No. 2 of 1961 on the Qatari Nationality (Repealed)," Al Meezan: Qatar Legal Portal, 2018, www.almeezan.qa/LawPage.aspx?id=2578&language=en.

24. The Twelver Shiʿi school of jurisprudence.

25. Teyseer is a security services company in Qatar.

26. "Haidar" is a 26-year-old Qatari who studied engineering in a well-known institution in Education City. Interviews with him were held in English during the fall of 2017. Haidar, interviewed by author, Education City, Doha, Qatar, 2017.

27. In the Gulf region, *ḥusayniyya* is also known as *maʾtam*, whereas in Pakistan and India the preferred term is *imāmbārgāh*.

28. Misba Bhatti, "COVID Restrictions and Sectarian Tensions in the Middle East," Center for International and Regional Studies (CIRS), Georgetown University in Qatar, May 7, 2020, https://cirs.georgetown.edu/news-analysis/covid-restrictions-and-sectarian-tensions-middle-east.

29. Toby Matthiesen, "The Coronavirus Is Exacerbating Sectarian Tensions in the Middle East," *Foreign Affairs*, March 23, 2020.

30. In Shiʿi Islam, Marjaʿ-e-Taqlīd are the highest-ranking authorities that are to be followed in their interpretations and jurisprudence.

31. Interviews with Jaʿfar were held in English during the spring of 2017: Jaʿfar, interviewed by author, 2017.

32. Sabrina Mervin, "ʿĀshūrāʾ Rituals, Identity and Politics: A Comparative Approach (Lebanon and India)," in *The Study of Shiʿi Islam: History, Theology and Law*, eds. Farhad Daftary and Gurdofarid Miskinzoda (London: I. B. Tauris, 2014), 528.

33. Shaykh Habīb, interviewed by author, the Bukshaisha Mosque, Doha, Qatar, 2018.

34. Islamweb, Homepage, www.islamweb.net/en.

35. "Mahmud" has been an Awqāf officer for more than a decade. He was 45 years old at the time of the two interviews in the spring of 2017. The interview was held in English.

36. "Masuma's" father is a Qatari Shiʿi man and her mother is an American woman who converted to Shiʿi Islam. The interview was held in English at the Student Center of Education City during the spring of 2017.

37. Mohammad Shoeb, "The Imam Muhammad Ibn Abdul Wahhab Mosque in

Doha!" Umm Maimoonah's Journal, December 17, 2011, https://ummmaimoo-nahrecords.blogspot.com/2011/12/imam-muhammad-ibn-abdul-wahhab-mosque.html.

38. "Qatar—Religion," GlobalSecurity, www.globalsecurity.org/military/world/gulf/qatar-religion.htm.

39. "State Mosque to be Named after Imam Abdul Wahhab," *Gulf Times*, December 14, 2011, www.gulf-times.com/story/31543/State-Mosque-to-be-named-after-Im%C4%81m-Abdul-Wahhab.

40. Steinberg underlines the fact that, as a movement, "the Wahhabiyya has been a violently anti-Shiʿi movement since its inception in the first half of the eighteenth century." See Guido Steinberg, "The Wahhabiyya and Shiʿism, from 1744/45 to 2008," in *The Sunna and Shiʾa in History: Division and Ecumenism in the Muslim Middle East*, eds. Ofra Bengio and Meir Litvak (New York, NY: Palgrave Macmillan, 2011), 163. However, it very much depended on the political needs of the House of Saud, which has relied heavily on the religious establishment. Thus, systematic discrimination against the Shiʿa in the Kingdom may increase or decrease but will not disappear.

41. James M. Dorsey, "The Gulf Crisis: Small States Battle it Out," SSRN, July 16, 2017, https://ssrn.com/abstract=3003598.

42. Allen James Fromherz, *Qatar: A Modern History* (London: I. B. Tauris, 2012), 20.

43. As the leading religious jurisconsult within a state, the Grand Mufti is often part of the centralized power structure and has significant leverage on the population. However, in Qatar, religious authority is not centralized, there is no Grand Mufti, and the Wahhabi establishment is separated from political circuits.

44. Jocelyn Sage Mitchell, "Beyond Allocation: The Politics of Legitimacy in Qatar" (PhD diss., Georgetown University, 2013), 229.

45. The last official figure presented by the Ministry of Development Planning and Statistics is 2,700,390, as of February 2018. See Ministry of Development Planning and Statistics, "Monthly Figures on Total Population," 2018.

46. Central Intelligence Agency, "Population of Qatar by Ethnicity Estimated in 2015," The World Factbook, 2019, www.cia.gov/library/publications/the-world-factbook/geos/qa.html.

47. Author's translation of Noura Al Mussaifri's poem titled "Qatar, Kaʿbat al-Maḍīūm," in *Al Arab*, July 16, 2017, http://bit.ly/2STyEg2: Verily, the covetous blame me for pursuing sublimity / And blames me whose affection is not mine / And we are the Mecca of the oppressed who fled / Only with his wellbeing and satisfaction we are satisfied / And we have a plateau in which we shelter who seeks refuge / Against the will of whom opposed and antagonized him / We sheltered in it whose rights were stripped / And they are at ease and opulence after what they had spent in tightness.

48. Fromherz, *Qatar: A Modern History*, 39.

49. Ramy Jabbour, "Qatar: The Annoying Gulf Emirate," *BullsEye*, October 7, 2017, www.bullseye-magazine.eu/article/qatar.

50. "Qatar Emir to Change Style but Keep Policy," *Gulf News Qatar*, June 27, 2013, https://gulfnews.com/world/gulf/qatar/qatar-emir-to-change-style-but-keep-policy-1.1202793.

51. Muhammad Al-Kubaysī, "Tajnis Ghayr al-Qaṭari" ["Naturalization of Non-Qataris"], *Al-Sharq*, November 9, 2014, http://bit.ly/2SRYlOb.

52. Islam Hassan, "The Ruling Family's Hegemony: Inclusion and Exclusion in Qatari Society," in *Sites of Pluralism: Community Politics in the Middle East*, ed. Firat Oruc (New York, NY: Oxford University Press, 2018), 63–85.

53. Fromherz, *Qatar: A Modern History*, 17.

54. Scott Cooper and Karen Exell, "Bin Jelmood House: Narrating an Intangible History in Qatar," in *The Routledge Companion to Intangible Cultural Heritage*, eds. Michelle L. Stefano and Peter Davis (New York, NY: Routledge, 2016), 373.

55. Justin Gengler, "The Political Economy of Sectarianism in the Gulf," Carnegie Endowment for International Peace, August 29, 2016, 9, https://carnegieendowment.org/files/Gengler_Sectarianism_Final.pdf.

56. Mitchell, "Beyond Allocation," 62–3.

57. There is a special consideration for Christians and Jews who belong to *ahl al-kitāb* (people of the book) or the Abrahamic tradition, whereas Buddhist and Hindu migrants are sometimes seen in derogatory terms.

58. Nasr, *The Shia Revival*.

59. Kamrava, *Qatar: Small State, Big Politics*, 123.

60. Hassan, "The Ruling Family's Hegemony," 77.

61. "Qatar National Vision 2030," General Secretariat for Development Planning, July 2008, 4, www.mdps.gov.qa/en/qnv1/Documents/QNV2030_English_v2.pdf.

62. Ibid., 7 and 10.

63. Bender and Klassen, *After Pluralism*, 17.

64. "Sajad" was 26 years old when the interview was conducted. He is from Lahore, Pakistan, and speaks fluent English. He came a few years ago in the quest for high-quality education in journalism, and a more open society since he had faced some hardship in the UAE. The interviews took place in different cafeterias in Education City: Sajad, interviewed by author, Education City, Doha, Qatar.

65. It is important to acknowledge that their responses about the royal family could be biased given the extra caution many exert when sharing political opinions in Qatar. Nevertheless, in most cases, I perceived genuine statements, strong arguments, and even enthusiasm when making a point regarding members of the royal family.

66. "Al-nas al-kamil li kalimat al-Shaykh Tamim bin Hamad al-Thani" [Full text of speech given by Sheikh Tamim Bin Hamad Al Thani], *Al Jazeera*, June 26, 2013, https://bit.ly/2YEHkIj.

67. Habib Toumi, "Sunni-Shiite Divide 'Driven by Politics'—Qatar," *Gulf News Qatar*, September 29, 2015, https://gulfnews.com/world/gulf/qatar/sunni-shiite-divide-driven-by-politics---qatar-1.1591905.

68. Kristian Coates Ulrichsen, *Qatar and the Arab Spring* (New York, NY: Oxford University Press, 2014).

69. Government of Qatar, "Information About Education, Economy, Health, IT and Tourism in Qatar," 2020, https://portal.www.gov.qa/wps/portal/topics/Religion+and+Community/Charity+Work.

70. Gengler, "Royal Factionalism, the Khawalid, and the Securitization," 58.

71. Fuller and Francke, *Arab Shi'a: The Forgotten Muslims*, 40.

72. Jure Snoj, "A Guide to the Most Powerful Families in Qatar," Priya DSouza Communications, February 24, 2017, http://priyadsouza.com/powerful-families-qatar-al-thani.

73. I personally attended the Muharram mourning sessions in 2017 and 2018, and listened to an Iraqi guest speaker at the Buharna *ma'tam* and an Indian guest speaker at the Imāmbārgāh.

74. In Shi'i Islam, it is the peak of the mourning period and remembrance of the martyrdom of Prophet Muhammad's grandson, Husayn Bin Alī (Imām Husayn), back in the year 61 of the Islamic calendar. It happened on the tenth day of the month of Muharram; each year, in a massive effort of collective memory, the Shi'a evoke and enact such historic event, seeking unity and solidarity against oppression—often from a "Sunni majority or regime."

75. "Qatar Unemployment Rate," Trading Economics, 2019, https://tradingeconomics.com/qatar/unemployment-rate.

6. THREATENING URBAN INFORMALITY IN THE MIDDLE EAST

1. David Sims, *Desert Dreams: Development or Disaster?* (Cairo: American University in Cairo Press, 2014).

2. Raf Sanchez, "Inside Egypt's Vast New Desert Capital, Far From Cairo's Traffic and the Threat of Revolution," *The Telegraph*, February 17, 2019, www.telegraph.co.uk/news/2019/02/17/inside-egypts-vast-new-desert-capital-far-cairos-traffic-threat.

3. Sustainable Development Strategy: Egypt Vision 2030, "Urban Development Pillar," http://sdsegypt2030.com/environmental-dimension/urban-development-pillar/quantitative-indicators-updates/?lang=en&lang=en.

4. Doaa A. Moneam, "Egypt Informal Settlement-Free by 2019, Quelling it Fully by 2030: Executive Director of ISDF Khaled Seddiq," *Daily News Egypt*, December 23, 2018, https://dailynewsegypt.com/2018/12/23/egypt-informal-settlement-free-by-2019-quelling-it-fully-by-2030-executive-director-of-isdf-khaled-seddiq.

5. Omnia Khalil, "From Community Participation to Forced Eviction in the Maspero Triangle," The Tahrir Institute for Middle East Policy, June 14, 2018, https://timep.

org/commentary/analysis/from-community-participation-to-forced-eviction-in-the-maspero-triangle.

6. United Nations High Commissioner for Human Rights (OHCHR), "Mandate of the Special Rapporteur on Adequate Housing as a Component of the Right to an Adequate Standard of Living, and on the Right to Non-Discrimination in this Context," February 26, 2016, www.ohchr.org/Documents/Issues/Housing/InformalSettlements/Egypt.pdf.

7. Duygu Parmaksizoglu, "Istanbul: The City of Resistance," in *Beyond the Square: Urbanism and the Arab Uprisings*, eds. Deen Sharp and Claire Panetta (New York, NY: Urban Research, 2016), 162–81.

8. Koenraad Bogaert, *Globalized Authoritarianism: Megaprojects, Slums, and Class Relations in Urban Morocco*, (Minneapolis, MN: Minnesota Press, 2018).

9. Valérie Clerc, "Informal Settlements in the Syrian Conflict: Urban Planning as a Weapon," *Built Environment* 40, no. 1 (2014): 34–51.

10. Ahmad Fallatah et al., "Mapping Informal Settlement Indictors Using Object-Oriented Analysis in the Middle East," *International Journal of Digital Earth* 12, no. 7 (2019): 802–24.

11. Abdulla Difalla, "Jeddah's Slum Areas: The Attempt to Redevelop Al-Nuzla Al-Yamania" (Master's thesis, Ball State University, 2015), http://cardinalscholar.bsu.edu/bitstream/handle/123456789/199892/DifallaA_2015-3_BODY.pdf?sequence=1&isAllowed=y.

12. Keith Hart, "Informal Income Opportunities and Urban Employment in Ghana," *The Journal of Modern African Studies* 11, no. 1 (1973): 61–89.

13. Richard Harris, "A Double Irony: The Originality and Influence of John F.C. Turner," *Habitat International* 27, no. 2 (2003): 245–69.

14. Debolina Kundu, "Urban Informality," in *The Wiley Blackwell Encyclopedia of Urban and Regional Studies*, ed. Anthony M. Orum (Hoboken, NJ: Wiley, 2019), 1–5.

15. OHCHR, "Mandate of the Special Rapporteur," 1.

16. Harris, "Modes of Informal Development," 267.

17. Richard Harris, "Modes of Informal Urban Development: A Global Phenomenon," *Journal of Planning Literature* 33, no. 3 (2017): 267.

18. Michael Waibel and Colin McFarlane, *Urban Informalities: Reflections on the Formal and Informal* (London: Routledge, 2012).

19. See for instance, "Global Economic Prospects: Darkening Skies," World Bank Group Report, 2019, https://blogs.worldbank.org/developmenttalk/global-economic-outlook-darkening-skies.

20. Harris, "Modes of Informal Urban Development," 272.

21. Medhat Mahfouz Hassan, "Culture, Behavior and Urban Form: A Study of Low-Cost Housing with Special Reference to Cairo, Egypt" (PhD diss., University of Sheffield, 1978).

22. Ibid.; Tarik Şengül, "On the Trajectory of Urbanization in Turkey: An Attempt at Periodization," *International Development Planning Review* 25, no. 2 (2003): 153–68.

23. Şengül, "On the Trajectory of Urbanization"; Hassan, "Culture, Behavior and Urban Form."

24. David Sims, *Understanding Cairo: The Logic of a City Out of Control* (Cairo: American University in Cairo Press, 2010), 74.

25. Hoda Tolba Sakr, "Underlying Collegial Relationships Controlling Project Implementation: Case Study in Egypt" (PhD diss., Massachusetts Institute of Technology, 1990), xi.

26. David Sims, *Understanding Cairo*, 64.

27. There is a vast scholarship on neoliberal urbanism in the Middle East. For an overview of this literature since the Arab uprisings, see Koenraad Bogaert, "Contextualizing the Arab Revolts: The Politics behind Three Decades of Neoliberalism in the Arab World," *Middle East Critique* 22, no. 3 (2013): 213–34.

28. Ibid., 51.

29. Abt Associates with Dames and Moore, General Organization for Housing, Building, and Planning Research, *Informal Housing in Egypt* (USAID, 1982).

30. Ibid.

31. Sims, *Understanding Cairo*, 66.

32. Ibid.

33. Ibid.

34. Walter Armbrust, *Martyrs and Tricksters: An Ethnography of the Egyptian Revolution* (Princeton, NJ: Princeton University Press, 2019).

35. Asef Bayat and Eric Denis, "Who is Afraid of Ashwaiyyat? Urban Change and Politics in Egypt," *Environment and Urbanization* 12, no. 2 (2000): 197.

36. Sims, *Understanding Cairo*.

37. James Napoli, "Egypt Remains Stable Despite 'Annus Horribilis' in 1992," *Washington Report on Middle East Affairs*, February 1993, www.wrmea.org/1993-february/egypt-remains-stable-despite-annus-horribilis-in-199.html.

38. W. J. Dorman, "Informal Cairo: Between Islamist Insurgency and the Neglectful State?," *Security Dialogue* 40, nos. 4–5 (2009): 419.

39. Asef Bayat, "Radical Religion and the Habitus of the Dispossessed: Does Islamic Militancy Have an Urban Ecology," *International Journal of Urban and Regional Research* 31, no. 3 (2007): 586.

40. Ibid.

41. Ibid., 583.

42. Ibid., 586.

43. Angel Rabasa et al., *Ungoverned Territories: Understand and Reducing Terrorism Risks* (RAND Project Air Force, 2007).

44. Ibid.

45. Bogaert, *Globalized Authoritarianism*, 22.

46. Ibid., 208.

47. Jennifer Keister, *The Illusion of Chaos: Why Ungoverned Spaces Aren't Ungoverned, and Why that Matters* (Washington, DC: Cato Institute Policy Analysis, 2015).

48. Timothy Mitchell, *The Rule of Experts: Egypt, Techno-Politics, Modernity* (Berkeley, CA: University of California Press, 2002), 273.

49. Ibid., 282.

50. Sims, *Understanding Cairo*, 79.

51. UN Habitat, "Egypt-Urban Issues," https://unhabitat.org/egypt/urban-issues.

52. Gregory Scruggs, "'Everything We've Heard about Global Urbanization Turns out to be Wrong'—Researchers," *Place*, July 10, 2018, www.thisisplace.org/i/?id=0150beca-e3f5-47e0-bc74-9ccc5ef1db8a.

53. Ibrahim Rizk Hegazy and Mosbeh Rashed Kaloop, "Monitoring Urban Growth and Land Use Change Detection with GIS and Remote Sensing Techniques in Daqahlia Governate Egypt," *International Journal of Sustainable Built Environment* 4, no. 1 (2015): 124.

54. Ibid.

55. Ibid.

56. Jack Shenker, *The Egyptians: A Radical History of Egypt's Unfinished Revolution* (London: Allen Lane, 2016), 99.

57. Deen Sharp, "Urbanism and the Arab Uprisings: Downtown Cairo and the Fall of Mubarak," *Jadaliyya*, August 6, 2012, www.jadaliyya.com/Details/26808.

58. Alison Brown, Nezar Kafafy, and Adnane Hayder, "Street Trading in the Shadows of the Arab Spring," *Environment and Urbanization* 29, no. 1 (2017): 283–98.

59. Joseph Dana, "In the Traffic of Cairo's DIY Highway Exit, an Urbanist Movement Grows," *Next City*, December 4, 2012, https://nextcity.org/daily/entry/in-the-traffic-of-cairos-diy-highway-exit-an-urbanist-movement-grows.

60. Nicholas Simcik Arese, "Urbanism as Craft: Practicing Informality and Property in Cairo's Gated Suburbs, from Theft to Virtue," *Annals of the American Association of Geographers* 108, no. 3 (2018): 620–37.

61. Ibid., 627.

62. Ibid., 632.

63. Ananya Roy and Nezar AlSayyad, *Urban Informality: Transnational Perspectives from the Middle East, Latin America and South Asia* (Lanham, MD: Lexington Books, 2004).

64. Arese, "Urbanism as Craft," 623.

65. Clerc, "Informal Settlements in the Syrian Conflict."

66. David Kilcullen and Nate Rosenblatt, "The Rise of Syria's Urban Poor: Why the War for Syria's Future Will be Fought over the Country's New Urban Villages," *Prism* 4 (2014): 32–42.

67. Maged Tamraz, "9864 shiqa jahiza li-istiqbal sukkan 'ashwa'iyyat al-qahira" ["9864 flats ready to receive the residents of Cairo's *ashwa'iyyat*"], *Sout Al-Ouma*, January 21, 2019, www.soutalomma.com/Article/854437/9864-ش-ققة-ةزهاج-ةلساستقباب-ال-سكان-عواشيائت-القاهرة.

68. "Third Meeting of the Municipalities," Egyptian Cabinet, www.cabinet.gov.eg/Arabic/MediaCenter/CabinetNews/Pages/Governors-meeting-No.-3.aspx, translation by the author.

7. VOLUNTARY ASSOCIATIONS AS SOCIAL MICROMOVEMENTS: THE CASE FOR GRADUAL SOCIOPOLITICAL CHANGE IN ALGERIA

1. Amaney A. Jamal, *Barriers to Democracy: The Other Side of Social Capital in Palestine and the Arab World* (Princeton, NJ: Princeton University Press, 2009), 4.

2. Although others argue the case for Tunisian "exceptionalism," see Safwan M. Masri, *Tunisia: An Arab Anomaly* (New York, NY: Columbia University Press, 2017).

3. Isabelle Werenfels, *Managing Instability in Algeria: Elites and Political Change Since 1995* (New York, NY: Routledge, 2007), 135.

4. Harry Verhoeven, "Introduction," in *Environmental Politics in the Middle East* (New York, NY: Oxford University Press, 2018), 1–26.

5. R. L. Bryant, "Power, Knowledge and Political Ecology in the Third World: A Review," *Progress in Physical Geography* 22, no. 1 (1998): 79.

6. Judith Scheele and James McDougall, "Introduction," in *Saharan Frontiers: Space and Mobility in Northwest Africa* (Bloomington, IN: Indiana University Press, 2012), 1–16.

7. Nejm L. Benessaiah and Irene Calis, "African Trysts: Rethinking the Saharan Divide," in *Postcolonial African Anthropologies*, eds. Rosabelle Boswell and Francis Nyamnjoh (Cape Town: HSRC Press Books, 2016).

8. Diana K. Davis, "Imperialism, Orientalism, and the Environment in the Middle East" in *Environmental Imaginaries of the Middle East and North Africa*, eds. Diana K. Davis and Edmund Burke (Athens, OH: Ohio University Press, 2011), 1–22.

9. Sylvia I. Bergh, "Traditional Village Councils, Modern Associations, and the Emergence of Hybrid Political Orders in Rural Morocco," *Peace Review* 21, no. 1 (2009): 45–53; and Judith Scheele, "A Taste for Law: Rule-Making in Kabylia (Algeria)," *Comparative Studies in Society and History* 50, no. 4 (2008): 895–919.

10. David Crawford, *Moroccan Households in the World Economy: Labor and Inequality in a Berber Village* (Baton Rouge, LA: Louisiana State University Press, 2008), 12.

11. Although there is not always intermixing between these categories, particularly men and women. By contrast, other categories do see intermixing such as peasant farmers and professional classes, as I observed in the M'zab.

12. Nejm L. Benessaiah, "Anomie and the Postcolonial State: Local Justice in the M'zab," in *Law and Property in Algeria: Anthropological Perspectives*, eds. Yazid Ben Hounet and B. Dupret (Leiden: Brill, 2018), 119–41.

13. Sarah Muir and Akhil Gupta, "Rethinking the Anthropology of Corruption: An Introduction to Supplement 18," *Current Anthropology* 59, S18 (2018): S4–S15.

14. Ahmed Amin Mohamed and Hadia Hamdy, *The Stigma of Wasta: The Effect of Wasta on Perceived Competence and Morality*, working paper no. 5 (New Cairo: The German University in Cairo, 2008).

15. Jessica Barnes, *Cultivating the Nile: The Everyday Politics of Water in Egypt* (Durham, NC: Duke University Press, 2014); and Nikhil Anand, *Hydraulic City: Water and the Infrastructures of Citizenship in Mumbai* (Durham, NC: Duke University Press, 2017).

16. Revised from James Mahoney and Kathleen Thelen, *Explaining Institutional Change: Ambiguity, Agency, and Power* (New York, NY: Cambridge University Press, 2010), 1–37.

17. Mehran Kamrava, *Beyond the Arab Spring: The Evolving Ruling Bargain in the Middle East* (London: Hurst, 2014).

18. Moha Ennaji, "The Feminist Movement and Counter-Movement in Morocco," in *Understanding Southern Social Movements* (Abingdon: Routledge, 2016), 66–78.

19. Marshall Sahlins, *Apologies to Thucydides: Understanding History as Culture and Vice Versa* (Chicago, IL: University of Chicago Press, 2004); Marshall Sahlins, *Islands of History* (Chicago, IL: University of Chicago Press, 2013); Marshall Sahlins, "The Return of the Event, Again: With Reflections on the Beginnings of the Great Fijian War of 1944 to 1955 between the Kingdoms of Bau and Rewa," in *Clio in Oceania: Toward a Historical Anthropology*, ed. Aletta Biersack (Washington, DC: Smithsonian Institution Press, 1991), 37–99.

20. David Lewis and Mark Schuller, "Engagements with a Productively Unstable Category: Anthropologists and Non-Governmental Organizations," *Current Anthropology* 58, no. 5 (2017): 634–51.

21. Saad Eddin Ibrahim, "The Troubled Triangle: Populism, Islam and Civil Society in the Arab World," *International Political Science Review* 19, no. 4 (1998): 373–85.

22. Andrea Liverani, *Civil Society in Algeria: The Political Functions of Associational Life* (New York, NY: Routledge, 2008).

23. Alexis de Tocqueville, *Democracy in America*, vol. 10 (Washington, DC: Regnery Publishing, 2003).

24. The Algerian civil war, also known as the "black decade," ensued due to a military coup which annulled the results of the 1991 democratic elections, in which the Islamist party gained the popular vote over the prevailing National Liberation Front (FLN) party. Some of the Islamists formed an armed guerilla organization, and the resulting brutality between the government and the Islamists resulted in an estimated 200,000 deaths. Luis Martinez, "Why the Violence in Algeria?" *The Journal of North African Studies* 9, no. 2 (2004): 14–27.

25. Vincent Durac and Francesco Cavatorta, *Civil Society and Democratization in the Arab World: The Dynamics of Activism* (New York, NY: Routledge, 2010), 7.

26. Jessica Ayesha Northey, "Associations and Democracy in Algeria," *Democratization* 24, no. 2 (2017): 209–25.

27. Nabila Amir, "Les députés relèvent des ambiguïtés et des atteintes à la liberté d'association" ["MEPs Raise Ambiguities and Violations of Freedom of Association"], *El Watan*, November 28, 2011, https://algeria-watch.org/?p=24825.

28. Liverani, *Civil Society in Algeria*, 7.

29. Ibid.

30. Charity Butcher, "Can Oil-Reliant Countries Democratize? An Assessment of the Role of Civil Society in Algeria," *Democratization* 21, no. 4 (2014): 722–42.

31. Ibid.

32. Northey, "Associations and Democracy in Algeria."

33. Ibid., 221.

34. Timothy Mitchell, "Carbon Democracy," *Economy and Society* 38, no. 3 (2009): 399–432.

35. "Coronavirus: Algeria Protests Called off for First Time in a Year," BBC, March 20, 2020, www.bbc.com/news/world-africa-51982703?intlink_from_url=https://www.bbc.com/news/topics/cy22g7n28mvt/algeria-protests&link_location=live-reporting-story.

36. Marc Daou and Tom Wheeldon, "Algeria Popular Movement Remains 'Strong'— But Fears 'Business as Usual,'" *France 24*, July 13, 2019, www.france24.com/en/20190713-algeria-protest-gaid-salah-bouteflika.

37. Mahoney and Thelen, *Explaining Institutional Change*, xi.

38. Veena Das, "On Singularity and the Event: Further Reflections on the Ordinary," in *Recovering the Human Subject*, eds. James Laidlaw, Barbara Bodenhorn, and Martin Holbraad (Cambridge: Cambridge University Press, 2018), 53–73.

39. Alain Badiou, *Being and Event*, trans. Oliver Feltham (London and New York: Continuum, 2005 [1988]), 294; and Pierre Bourdieu, *Outline of a Theory of Practice* (Cambridge: Cambridge University Press, 1977).

40. Das, "On Singularity and the Event."

41. Antonio Gramsci, *A Gramsci Reader: Selected Writings, 1916–1935*, ed. David Forgacs (New York, NY: New York University Press, 2000).

42. See, for example, instance, Steven M. Southwick and Dennis S. Charney, *Resilience: The Science of Mastering Life's Greatest Challenges* (Cambridge: Cambridge University Press, 2018).

43. Frances R. Westley et al., "A Theory of Transformative Agency in Linked Social-Ecological Systems," *Ecology and Society* 18, no. 3 (2013): 27.

44. Mahoney and Thelen, *Explaining Institutional Change*, 28.

45. Marshall Sahlins, *How "Natives" Think: About Captain Cook, For Example* (Chicago, IL: University of Chicago Press, 1995).

46. Sahlins, "The Return of the Event, Again," 37–99; Sahlins, *Apologies to Thucydides*.

47. Sahlins, *Apologies to Thucydides*, 69.

48. Joel Robbins, "How Long is a *Longue Durée?* Structure, Duration, and the Cultural Analysis of Cultural Change," in *A Practice of Anthropology: The Thought and Influence of Marshall Sahlins*, eds. Alex Golub, Daniel Rosenblatt, and John D. Kelly (Montreal: McGill-Queen's Press, 2016), 51.

49. William H. Sewell, *Logics of History: Social Theory and Social Transformation* (Chicago, IL: University of Chicago Press, 2005).

50. Robbins, "How Long is a *Longue Durée?*," 53.

51. Benessaiah, "Anomie and the Postcolonial State," 120.

52. Valerie Jon Hoffman, *The Essentials of Ibadi Islam* (Syracuse, NY: Syracuse University Press, 2012).

53. Benessaiah, "Anomie and the Postcolonial State."

54. Sergio Cristancho and Joanne Vining, "Culturally Defined Keystone Species," *Human Ecology Review* 11, no. 2 (2004): 153–64.

55. Nourredine Ben Saadoun and Nordine Boulahouat, *Le palmier dattier: raconté par un cultivateur* (France: BEDE, 2010).

56. Verweij et al., "Clumsy Solutions for a Complex World: The Case of Climate Change," *Public Administration* 84, no. 4 (2006): 817–43.

57. Bechir, local student, interview with author. Interviews conducted in Algerian colloquial Arabic have been translated into English by the author. Other interviews were conducted in English, September 29, 2013.

58. Nejib, interview with author, November 26, 2013.

59. Mohamed Brik, interview with author, April 2, 2013.

60. Ibid.

61. Aradhana Sharma and Akhil Gupta, "Introduction: Rethinking Theories of the State in an Age of Globalisation," in *The Anthropology of the State: A Reader*, eds. Aradhana Sharma and Akhil Gupta (Oxford: Blackwell, 2006), 1–42.

62. James C. Scott, *Seeing Like a State: How Certain Schemes to Improve the Human Condition Have Failed* (New Haven, CT: Yale University Press, 1998); and Asef Bayat, *Life as Politics: How Ordinary People Change the Middle East* (Stanford, CA: Stanford University Press, 2013).

63. Paul Stoller, "Slow Politics, Slow Media and Slow Teaching: Toward a More Perfect Union," *Huffington Post*, September 13, 2016, www.huffingtonpost.com/paul-stoller/slow-politics-slow-media_b_11985702.html.

64. Charles Tilly and Lesley J. Wood, *Social Movements 1768–2012* (New York, NY: Routledge, 2015).

65. Mahoney and Thelen, *Explaining Institutional Change*.

66. Robbins, "How Long is a *Longue Durée?*"

67. UNESCO, "M'Zab Valley," UNESCO World Heritage Centre, 2019, https://whc.unesco.org/en/list/188.

68. Pierre Bourdieu, *The Algerians* (Boston, MA: Beacon Press, 1962).

69. See Ulf Hannerz, "Being There ... and There ... and There!: Reflections on Multi-Site Ethnography," *Ethnography* 4, no. 2 (2003): 201–16; James L. Watson, *Golden*

Arches East: McDonald's in East Asia (Stanford, CA: Stanford University Press, 2006).

70. Joel Robbins, *Becoming Sinners: Christianity and Moral Torment in a Papua New Guinea Society*, vol. 4 (Berkeley, CA: University of California Press, 2004), 4–5.

71. Jean-Loup Amselle, *Mestizo Logics: Anthropology of Identity in Africa and Elsewhere* (Stanford, CA: Stanford University Press, 1998).

72. Lara Deeb, *An Enchanted Modern: Gender and Public Piety in Shi'i Lebanon* (Princeton, NJ: Princeton University Press, 2011), 14; and Saba Mahmood, *Politics of Piety: The Islamic Revival and the Feminist Subject* (Princeton, NJ: Princeton University Press, 2011), 155.

73. John Pierre Entelis, *Algeria: The Revolution Institutionalized* (Boulder, CO: Westview Press, 1986), 13.

74. Bayat, *Life as Politics*.

75. Sylvia I. Bergh, *The Politics of Development in Morocco: Local Governance and Participation in North Africa* (London and New York: I.B. Tauris, 2017).

76. James Nwannukwu Kerri et al., "Studying Voluntary Associations as Adaptive Mechanisms: A Review of Anthropological Perspectives [and Comments and Reply]," *Current Anthropology* 17, no. 1 (1976): 23–47.

77. Paul Pascon, *Capitalism and Agriculture in the Haouz of Marrakesh*, ed. John R. Hall (London: KPI, 1986), 20.

78. Marshall Sahlins, "On the Anthropology of Modernity, or, Some Triumphs of Culture over Despondency Theory," in *Culture and Sustainable Development in the Pacific*, ed. Antony Hooper (Canberra: The Australian National University, 2000), 44–61.

8. PERILOUS ADVENTURES: WOMEN AND CIVIL SOCIETY PARTICIPATION IN IRAN

1. Author's note: I am grateful to Mehran Kamrava, Director of the Center for International and Regional Studies (CIRS), and Zahra Babar, the Center's Associate Director for Research. I thank Suzi Mirgani, CIRS Assistant Director for Publications, for her perceptive editorial comments; and to Clemens Chay, Michelangelo Guida, Paulino R. Robles Gil Cozzi, Islam Hassan, Charles Schmitz, and Deen Sharp, for their constructive comments on an earlier draft of this chapter. I am also grateful to Elham Rahmatabadi who graciously introduced me to several female heads of NGOs, and assisted me with data collection in Tehran. Additionally, I wish to express my deep appreciation to Leila Arshad, Shahin Oliyaee Zand, Akram Movaghari, and Mina Keshavarz.

2. Saeed Moidfar quoted in Fariba Sahraei, "Iranian University Bans on Women Causes Consternation," *BBC News*, September 22, 2012, www.bbc.com/news/world-middle-east-19665615.

3. *Setare dar* (tagged) college students are barred from attending college and continuing their education, and maybe held in limbo for years.

4. Parvaneh Salahshouri, "Speech to the Parliament," YouTube, September 4, 2018, www.youtube.com/watch?v=wucwvKYww88. Unless otherwise stated, all translations from Persian are mine.

5. Research for this study was done in 2018 prior to the outbreak of global COVID-19 pandemic. It has obviously impacted the functioning of the state and society, including those of the NGOs mentioned in this chapter.

6. Daryush Shayegan argues that, while "our culture" is rich, its structures are "medieval," i.e., backward; *Cultural Schizophrenia: Islamic Societies Confronting the West* (New York, NY: Syracuse University Press, 1992), 123.

7. Iranian women are neither monolithic in their class and ethnicity, in their educational and professional backgrounds, nor in their relationship with the state and civil society. Further, women's political and legal objectives are diverse, covering the whole range of religious and political spectrums.

8. Noushin Ahmadi Khorasani, *Iranian Women's One Million Signatures Campaign for Equality: The Inside Story* (Women's Learning Partnership Translation, 2010). See also https://tavaana.org/en/content/noushin-ahmadi-khorasani-two-decades-struggle-womens-rights.

9. Rakhshan Banietemad's *Blue Scarf* (1995) and *Nargues* (1992), and Tahmineh Milani's *Two Women* (1999) and *The Fifth Reaction* (2003), are but a few examples.

10. See Noushin Ahmadi Khorasani, "Bahar-i junbish-i zanan" ["Spring of Women's Movement"] (2018): 57 and 71, http://bit.ly/31PqxV0.

11. Under the Family Protection Law of 1967 and 1975, polygyny was restricted, subject to the first wife's consent—but not her permission. The legal status of *sigheh* or *mut'a* (temporary marriage) was never directly addressed in the FPL, and this form of marriage, though marginalized and stigmatized, continues to be practiced in urban centers in Iran. See Shahla Haeri, *Law of Desire: Temporary Marriage in Shi'i Iran*, revised edition (New York, NY: Syracuse University Press, 2014).

12. As the Secretary General of Iran's National Committee for World Literacy Program (1975–79), G. R. Afkhami led the Shah's national literacy campaign. See *The Life and Times of the Shah* (Berkeley, CA: University of California Press, 2009), 225. On December 27, 1980, Ayatollah Khomeini issued a decree establishing the Literacy Movement Organization. For more information, see Golnar Mehran, "Social Implications of Literacy in Iran," *Comparative Education Review* 36, no. 2 (1992): 194–6.

13. All candidates, however, must be "qualified" by the Guardian Council, a highly conservative all-male body, before they can actually run for an office.

14. This law, however, may be overridden if a married women wishes to make the hajj pilgrimage to Mecca. The ruling does not apply to widows and divorced women.

15. In 2018, as the divorce rate climbed ever higher over the previous fifty-one years, the rate of marriage decreased precipitously. Correspondingly, the number of cou-

ples living together without formal marriage contract, locally known as "white marriage," has increased, despite the state's restrictions on this form of union. See "Ba'ad az so'ud-e talaq, amar-i izdevaj soqout kard" ["As Divorce Rose, Marriage Fell"], *Alef News*, May 4, 2018, www.alef.ir/news/3970204052.html.

16. For similar examples in the Middle East, see Suad Joseph and Susan Slyomovics, *Women and Power in the Middle East* (Philadelphia, PA: University of Pennsylvania Press, 2001).

17. In 2018, President Donald Trump withdrew the US from the 2015 internationally supported nuclear treaty, subjecting Iran to punishing unilateral sanctions, with the threat of war and aggression hanging over the nation.

18. Joseph Schacht, "Foreign Elements in Islamic Law," *Journal of Comparative Legislation and International Law* 32, nos. 3/4 (1950): 9–17. My argument here is based on an earlier paper, Haeri, "Ambivalence toward Women in Islamic Law and Ideology," *The Middle East Annual* 5 (1986): 45–67.

19. Schacht, "Foreign Elements in Islamic Law."

20. While removing this legal disparity faced stiff opposition from the Guardian Council, it has since been changed and presently children under the age of eighteen are granted Iranian citizenship. See Radio Farda, "Children With Iranian Mothers, Foreign Fathers to Receive Citizenship," June 4, 2020, https://en.radio-farda.com/a/children-with-iranian-mothers-foreign-fathers-to-receive-citizenship-/30652718.html.

21. See also Suad Joseph, "Gender and Citizenship in Middle Eastern States," *Middle East Report* 198 (1996): 4–10.

22. Peter Loizos, "How Ernest Gellner Got Mugged on the Streets of London. Or: Civil Society, the Media and the Quality of Life," in *Civil Society: Challenging Western Models*, eds. Elizabeth Dunn and Chris Hann (London: Routledge, 1996), 47.

23. For a comprehensive discussion of guilds, see Ahmad Ashraf, "Nizam-sinfi, jami'ih madani va dimokrasi dar Iran" ["Order of Guilds, Civil Society and Democracy in Iran"], *Goftogu* 14 (1997): 17–47.

24. Mehran Kamrava, "The Civil Society Discourse in Iran," *British Journal of Middle Eastern Studies* 28, no. 2 (2001): 166.

25. Ibid., 167.

26. Ibid., 184.

27. Amaney Jamal, "Introduction: Democratic Outcomes and Associational Life," in *Barriers to Democracy: The Other Side of Social Capital in Palestine and the Arab World* (Princeton, NJ: Princeton University Press, 2007), 1.

28. Ibid., 3.

29. Ibid.; see also Afshan Jafar, "Engaging Fundamentalism: The Case of Women's NGOs in Pakistan," *Social Problems* 54, no. 3 (2007): 256–73.

30. Kamrava, "The Civil Society," 179.

31. Ibid., 167.

32. Ahmadi-Khorasani, *Bahar-i junbish-i zanan*, 57 and 71; Maryam Husain Khah, "*Mahfilha-yi zanan dar daheh-hay-i 1360s and 70s: atash zir-i khakistar*" ("Women's Gatherings of the 1980s and 90s: Fire under the Ashes"), October 17, 2018, www.aasoo.org/fa/articles/1781.

33. Negar Katirai, "NGO Regulations in Iran," *The International Journal of Not-for-Profit Law* 7, no. 4 (2005): 28–42.

34. M. Barari, Asl Motahari, and Razavi Khorasani, "Impact of NGOs on the Socioeconomic Wellbeing of Woman-Headed Households," *Sociology of Women's Quarterly* 3, no. 1 (2012): 160; Masoumeh Dejman et al., "Barnameh ijtima'i-mihvar mosharekati murtabet ba salamat dar jumhuri Islami Iran" ("Community-based Participatory Programs Related to Health in Islamic Republic of Iran: Strengths, Challenges and Lessons Learnt"), *Hakim Research Journal* 15, no. 3 (2012): 185–91.

35. Ahmadi-Khorasani, *Bahar-i junbish-i zanan*, 69.

36. Afsaneh Najmabadi, *Bibi Khanum Esterabadi, Mayib al-Rejal* ["Men's Defects"] (Tehran: Roshangaran Publisher, 1985).

37. I wish to thank Sassan Tabatabai and Farzaneh Milani for their translations of this poem. In English transliteration: "Be hich mabhas-o dibachehi qaza nanivisht/ baray mard kamal-o baray zan nuqsan." See Parvin Etisami, "*Divan-i 'Ashar*" [poetry compendium], https://ganjoor.net/parvin/divanp/mtm/sh102.

38. Ibid., "Chishm-o dil ra pardeh mibayast amma az ifaf/ chadur-i pusideh bunyad-i musalmani nabud."

39. The Friday prayer imam of Behshahr commanded women to stay home and not walk aimlessly in the streets and bazaars, and thus "deviate from the right path." He wanted the state to oblige women to stay home, as in the past, learn embroidery, mend socks, and busy themselves with such traditional crafts. See Maryam Mohseni, "Khanumha az masir kharij nashavand" ["Women, Do Not Deviate from the (Right) Path"), *Jahanezanan*, January 17, 2016, https://jahanezan.wordpress.com/2016/01/17/12345–4558.

40. In the past few years, however, women have objected publically to forced veiling, prompting the state tighten its anti-loose veiling, "bad hijabi," and implement more punitive policies.

41. Ali Banuazizi, "Faltering Legitimacy: The Ruling Clerics and Civil Society in Contemporary Iran," *International Journal of Politics, Culture, and Society* 8, no. 4 (1995): 563–78. For the 2013 presidential cycle, the Guardian Council disqualified Rafsanjani's candidacy for presidency.

42. Khatami's unexpected victory was characterized as *himasi* (epic) by his followers.

43. Vali Nasr, "Dalili baraye democracy zamani baraye solh" ["A Reason for Democracy, A Time for Peace"], *Shargh*, February 25, 2006. After the election, *Shargh*, a daily newspaper, published a series of articles in which several authors discussed issues

of democracy, human rights, peace, and international relations from various perspectives (2006/1384, No. 706). As a progressive and popular newspaper, *Shargh*
has been censored several times, though after a period of suspension, it has resumed
publication, http://sharghdaily.com/fa/main/archive.

44. While the title of this journal is a tribute to Simone de Beauvoir's classic book, *The
Second Sex*, it intends to highlight women's second-class citizenship in Iran. This
journal was meant to be a quarterly, but because of its controversial title and feminist content, Ahmadi Khorasani was obliged to publish it as a book. This required
going to the Ministry of Guidance to obtain permission for the publication of
every single issue. Faced with so many restrictions and obstacles, *Second Sex* eventually ceased publication in 2004.

45. Ahmadi Khorasani, *Bahar-i junbish-i zanan*, 63.

46. Ashraf, "Nizam-sinfi, jami'ih madani va dimokrasi dar Iran", 17–47.

47. For more detail on the structure and function of SAMANS or NGOs, see *Site-i
marja'-i sazmanhay-i mardum nahad* ["Resource Site of Non-Governmental
Organizations"]; Government of Iran, "Chapter 2, Article 26," Constitution of
the Islamic Republic Of Iran, 2019, www.constituteproject.org/constitution/
Iran_1989.pdf?lang=en; and Seyed Mohammad Moghimi, "The Relationship
between Environmental Factors and Organizational Entrepreneurship in Non-
Governmental Organizations (NGOs) in Iran," *Iranian Journal of Management
Studies* 1, no. 1 (2007): 39–55.

48. Katirai, "NGO Regulations in Iran," 28–42.

49. Ahmadi Khorasani, *Bahar-i junbish-i zanan*, passim.

50. Negar Katirai, "NGO Regulations in Iran," 28–42.

51. The OWP was renamed as the Center for Women's and Family Affairs under
President Ahmadinejad's administration.

52. Sussan Tahmasebi, "NGOs Take on New Roles in Iran," *Alliance*, June 1, 2001,
www.alliancemagazine.org/analysis/ngos-take-on-new-roles-in-iran.

53. Ibid.

54. Katirai, "NGO Regulations in Iran," 40.

55. The "registration of a new NGO in Iran can take from several months to several
years. This means that many modern NGOs have begun their activities despite
the fact that their application for registration may be pending," Sussan Tahmasebi,
"NGOs Take on New Roles in Iran," *Alliance Magazine*, June 1, 2001, www.alli-
ancemagazine.org/analysis/ngos-take-on-new-roles-in-iran. However, they also
leave themselves open to state harassment and prosecution.

56. For Mirhadi's life and legacy, I interviewed her son Pirouz Valiki, who is a friend
and also a colleague at Boston University. I wish to thank him sincerely.

57. Masoud Miralaei, *Goft-o gou ba zaman: majmoueh goft-o gouhay-i* touran-i mirhadi
["Conversations with Touran Mirhadi"] (Tehran: Intisharat-i moa'seseh-i pajuhesh-
i tarikh-i adabiyat-i koudakan, 2013).

58. See the impact of COVID-19 on this particular school, https://bit.ly/2ZJmqeu.

59. Leila Arshad sent me the link to the following article by Mehdi Najafi Khah, "Inja kasi az aids nemitarsad" ["No One Is Afraid of AIDS Here"], *IRNA*, October 7, 2018, www.irna.ir/fa/News/83051482. It highlights the work of a few dedicated dentists who periodically visit The House and treat its women clientele free of charge. Many of these women have lost their teeth due to addiction.

60. See "Ti'dad-i khanehay-i amn be 30 bob afzayesh miyabad" ["The Number of Safe Houses Will Increase to 30"], *IRNA*, July 23, 2017, www.irna.ir/fa/News/82628607.

61. Shahin Oliyaee Zand autographed a copy of the book for me.

62. Her research is ongoing.

63. In a lecture that was pointedly entitled, "Children: The Forgotten Victims of Sexual Abuse," and presented at Ferdausi University in the very conservative city of Mashhad (northeast Iran), she highlighted the devastating impact of child sexual abuse, particularly on boys, https://bit.ly/3c6HiSa.

64. Mina Keshavarz, *Dar Mina-i Amvaj* ["Braving the Waves"], 2016.

65. *Zanan* magazine was banned by President Ahmadinejad in 2007. It resumed publication in 2014 when President Rouhani took office, renamed as *Zanan-i Emruz* ["Today's Women"].

66. She passed away in October of 2019.

67. Haeri Shahla, *Mrs. President: Women and Political Leadership in Iran*, Films for the Humanities and Sciences, 2002, www.films.com/ecSearch.aspx?q=shahla+haeri.

68. Ibid.

69. Shahla Haeri, "Women, Religion, and Political Agency in Iran," in *Contemporary Iran: Economy, Society, Politics*, ed. Ali Gheissari (New York, NY: Oxford University Press, 2009),136.

70. Rebecca Barlow and Fatemeh Nejati, "Impact and Significance of the 2016 'Campaign to Change the Male Face of Parliament' in Iran," *Social Movement Studies* 16, no. 3 (2017): 361.

71. Ibid.

72. Ibid., 364.

73. Rakhshan Banietemad and Mojtaba Mirtahmasb, *Touran Khanom*, 2018, www. amazon.com/Touran-Khanom-Rakhshan-Banietemad/dp/B08192GPKR.

74. *Hayat Khalvat-i Haneh Khorshid* ["Angels of the House of Sun"], dir. Rakhshan Banietemad, written by Naghmeh Samini, 2009.

75. Rakhshan Banietemad, email to author, September 20, 2017.

76. Faced with the scourge of COVID-19, a few Iranian NGOs, including Karestan, collaborated with two Iranian women NGOs in California—Keep Children in School (KCIS) and Mothers Against Poverty (MPA)—to raise money to procure PPE for Iranian doctors, nurses, and frontline responders. On June 7, 2020, they organized an international Zoom webinar to give a report of their charitable activities.

77. Bayat in Nayereh Tohidi, "Women's Rights and Feminist Movements in Iran," *SUR-International Journal on Human Rights* 13, no. 24 (2016): 80.

78. Mark Ryan Goodale, "Leopold Pospisil: A Critical Reappraisal," *The Journal of Legal Pluralism and Unofficial Law* 30, no. 40 (1998): 126.

79. In practice, one's wealth and connections could—and often do—override the law.

80. Ahmadi Khorasani, *Iranian Women's One Million Signatures Campaign* (2010).

9. POST-2013 EGYPT: DECLINING FORMAL POLITICS AND RESILIENT SOCIAL ACTIVISM

1. Mohamed al-Sudani, "'Admen Kolenā Khāled Saʿīd Yaʿūd Baʿd Ghiyāb wa Yoṭāleb be-Tawhod Qūwa Thawrat Yanāyar" ["Admin of Khaled Said's Facebook Page Returns after Absence and Demands Unity among the January Revolution's Forces"], *Miṣr al-ʿArabiya*, May 20, 2015, ‏ى-قوو-د-حوت-ب-ب-لطاي-و-باي-غ-د-عب-دوع-ي-دي-عس-،‏ ثورة-ياني-ر.

2. "Arbaʿa Aʿwām ʿala Majazret Māsbīru wa Lāzāl al-Motawaretīn fī Ghiyāb men al-ʿAdāla" ["Four Years since the Maspiro Massacre and Those Implicated Remain Away from Justice"], *Human Rights Monitor*, October 9, 2015, http://humanrightsmonitor.org/Posts/ViewLocale/18283#.WMdkCBhh3Vo.

3. ʿAlyaaʾ Mosalam, "ʿAn Ḥob al-Ḥayāt wa Ḥabs ʿAlāʾ" ["On Loving Life and Alaa's Imprisonment"], Al-Ḥoriyya Lel-Jedaʿān, Facebook, February 22, 2105, www.facebook.com/Al7oriallgd3an/photos/a.110216819090186.15443.1101744690944 21/650145251764004/?type=1&theater.

4. Ahmed al-Fakharani, "Miṣr: Ḥamlat al-Ḥorīya lel-Jedaʿān.. La Tuwqef al-Iʿteqālāt" ["Egypt: Freedom for the Brave Campaign Does Not Stop Arrests"], *al-Modon*, February 8, 2014, www.almodon.com/arabworld/2014/2/8/مصر-ة-حملة-الحرية-‏ الجدعان-ال-توقف-اعتقالات.

5. Najwa Mostafa, "Al-Ḥorīya lel-Jedaʿān.. Ḥamla le-Noshaṭāʾ Miṣrīyyn lel-Moṭālaba bel-Ifrāj ʿan al-Moʿtaqlīyn al-Siyāsīyyn" ["Freedom for the Brave: A Campaign by Egyptian Activists to Demand the Release of Political Prisoners"], *Raʾay al-Yum*, February 6, 2014, www.raialyoum.com/?p=50160.

6. Mahmud Hassuna, "Al-Ḥorīya lel-Jedaʿān: 163 Ḥālat Ikhtefāʾ Qasrī wa Iḥtejāz Dun Taḥqīq Mondho Abrīl" ["Freedom for the Brave: 163 Cases of Forced Disappearances and Detentions Without Legal Proceedings"], *al-Watan*, June 8, 2015, www.elwatannews.com/news/details/746597.

7. "Al-Ḥorīya lel-Jedaʿān Totleq Ḥamlat ʿLā lel-Ḥabs al-Inferādī'" ["Freedom for the Brave launches 'No to Solitary Confinement' Campaign"], *The Arabic Network for Human Rights Information*, June 9, 2016, http://anhri.net/?p=166611.

8. "Al-Ḥorīya lel-Jedaʿān: Zanāzīn al-Zolm Hābsa al-ʿEīd" ["Freedom for the Brave: Prison Cells Full of Injustice Undermine Religious Feast's Happiness"], *al-Miṣriyyun*, October 3, 2014, https://almesryoon.com/فترت-أحوال-ال-طولن/568347-الحرية-‏ الجدعان-زنازين-الظلم-حابسة-العيد.

9. Amr Hamzawy, "Legislating Authoritarianism: Egypt's New Era of Repression," Washington, DC: Carnegie Endowment for International Peace, March 16, 2017, http://carnegieendowment.org/2017/03/16/legislating-authoritarianism-egypt-s-new-era-of-repression-pub-68285.

10. Ahmed Jamal Ziyada, "Waqāʼeʻ ʻOmūmīyat al-Karāma'" ["Proceedings of the 'Dignity's General Assembly'"], *Mada Miṣr*, February 12, 2016, www.madamasr. com/ar/2016/02/12/feature/سياسة/وقائع-عمومية-الكرامة-ع-دان-الداخلية-ي; Biysan Kassab, "'Ayna Taqef al-Neqābāt al-Mehanīya men 'Azmat al-Ṣaḥafiyyn?" ["Where Do Professional Associations Stand with Regard to the Crisis of the Syndicate of Journalists?"], *Mada Miṣr*, May 3, 2016, www.madamasr.com/ar/2016/05/03/feature/سياسة/أي-تقف-النقابات-المهنية-من-أزمة-الصحف.

11. Sasa Post—Working Group, "Ṣerāʻ al-Neẓām wa al-Neqābāt al-Mehanīya fi Miṣr: Men Mubārak 'Ila al-Sīsī" ["The Conflict between the Regime and Professional Associations in Egypt: From Mubārak to Sīsī"], *Sasa Post*, February 12, 2016, www.sasapost.com/the-conflict-between-egyptian-regime-and-syndicates;
"al-'Ikhwān wa al-Neqābāt fī ʻAhd Mubārak" ["The Brotherhood and the Professional Associations during Mubārak's Era"], *Ikhwan Wiki*, no date, accessed on March 30, 2017, www.ikhwanwiki.com/index.php?title=الإخوان_والنقابات_في_عهد_مبارك.

12. As per the narrative of the doctors' syndicate, one of the police officers assaulted Ahmed Mahmud al-Tayeb, the resident doctor in the surgery department in the Matariya hospital, after the doctor refused the request of the police officer to prove unreal injuries in his medical report. As a result, the police officer attacked the doctor and the administrative deputy at the hospital with the help of another police officer that was with him, and then they took them over to the Matariya police station to continue abusing and assaulting their dignity. However, the police officer has released them and returned them to the hospital. See: Ahmed Mohamed ʻAbdel Baset, "Bel-Ṣewar: 'Aṭebā' Miṣr.. Men Yokhaīyeṭ Jirāḥahom?" ["In Pictures: Egypt's Doctors.. Who Can Heal their Injuries?"], *al-Watan*, February 12, 2016, www.elwatannews.com/news/details/969748.

13. Ibid.

14. Ibid.

15. "Neqābat Aṭebā' Miṣr Tadʻū 'A'ḍā'eha le-Ḥodūr al-Jamʻīya al-ʻOmūmīya al-Ṭāreʼa al-Jomeʻa 12 Fibrāyir" ["Egyptian Doctors' Syndicate Calls Its Members to Attend the Exceptional General Assembly on February 12"], *Egyptian Medical Syndicate*, February 5, 2016, www.ems.org.eg/our_news/details/3895.

16. "Jamʻ Tārīkhī Ḥāshed lel-'Aṭebā' fi Miṣr Iḥtijājan ʻala Iʻtedā'āt al-Shorṭa ʻAliyhom" ["Historic Assembly for Doctors in Egypt Protesting Police Attacks on Them"], *BBC Arabic*, February 13, 2016, www.bbc.com/arabic/middleeast/2016/02/160212_egypt_doctors_protest.

17. Osama Jaʻfer, "Bel-Ṣuwar: Waqafāt al-Karāma fi Jamīʻ Mostashfayāt al-Jomhurīya"

["In Pictures: Dignity Rallies in All Hospitals across the Republic"], *Egyptian Medical Syndicate*, Feburary 20, 2016, www.ems.org.eg/our_news/details/3956.

18. Ahmed Ghonim, "Ra'īs al-Wuzarā' Yuwājeh be-Mo'āqabat al-Modānīn fī 'Azmat 'Aṭebā' al-Maṭarīya" ["The Prime Minister Orders the Punishment of Those Accused in the Matariya Doctors' Crisis"], *al-Watan*, February 12, 2016, www.elwatannews.com/news/details/969859.

19. "Ra'īs al-Wuzarā': Sa'ajtame' ma'a al-'Aṭebā' wa Wazīr al-Ṣeḥa Qarīban le-Ḥal 'Azmat al-Matarīya" ["The Prime Minister: I Will Meet with the Doctors and the Minister of Health Soon to Solve the Matariya Crisis"], *al-Watan*, February 15, 2016, www.elwatannews.com/news/details/974992.

20. Dr. Mai Hassan Khalil, member of the elected board of the Egyptian Doctors' Syndicate, phone interview by Nihad Abboud, the author's research assistant in the fall of 2016.

21. "Ta'jīl Moḥākamat 9 'Omanā' Shorṭa fī 'Aḥdāth Mostashfa al-Maṭarīya 'Ila 20 Sibtambar" ["Adjournment of Court Proceedings against 9 Policemen Implicated in the Matariya Hospital's Incident to September 20"], *Aṣwat Miṣriya*, July 19, 2016, www.aswatmasriya.com/news/details/65735.

22. For example, the administrative judiciary issued a ruling in the fall of 2015 that entails the legitimacy of the doctors who work in the public hospitals and facilities to have an "infection compensation" of 1,000 EGP per month. However, the regime abstained from carrying out and implementing the decision, and it stretched the negotiations with the doctors' syndicate until the latter decided to end the negotiations in the fall of 2016. See Hadir al-Khodari, "Naqābat al-'Aṭebā' Tuwqef Mofāwaḍāt Badl al-'Adawa ma'a al-Ḥokūma" ["Doctors' Syndicate Stops Negotiations with the Regime Regarding the Infection Compensation"], *Aṣwat Miṣriya*, October 17, 2016, www.aswatmasriya.com/news/details/68875.

23. Raniya 'Omar, "Tashwīh Ṣowrat al-'Aṭebā'.. Jadīd al-'I'lām al-Miṣrī" ["Defamation of Doctors.. A New Trend in the Egyptian Media"], *al-'Arabi al-Jadīd*, February 19, 2016, www.alaraby.co.uk/medianews/2016/2/19/تشويه-صورة-الأطباء-جديد-الإعلام-المصري.

24. "Moḥām: Ḥefẓ al-Taḥqiqāt ma'a Mona Mina fī Itehāmeha be-Nashr 'Akhbār Kādheba" ["Lawyer: Interrogations of Mona Mina in the Accusation of Propagating False News Are Stopped"], *Aṣwat Miṣriya*, March 12, 2017, www.aswatmasriya.com/news/details/73824.

25. "China, Egypt Imprison Record Numbers of Journalists," Committee to Protect Journalists (CPJ), December 15, 2015, www.cpj.org/reports/2015/12/china-egypt-imprison-record-numbers-of-journalists-jail.php; "2016 Prison Census: 259 Journalists Jailed Worldwide," CPJ, December 1, 2016, https://cpj.org/imprisoned/2016.php.

26. "Taqrīr Dawlī: Miṣr Thānī Aswa' Dawla fī Ḥabs al-Ṣaḥafiyyn bel-'Ālam" ["International Report: Egypt Is the Second Worst Country in Jailing Journalists

Worldwide"], *Aswat Miṣriya*, December 15, 2015, www.aswatmasriya.com/news/details/52625.

27. "'Fī Jomaʿat al-'Arḍ'.. al-Qabḍ ʿala Motaẓāhirīyn fī al-Ismāʿīlīya wa al-Manṣūra.. Wa Taẓāhorat Moḥīt al-Ṣaḥafiyyn Mostamera Raghm al-Taḍīyyq al-'Amnī" [On the "Land Friday" ["Arrests of Demonstrators in Ismaʿiliya and Mansura. Demonstration around the Syndicate of Journalists Continues Despite Security Restrictions"], *Mada Miṣr*, April 15, 2016, www.madamasr.com/ar/2016/04/15/news/u/ال.يف-ني-نهاظهر-ةملعى-ضض-قبلال-ض.رألا-ةعمج-ج-ي-في.

28. "Bel-'Asmā'.. al-Mushārekūn fī Moẓāharāt ʿal-'Ard Hīya al-'Ard'" ["In Names.. Participants in the 'Land is Honor' Demonstrations"], *al-Miṣriyyun*, April 14, 2016, https://almesryoon.com/دفترت-أحاوو/876448-نطولال-راشملا-ءامسألاب. كون-ف-ي-مهاظهارات-»ألأر.ض-هـ-ي-لعرض«.

29. "'Jomaʿat al-'Ard' Tataṣāder Twitter fī al-ʿĀlam" ["'Land is Honor' Friday Leads Twitter Feeds Worldwide"], *CNN Arabic*, April 15, 2016, http://arabic.cnn.com/middleeast/2016/04/15/egypt-tiran-sanafir-25th-january.

30. "Al-'Amn Yaʿtaqel al-ʿAsharāt wa Yofareq Taẓāhorāt ʿal-Ard' bel-Khartūsh wa al-Ghāz" ["Security Arrests Dozens and Disbands 'Land is Honor' Demonstrations Using Rubber Bullets and Teargas"], *Mada Miṣr*, April 25, 2016, www.madamasr.com/ar/2016/04/25/feature/ايسايةنمألا/ة-يي-لقت علال-تارشعلا-تو-يفرق-ت-هاظهر. ال-تا.

31. "Jabhat al-Defaʿ ʿan Motaẓāhirī al-'Ard: Moʿtaqalūw Iḥtejajat Tīrān wa Sanāfir 100 Motaẓāhirīn" ["Front for the Defense of Land Demonstrators: 100 Arrested in Tiran and Sanafir Protests"], *al-Qods al-'Arabi*, April 15, 2016, www.alquds.co.uk/?p=517028.

32. Suzan ʿAbdel Ghani, "Nanshor Asmāʾ 230 Moʿtaqalān men Motaẓāhirī 25 Abrīl" ["We Publish the Names of 230 Arrested Demonstrators on April 25"], *al-Bedaya*, April 27, 2016, http://albedaiah.com/news/2016/04/27/112063; "Egypt: Fearing Protests, Police Arrest Hundreds. Journalists, Lawyers among those Apprehended," Human Rights Watch, April 27, 2016, www.hrw.org/news/2016/04/27/egypt-fearing-protests-police-arrest-hundreds.

33. "Maḥmūd al-Saqqa le-CNN: al-Neẓām Yuʾadeb Thawrat Yanāyir" ["Mahmud al-Saqqa to CNN: The Regime Disciplines the January Revolution"], *CNN Arabic*, October 2, 2016, http://arabic.cnn.com/middleeast/2016/10/02/egypt-mahloud-saqqa-interview; Ibrahim al-Hawari, "Maṣdar 'Amnī: ʿAmr Badr wa Maḥmūd al-Saqqa Ṣāder Lahomā 'Amr Ḍabṭ wa Iḥdar be-Tohmat al-Tajamhor wa al-Taḥrīḍ ʿala al-Taẓahor" ["Security Source: An Arrest Warrant Has been Issued Against Amr Badr and Mahmud al-Saqqa with Unlawful Assembly and Inciting to Demonstrate Charges"], *Sada al-Balad*, May 1, 2016, www.elbalad.news/2174518.

34. Mohamed ʿAtef, "'Amr Badr wa al-Saqqa Yadkholān fī Iʿteṣām Maftūḥ be-Neqābat al-Ṣaḥafiyyn Iʿteraḍan ʿala Ḍabṭehem wa Iḥḍarehem wa Iqtehām Manāzelehem" ["Amr Badr and al-Saqqa Begin an Open Sit-In in the Journalists' Syndicate

Protesting their Arrest Warrant and the Storming of their Homes"], *al-Bedaya*, April 30, 2016, http://albedaiah.com/news/2016/04/30/112210.

35. "Le-'Awal Mara fi Tārīkh al-Neqāba Quwāt al-'Amn Taqtaḥem Neqābat al-Ṣaḥafiyyn wa Tolqī al-Qabḍ 'ala Badr wa al-Saqqa" ["For the First Time in the Syndicate's History Security Forces Storm the Journalists' Syndicate and Arrest Badr and al-Saqqā"], *Miṣr al-'Arabiya*, May 1, 2016, www.masralarabia.com/ قلتو-نييينيفصحصلا-ةباقن-نتتقحتم-تاقوا/1040213-ةيسايسلا-ةياي حلا ي-لقبقلا-ضىلع-ردرو-لاسقا.

36. Samar Medhat, "Fī Dhekra Taʾsīsaha.. 5 Maḥtat Hama be-Tārīkh Neqābat al-Ṣaḥafiyyn" ["On Its Anniversary.. 5 Significant Milestones in the History of the Syndicate of Journalists"], *al-Wafd*, March 31, 2016, https://alwafd.org/خاب ار-ةباقن-خيرات-ب-ةمامه-تاطحم-5-اهسيسأت-ىركذ-يف-1103331/ريراقيرو صلا-نييفص».

37. Mohamed Qasem, "Bel-Ṣewār.. Tafāṣīl Itehām 'Amr Badr wa Maḥmūd al-Saqqa bel-Taḥarīḍ 'ala al-Taẓāhor" ["In Pictures.. Details of Accusing Amr Badr and Mahmud al-Saqqa of Inciting Demonstrations"], *al-Yum al-Sabae'*, May 2, 2016, www.youm7.com/story/2016/5/2/باروصلا-ليصافت-ماهت ا-ورمع-ردب-ومحمو 2701144/رهاظتلا-ىلع-ضيرحتلاب-اقسلا-د-د.

38. Samir Hosni, "Qlāsh: al-'Amn Iqtaḥam Neqābat al-Ṣaḥafiyyn lel-Mara al-'Awla bel-Tārīkh wa 'Onāshed al-Ra'īs al-Tadakhol" ["Qalash: Security Forces Stormed the Journalists' Syndicate for the First Time Ever and I Call on the President to Interfere"], *al-Yum al-Sabae'*, May 1, 2016, www.youm7.com/story/2016/5/1/ رلا-دشانأو-خيرات لاب-ىلوألا-ةرملل-نييفحصلا-ةباقن-محتقا-نمألا-الشالق ئيس/2699928.

39. Yara Saleh, "Jamāl 'Abdel Raḥīm Yoṭāleb be-'Azl Wazīr al-Dākhelīya wa Yoḥamel al-Sīsī Mas'ūlīyat Iqtehām al- Ṣaḥafiyyn" ["Jamāl 'Abdel Raḥīm Demands the Dismissal of the Minister of the Interior and Blames Sīsī for the Storming of the Journalists' Syndicate"], *al-Bedaya*, May 2, 2016, http://albedaiah.com/news/ 2016/05/02/112357.

40. 'Abdallah Bedair, "Khāled al-Balshī: Iqtehām Neqābat al-Ṣaḥafiyyn I'tedā' Ghāshem wa Ghayr Masbūq" ["Khaled el-Balshy: Storming the Journalists' Syndicate Is a Violent and Unprecedented Aggression"], *Miṣr al-'Arabiya*, May 1, 2016, www.masralarabia.com/سوشيدي-يايدي م-لادلا-خاد-1040291/يش لبلا-يقاقتح م-نقابة لا-نييفحص عادءاع نيي-ش مشغ-غ وريم س بوق..

41. Ingy Taha, "Maḥmūd Kāmel Mo'leqqan 'ala Iqtehām al-Ṣaḥafiyyn: al-Dākhelīya Tasir bel-Watan le-Ḥāfat al-Hāwīa" ["Mahmud Kamel Commenting on the Storming of the Journalists' Syndicate: The Ministry of the Interior Pushes the Nation to the Brink"], *al-Wafd*, May 1, 2016, https://alwafd.org/اقتحام-صحفيين-نيد لادلا-ريست-ةيلخاد-نطولاب-لحفاف-ةلاوها.ةيو.

42. Mohamed al-Sayyid, "Nanshor Qarārāt al-Jam'īya al-'Omumīya lel-Ṣaḥafiyn Radan 'ala Azmat Iqtehām al-Neqāba" ["We Publish the Decisions of the General

Assembly of the Journalists' Syndicate in Response to the Crisis Following the Storming of the Syndicate"], *al-Yum al-Sabae'*, May 4, 2016, www.youm7.com/story/2016/5/4/2703692/نشر-قرارات-الجمعية-العمومية-للصحفيين-ردا-على-أزمة-اقتحام-النقابة.

43. Wagih al-Saqqar et al., "Kol al-'Ajyal wa al-Itejāhāt fi Ijtemā' 'al-'Osra al-Ṣaḥafiya' bel-Ahrām" ["All Generations and Directions in Attendance in the 'Press Family' Meeting in Ahram"], *Ahram*, May 9, 2016, www.ahram.org.eg/NewsPrint/510614.aspx.

44. Al-Ahram, "Bayan Ijtemae' al-Osra al-Sahafiya Bel-Ahram" ["Statement of the 'Press Family' Meeting in Ahram"], *Ahram*, May 8, 2016, http://shabab.ahram.org.eg/News/48053.aspx.

45. Mina Ghali, "Isted'aa' Qalash Wa al-Balshi Wa 'Abdel Rahim Lel-Tahqiq fi Waqe'at 'Badr Wa al-Saqqa' al-Ahad" ["Citing Qalash, Balshy, and Abdel Rahim for Interrogation in the Incident of 'Badr and al-Saqqa' on Sunday"], *al-Miṣri al-Yum*, May 28, 2016, www.almasryalyoum.com/news/details/955793.

46. "Al-Neyaba Tohil Naqib al-Sahafiyyin al-Miṣriyyin Wa Ithnayn Men al-A'daa' Le-Mohakama 'Ajela" ["Prosecution Refers Head of the Elected Board of the Journalists' Syndicate and Two Members to an Expedited Trial"], *BBC Arabic*, May 31, 2016, www.bbc.com/arabic/worldnews/2016/05/160530_egypt_journalists_detention.

47. "Mahkama Miṣriya Taqdi Be-Habs Naqib al-Sahafiyyin Wa 'Odawin fi Majles al-Neqaba Le-'Amayn" ["An Egyptian Court Sentences Head of the Elected Board of the Journalists' Syndicate and Two Members to Two Years in Imprisonment"], *BBC Arabic*, November 19, 2016, www.bbc.com/arabic/middleeast-38038271.

48. Mo'taz Shams al-Din, "Tazamonan Ma'a Hadith al-Sīsī 'Aan Horiyyat al-I'lam.. Akbar Hamlat Dabt Wa Ihedar Lel-Sahafiyyin Wa Modahamt 6 Maqarat I'lamiya Qabl 11 Nufamber" ["Coinciding with Sīsī's Talk about Media Freedom.. Biggest Campaign to Arrest Journalists and Storming of 6 Media Facilities Prior to November 11"], *Huffington Post Arabic*, October 27, 2016, www.huffpostarabi.com/2016/10/27/story_n_12669428.html.

49. 'Abdel Rahman Riyad, "al-Haraka al-Tolabiya: Ghiyab al-Qadiya Wa Aulawiyat al-Sera'" ["The Student Movement: Absent Cause and Struggle Priorities"], *Mada Miṣr*, March 18, 2015, www.madamasr.com/ar/2015/03/18/opinion/u/الحركة-الطلابية-غياب-القضية-وأولويات.

50. Mohamed Hamama, "'Alamat Istefham Hawl Ta'dilat 'La'ehat al-Itehadat al-Tolabiya" ["Questions Marks about the Amendments of the Bylaws of Student Unions"], *Mada Miṣr*, October 20, 2015, www.madamasr.com/ar/sections/politics/علامات-استفهام-حول-تعديل-لائحة-الاتحادات-الطلابية.

51. Mu'asaset Mu'asher al-Dimuqratiya, "1677 Ihtejaj Tolabi Khelal al-Fasal al-Derasi al-Aual Le-'Aam 2013–2014" ["1677 Student Protests During the First Semester of the Academic Year 2013–2014"], *Mu'asaset Mu'asher al-Dimuqratiya*, no date,

accessed on March 30, 2017, http://demometer.blogspot.ch/2014/03/1677–2013–2014_31.html.

52. According to the Democracy Index Institution, the number of students who have been deprived of their freedom reached 1,326 within the first semester of the 2013–14 academic year, and dozens were killed due to the excessive force of the security apparatuses. See Mu'asaset Mu'asher al-Dimuqratiya, "1677 Ihtejaj Tolabi Khelal al-Fasal al-Derasi al-Aual Le-'Aam 2013–2014."

53. Sherihan Ashraf, "'Audat al-Dabtiya al-Qada'iya Dakhel al-Jame'at Tonzer Be-Qame' al-Fasaa'el al-Siyasiya al-Tolabiya" ["Legalizing Arresting Students on Campuses Again Threatens to Repress All Student Political Groupings"], al-Badil, September 5, 2013, http://elbadil.com/2013/09/عودة-الضبطية-القضائية-داخل-الجامعا.

54. Mu'asaset Horiyyat al-Fekr Wa al-Ta'bir, "Hokm al-Mahkama al-Ideariya al-'Olya fi Qadiyat al-Haras al-Jame'i" ["The Ruling of the Supreme Administrative Court in the University Guard's Case"], Mu'asaset Horiyyat al-Fekr Wa al-Ta'bir, October 26, 2010, http://afteegypt.org/academic_freedom/2010/10/26/177-afteegypt.html.

55. In the 2014–15 academic year, Egyptian universities signed contracts with private security companies to carry out security business on campuses, which has resulted in some of the violent clashes between the protesting students and the private security companies' personnel. See Bassant Rabie', "Mo'dalat Taa'min al-Haram al-Jame'i" ["The Dilemma of Security University Campuses"], Mada Miṣr, December 3, 2014, www.madamasr.com/ar/2014/12/03/feature/سياسة/معضلة-تأمين-الحرم-الجامعي.

56. Hesham al-Miyani, "Qarar Jomhuri Be-Tamkin Ru'asaa' al-Jame'at Men Tawqie' 'Oqubat al-Fasl 'Ala al-Tolab al-Lazina Yomaresun A'malan Takhriyebiya" ["Presidential Decree to Empower University Presidents to Dismiss Students Involved in Destructive Actions"], Ahram, February 18, 2014, http://gate.ahram.org.eg/News/458004.aspx; Do'aa' 'Adel, "Ta'liqan 'Ala Qanun al-Jame'at.. 'Omadaa' Koliyat: Yahtaj Tawdihat Wa Men Haq al-Tolab al-Tazalom Ded Qararat al-Jame'a" ["Commenting on the Universities' Law.. Deans of Different Faculties: It Warrants Explanations and Students Have the Right to Appeal University Decisions"], al-Watan, February 19, 2014, www.elwatannews.com/news/details/421336.

57. Abdel Rahman Mosharaf, "Qanun Tanzim al-Jame'at Yatasada Lel-Mokharebin Men Tolab al-Irhabiya Ma'a Beda' al-'Aam al-Dirasi" ["Universities' Law Confronts Rogue Students of the Terrorist Muslim Brotherhood at the Beginning of the New Academic Year"], al-Yum al-Sabae', October 11, 2014, www.youm7.com/story/2014/10/11/1901388/قانون-تنظيم-الجامعات-يتصدى-للمخربين-من-الطلاب-الإرهابية-مع-بدء/1901388.

58. Mu'asaset Mu'asher al-Dimuqratiya, "1677 Ihtejaj Tolabi Khelal al-Fasal al-Derasi al-Aual Le-'Aam 2013–2014."

59. 'Ali Jamal al-Din, "Miṣr: Tolab Mafsulun Men al-Jame'at Yakhshun Dayae'

Mostaqbalehem" ["Egypt: Students Dismissed from Universities Fear a Future Career Loss"], *BBC Arabic*, November 20, 2014, www.bbc.com/arabic/middlee-ast/2014/11/141120_egypt_expelled_students.

60. "1677 Ihtejaj Tolabi Khelal al-Fasal al-Derasi al-Aual Le-'Aam 2013–2014."

61. "572 Ihtejaj Tolabi Khelal al-Fasal al-Derasi al-Aual 2014–2015" ["572 Student Protests During the First Semester of the Academic Year 2014–2015"], *Mu'asaset Mu'asher al-Dimuqratiya*, http://demometer.blogspot.ch/2015/04/572–2014–2015.html.

62. Besha Majed and Mai Shams al-Din, "30 Yūnyū Ba'd 3 Sanawat: al-Dawla Wa al-Jame'at—Mohawalat al-Dawla Le-'Adam Tasyis al-Jame'at Tantahi Bel-Fashal" ["June 30, 3 Years On, The State and The Universities—Attempts by the State to Depoliticize the Universities Are Failing"], *Mada Miṣr*, June 30, 2016, www.mad-amasr.com/ar/2016/06/30/feature/سياسة/30-يونيو-ب-ع-د-3-سنوات-الدولة-والجامعات.

63. Mohamed 'Abdel Salam, "Man Yaqtol al-Tolab fi al-Jame'at al-Miṣriya?" ["Who Is Killing Students in Egyptian Universities?"], *al-'Arabi al-Jadid*, August 6, 2015, www.alaraby.co.uk/supplementyouth/2015/8/6/من-يقتل-الطلاب-في-الجامعات-المصرية-.

64. "572 Ihtejaj Tolabi Khelal al-Fasal al-Derasi al-Aual 2014–2015."

65. "Haraka 'Ala Istehiyaa' Wa Intehakat Mostamera.. Taqrir Hawl al-'Aam al-Dirasi 2015/2016" ["Limited Movement and Sustained Violations.. A Report about the Academic Year 2015/2016"], *Mu'asaset Horiyyat al-Fekr Wa al-Ta'bir*, August 16, 2016, http://afteegypt.org/academic_freedom/2016/08/16/12390-afteegypt.html.

66. Ibid.

67. Ibid.

68. The student unions' bylaws were amended by the regime of former president Morsi in 2012 and frozen after the coup in 2013. Student union elections did not take place in the 2013–14 and 2014–15 academic years. See Islam Salah al-Din, "al-Itehadat al-Tolabiya.. Tariykh Men Mosadamat al-Hokam" ["Student Unions.. A History of Confrontation with Egypt's Rulers"], *Shafaf*, October 22, 2015, www.shafaff.com/article/9680.

69. Hamama, "'Alamat Istefham Hawl Ta'dilat 'La'ehat al-Itehadat al-Tolabiya."

70. Ibid.

71. Mohamed Metwalli, "Nanshor al-Nataa'ej al-Kamela Le-Intekhabat al-Itehadat al-Tolab fi al-Jame'at" ["We Publish the Complete Results of Student Unions' Elections in Universities"], *Miṣr al-'Arabiya*, November 17, 2015, www.masralar-abia.com/شباب-وجامعات/796683-نننشر-النتائج-الكاملة-لانتخابات-اتحاد الطلاب-في-الجامعات.

72. Mai Shams al-Din, "Fī Intekhabat Itehadat al-Tolab Bel-Jame'at.. al-Siyasa Tahtader" ["In Student Unions Elections in Universities.. Politics Is Dying"], *Mada Miṣr*,

November 11, 2015, www.madamasr.com/ar/2015/11/11/feature/ةيساي/
في-ان ناختاباتات-احداتات-الطلبال-بالجماعات.

73. Shababik, "'Abdallah Anwar Ra'is Itehad Tolab Miṣr" ["Abdallah Anwar President of Egypt's Student Union"], *Shababik*, http://shbabbek.com/SH-27101.

74. Shababik, "Fawz al-Taleb 'Amr al-Helew Be-Manseb Amin Itehad Tolab Jame'at Tanta" ["Student Amr al-Helew Wins Vice-Chairmanship of the Student Union in Tanta University"], *Shababik*, http://shbabbek.com/SH-21846; Shababik, "'Abdallah Anwar Ra'is Itehad Tolab Miṣr."

75. Mai Shams al-Din, "Fī Intekhabat Itehadat al-Tolab Bel-Jame'at.. al-Siyasa Tahtader."

76. Yussef Mohamed, "al-Shihi: Itehad Tolab Miṣr Ghayr Mo'taraf Behi Ila fi Hazehi al-Hala" ["Minister of Higher Education al-Shihi: Egypt's Student Union Will not be Recognized Except under One Condition"], *Dot Miṣr*, December 14, 2015, www.dotmsr.com/details/الشيحي-احتاد-بالطلب-مصر-غ-ري-مع-فرتع-هب-الإ-ال-ف ي-هذه-الحال-ة.

77. Wa'el Rabie'I and Ahmed Hosni, "Monzamat Hoquqiya Todin Ilghaa' Natijat Intekhabat Ra'is Itehad Tolab Miṣr wa Na'ebehe" ["Rights Organization Condemn the Annulling of the Results of Electing the Chairman and Vice-Chairman of Egypt's Student Union"], *al-Yum al-Sabae'*, December 28, 2016, www.youm7. com/story/2015/12/28/2512483/منظمات-حقوقية-تدين-إلغ-ان-تيتجة-انت خاباتات-رئيس-احتاد-طلب-مصر.

78. "Haraka 'Ala Istehiyaa' Wa Intehakat Mostamera.. Taqrir Hawl al-'Aam al-Dirasi 2015/2016."

79. Yara Saleh, "Ha'ulaa' Dafa'u Thamn al-Defae' 'Aan Tiran Wa Sanafir" ["Those Paid the Price for Defending Tiran and Sanafir"], *al-Bedaya*, April 22, 2016, http:// albedaiah.com/news/2016/04/22/111666; Majed and Shams al-Din, "30 Yūnyū Ba'd 3 Sanawat: al-Dawla Wa al-Jame'at—Mohawalat al-Dawla Le-'Adam Tasyis al-Jame'at Tantahi Bel-Fashal."

80. Ahmed Abdalla, *The Student Movement and National Politics in Egypt, 1923–1973* (Cairo: The American University Press, 2008).

81. 'Abdel Rahman Naser, "al-Haraka al-Tolabiya fi Miṣr Monzo al-Qarn al-Madi" ["Student Movement in Egypt Since the Last Century"], *Sasa Post*, October 18, 2014, www.sasapost.com/the-student-movement-in-egypt-since-the-last-century; Mohamed 'Atef, "al-Haraka al-Tolabiya al-Miṣriya—al-Sedam Bayn al-Talaba Wa al-Solta" [The Egyptian Student Movement—The Clash Between the Students and the Regime"], *Sasa Post*, March 6, 2016, www.sasapost.com/opinion/the-student-movement-egyptian.

82. Lina 'Atallah, "Miṣr 2015: Kuz al-Mahba Itkharam" ["Egypt 2015: Accord Coming to an End"], *Mada Miṣr*, December 31, 2015, www.madamasr.com/ar/2015/12/31/ feature/ةيساي/مصر-2015-زوك-المحبة-اتخرم; Ahmed Mohamed Mostafa and Hayat al-Ya'qubi, "al-Dawr al-Siyasi Lel-Neqabat al-'Omaliya al-'Arabiya fi Zel Thawarat al-Rabie' al-'Arabi" ["The Political Role of Arab Labor Unions Amid

the Revolutions of the Arab Spring"], *Friedrich Ebert Stiftung*, 2015, http://fes-tunis.org/media/2016/pdf/Le_role_politique_des_syndicats-en_arabe.pdf.

83. For the Egyptian Center for Economic and Social Rights (al-Markaz al-Miṣri Lel-Hoquq al-Iqtesadiya Wa al-Ijtema'iya), see http://ecesr.org, and for the Democracy Index Institution (Mu'asaset Mu'asher al-Dimuqratiya) see http://demometer.blogspot.com. Both publish periodic statistics for labor protests in Egypt and their qualitative and quantitative distribution.

84. "493 Ihtejajan 'Omaliyan Khelal 4 Ashahor Yanayir—Abril 2016 Be-Motawaset 6 Ihtejajat Yumiyan Be-Ziyada 25% 'Aan al-'Aam al-Madi" ["493 Labor Protests During the Four Months January—April 2016, An Average of 6 Daily Protests, a 25% percent Increase Compared to the Last Year"], *Mu'asaset Mu'asher al-Dimuqratiya*, http://demometer.blogspot.com.eg/2016/04/493–4–6–25.html.

85. "Taqrir al-Ihtejajat al-'Omaliya Le-'Aam 2014" ["Report on Labor Protests in 2014"], *al-Markaz al-Miṣri Lel-Hoquq al-Iqtesadiya Wa al-Ijtema'iya*, May 1, 2015, http://ecesr.org/2015/05/01/2014/تقرير-الاحتجاجات-العمالية-لعام-; "493 Ihtejajan 'Omaliyan Khelal 4 Ashahor Yanayir."

86. 'Emad 'Anan, "Fī Miṣr.. 1736 Ihtejajan Khelal 'Aam wa Tahazirat men Ghadba Sha'abiya Qadema" ["In Egypt.. 1736 Protests in a Year and Warnings that Popular Anger is Rising"], *Noon Post*, December 29, 2016, www.noonpost.net/content/15899.

87. "493 Ihtejajan 'Omaliyan Khelal 4 Ashahor Yanayir."

88. "1117 Ihtejajan Lel-Motalaba Be-Hoquq al-'Amal Khelal 2015" ["1117 Protests to Demand Labor Rights During 2015"], *Mu'asaset Mu'asher al-Dimuqratiya*, http://demometer.blogspot.com/2016/01/1117–2015.html.

89. In 2015, the number of workers and employees who were arrested because of protesting or calling for protests reached almost seventy workers. See "1117 Ihtejajan Lel-Motalaba Be-Hoquq al-'Amal Khelal 2015." Also, in 2015, more than eighty workers and employees were arbitrarily dismissed in both the public and private sectors. See: Ibid.

90. Ibid.

91. Ibid.

92. "493 Ihtejajan 'Omaliyan Khelal 4 Ashahor Yanayir."

93. Nehal 'Abdel Ra'uf, "Ihalat Da'wa Hal al-Neqabat al-Mostaqela Ila al-Dosturiya al-'Olya" ["Referral of the Petition to Dissolve Independent Unions to the Supreme Constitutional Court"], *Miṣr al-'Arabiya*, June 26, 2016, www.masralarabia.com/حوادث/1126944-إحالة-دعوى-حل-النقابات-المستقلة-إلى-الدستورية-العليا.

94. Hassan 'Abdel Bar, "Qanun al-Neqabat al-'Omaliya..Geh Yekahalha 'Ammaha" ["Labor Unions' Law.. Dramatic Deterioration Instead of Improvement"], *al-Badil*, July 27, 2016, http://elbadil.com/2016/07/قانون-النقابات-العمالية-جهـ-يكهلها-عـم.

95. Ahmed al-Bora'i, "Shar'iyat al-Neqabat al-Mostaqela" ["On the Legitimacy of

Independent Unions"], *Tahrir*, May 23, 2015, www.tahrirnews.com/posts/
197555/أح‏مد‏+ال‏بربر‏ي‏+++ال‏ن‏قاب‏ات‏+ال‏عم‏ال‏ية‏+++ال‏ت‏ضامن‏+ال‏تج‏ام‏عي‏+++
وي‏كي‏لي‏كس‏+ال‏بربر‏لم‏ان.

96. The Parliament approved the civil service law in October 2016. See "Al-Barlaman
    Yuwafeq Be-Shakl Nehaa'i 'Ala Qanun al-Khedma al-Madaniya" ["Parliament
    Approves the Civil Service Law"], *Aswat Miṣriya*, October 4, 2016, www.aswat-
    masriya.com/news/details/68439.

97. "1117 Ihtejajan Lel-Motalaba Be-Hoquq al-'Amal Khelal 2015."

98. "Al-Idrab al-Selmi Haq Le-Kol Muwaten" ["Peaceful Strike Is a Citizen's Right"],
    Montada Qawanin al-Sharq, February 18, 2015, www.eastlawsacademy.com/
    ForumPostView.aspx?I=118.

99. Al-Ishteraki, "Tadamonan Ma'a 'Omal 'al-Iskandariya Lel-Ghazel Wa al-Nasij"
    ["In Solidarity with the Workers of Alexandria Spinning and Weaving Company"],
    al-Ishteraki, September 16, 2014, http://revsoc.me/statements/30886/.

100. "Al-Idrabat al-'Omaliya Tajtah al-Mohafazat" ["Labor Strikes Storm Gover-
     norates"], *al-Miṣriyyun*, September 2, 2016, https://almesryoon.com/‏دفترت‏-
     أح‏واال‏-ل‏وطن‏/920212-إل‏ا‏ض‏راب‏ات‏-ال‏عم‏ال‏ية‏-تج‏ت‏اح‏-ال‏مح‏اف‏ظات‏.

101. Karem Yahaya, "Mehnat 'Omal Tersanat al-Iskandariya" ["The Plight of the
     Alexandria Shipyard Workers"], *al-Bedaya*, July 19, 2016, http://albedaih.com/
     news/2016/07/19/116995.

102. Karem Yahaya, "Hona al-Iskandariya: al-Tabaqa al-'Aamela.. Tazhab Ila al-Mah-
     kama al-'Askariya" ["Here Is Alexandria: The Working Class Goes to the Military
     Court"], *al-Bedaya*, July 13, 2016, http://albedaih.com/news/2016/07/
     13/116581.

103. "Taqrir: 'Omal al-Tersana al-Bahariya Bayn Siyasat al-Tajuwie' Wa al-Mohaka-
     mat al-'Askariya" ["Report: The Alexandria Shipyard Workers Between Starving
     Policies and Military Trials"], *al-Markaz al-Miṣri Lel-Hoquq al-Iqtesadiya Wa
     al-Ijtema'iya*, October 18, 2016, http://ecesr.org/2016/10/18/‏تق‏رير‏-ع‏مال‏-
     ال‏ت‏رس‏انة‏-ال‏بح‏رية‏-ب‏ين‏-س‏ياس‏ا.

104. Hadir al-Mahdawi, "al-Ta'zib Wa al-Ikhtefaa' al-Qasri fi Miṣr.. Qeses Ma Waraa'
     al-Arqam" ["Torture and Forced Disappearance in Egypt.. The Stories Behind
     the Numbers"], *Mada Miṣr*, May 12, 2016, www.madamasr.com/ar/2016/05/12/
     feature/‏س‏ياس‏ة/ال‏تع‏ذي‏ب‏-وال‏اخ‏تف‏اء‏-ال‏قص‏ري‏-مص‏ر‏-ما‏-ورا‏ء‏-ا‏; "Ahkam Bel-
     Sejn al-Moshadad Wa al-Habs Le-Dabet Wa 5 Omanaa' Shorta fi Maqtal Tal'at
     Shabib Bel-Oqsor" ["Imprisonment and Detention Sentences for a Police Officer
     and 5 Policemen in the Killing of Tal'at Shabib in Luxor"], *Mada Miṣr*, July 12,
     2016, www.madamasr.com/ar/2016/07/12/news/u/أح‏كام‏-بال‏س‏جن‏-ال‏مش‏دد-
     وال‏ح‏بس‏-ل‏ض‏اب‏ط-و5-أم‏ن. The cases of outlaw killings and torture and viola-
     tions that were most prominent in the media were linked to the police officers
     torturing the citizen 'Emad al-Kabir in Giza Governorate (2006), the physical
     violence that led to the death of the Alexandrian citizen Khaled Said (2010), and

the detention and torturing and killing of the Alexandrian citizen Sayyid Belal (2011). See "Egypt: Bus driver raped by police forces faces new risk of torture," *Human Rights Watch*, January 12, 2007, www.hrw.org/ar/news/2007/01/12/231913; Shaher 'Ayyad, "Khaled Sa'id Men Daheyat Ta'zib Ila Mofajer Thawrat al-Qasas Men al-Dakheliya" ["Khaled Said From a Torture Victim to the Catalyst of the Revenge Revolution Against the Ministry of the Interior"], *al-Miṣri al-Yum*, October 28, 2011, www.almasryalyoum.com/news/details/121627; Mohamed al-Sayyid, "Jenayat al-Iskandariya: al-Sejn 3 Sanawat Le-Dabet Sabeq Be-Amn al-Dawla fi Qadiyat Ta'zib Wa Qatl Sayyid Belal" ["A Criminal Court in Alexandria: 3 Years Imprisonment for a Former Officer of the State Security in the Torturing and Killing of Sayyid Belal"], *al-Bedaya*, March 27, 2016, http://albedaiah.com/news/2016/03/27/109851.

105. Khaled Hassan, "Hal Taa'yyid al-Qadaa' Moraqabet al-Dakheliya Le-Mawaqae' al-Tawasul al-Ijtema'i Qame' Lel-Horiyyat Am Hefaz 'Ala al-Amn al-Qawmi?" ["Is the Judicial Approval of Security Surveillance of Social Media an Act of Repressing Freedoms or an Act of Preserving the Country's National Security?"], *Al-monitor*, October 5, 2016, www.al-monitor.com/pulse/ar/originals/2016/10/egypt-court-support-decision-monitor-social-media-facebook.html.

106. Ahmed 'Abdo, "Bel-Sura.. 'Mafish Haten Be-Yethakem'.. Gerafiti Be-Shawarae' al-Oqsor Ba'd Itehamat Lel-Shorta Be-Tawarot fi maqtal Muwaten" ["In Picture.. 'No Policeman on Trial'.. Graffiti in the Streets of Luxor after Accusations of the Police Implication in the Killing of a Citizen"], *al-Bedaya*, November 27, 2015, http://albedaiah.com/news/2015/11/27/101376.

107. "Ihalat 4 Dobat Wa 5 Omanaa' Shorta Lel-Jenayat Be-Tohmat Ta'zib 'Tal'at Shabib' Hata al-Mawt Bel-Oqsor" ["Referral of 4 Police Officers and 5 Policemen to the Criminal Court with the Charge of Torturing to Death Tala'at Shabib"], *al-Bedaya*, December 10, 2015, http://albedaiah.com/news/2015/12/10/102258.

108. Rajab Adam, "al-Sejn al-Moshadad 7 Sanawat Le-Dabet Be-Tohmat Qatl 'Tala'at Shabib'" ["7 Years Imprisonment for an Officer in the Killing of 'Tala'at Shabib'"], *al-Watan*, July 12, 2016, www.elwatannews.com/news/details/1257885; Ahmed 'Abdo, "al-Sejn 7 Wa 3 Sanawat Le-Dabet Wa 5 Omanaa' fi Qatl Wa Ta'zib 'Tala'at Shabib' Wa Ilzam al-Dakheliya Be-Meliyun Wa Nasef Ta'wid Muw'aqt" ["7 and 3 Year Imprisonment Sentences for an Officer and 5 Policemen in the Killing and Torture of 'Tala'at Shabib' and Obligating the Ministry of the Interior to One and a Half Million Pounds Temporary Reparation"], *al-Bedaya*, July 12, 2016, http://albedaiah.com/news/2016/07/12/116488.

109. Ahmed Abu 'Arab, "Hesar Modiriyyat Amn al-Qahira Ba'd Maqtal Shab 'Ala Yad Amin Shorta" ["Siege of the Cairo Security Directorate after the Killing of a Young Man by a Policeman"], *Miṣr al-'Arabiya*, February 18, 2016, www.masralarabia.com/وش-كوت/934243-فيديو-مواطن-نون-محاصرون-مدني-مصرية-أمن-القاهرة-دعب-د-مقتل-شاب-علي-أدي-أمين-شرطة.

110. Basel Basha, "al-Me'at Men Ahali al-Darb al-Ahmar Yatazaharun Amam

Modiriyyat Amn al-Qahira Ba'd Qatl Amin Shorta Saa'eq 'Tuk Tuk'" ["Hundreds
of Citizens from al-Darb al-Ahmar Demonstrate in Front of the Cairo Security
Directorate after a Policeman Kills a Rickshaw Driver"], *al-Bedaya*, February 18,
2016, http://albedaiah.com/news/2016/02/18/107361.

111. "Hashtag al-Darb al-Ahmar Yajtah Twitter" ["# al-Darb al-Ahmar Storms
Twitter"], *al-Miṣriyyun*, February 19, 2016, https://almesryoon.com/
story/857678/رتيوت-حاتجيج-رمرأحألا-بردلا-جاتشاهد.

112. "Le-Aual Mara fi I'tezar 'Alani.. Wazir al-Dakheliya al-Miṣri: Noqabel Raa's Kol
Muwatan Ta'arad Lel-Isaa'a" ["For the First Time in a Public Apology.. The
Egyptian Minsiter of the Interior: We Apologize to Every Citizen Who
Confronted Bad Treatment"], *Huffington Post Arabic*, February 22, 2016, www.
huffpostarabi.com/2016/02/22/---_n_9290214.html.

113. Mohamed Mostafa, "Beda' Mohakamat Amin al-Shorta al-Motaham Be-Qatl
Saa'eq al-Darb al-Ahmar" ["The Trial of the Policeman Implicated in the Killing
of al-Darb al-Ahmar's Driver Begins"], *al-Wafd*, March 5, 2016, https://alwafd.
org/لت-ققب-مهمهتها-ةطرشلا-نيمأ-ةمكاحم-ءدب-1067710/اياضيقق-و-ثداوح
رمحألأ-بردلا-قىئاس.

114. "Al-Mu'abad Le-Raqib Shorta Motaham Be-Qatl Saa'eq al-Darb al-Ahmar" ["Life-
Long Imprisonment for the Policeman Implicated in the Killing of al-Darb al-
Ahmar's Driver"], *Aswat Miṣriya*, April 2, 2016, www.aswatmasriya.com/news/
details/61224.

115. "Halat al-Qatl Kharej Itar al-Qanun Wa al-Ikhtefaa' al-Qasri fi Aghostos 2015..
79 Halat Qatl fi Miṣr Wathaqatha Human Rights Monitor Khelal Shahr Aghostos
2015" ["Cases of Outlaw Killings and Forced Disappearances in August 2015..
79 Cases of Killing in Egypt during August 2015 Documented by Human Rights
Monitor"], Human Rights Monitor, September 4, 2015, http://humanrights-
monitor.org/Posts/ViewLocale/16289#.WMhc7Rhh3R0.

116. Hadir al-Mahdawi, "al-Ta'zib Wa al-Ikhtefaa' al-Qasri fi Miṣr.. Qeses Ma Waraa'
al-Arqam" ["Torture and Forced Disappearance in Egypt.. The Stories behind
the Numbers"], *Mada Miṣr*, May 12, 2016, www.madamasr.com/ar/2016/05/12/
feature/ةسايس/لاعتلا-يذيب-والاو-خاتفاء-ف-مصص-رصم-ف-ماو-ءارو-ءا; "Hasad al-
Qahr fi 'Aam 2015" ["Oppression Balance Sheet in 2015"], *Markaz al-Nadim
Le-Taa'hil Dahayya al-'Onf Wa al-Ta'zib*, January 10, 2016, www.alnadeem.org/
content/2015حداص-لا-رهقلا-يف-ماع-.

117. On March 7, 2017, limited bread riots were reported in various Egyptian governorates. See "Misrawy Yarsod Intefadat al-Khobz fi al-Mohafazat Wa Taklefatha
al-Iqtesadiya (Taghtiya Khasa)" ["Masrawy Captures the Bread Uprising in the
Governorates and its Economic Cost (Special Coverage)"], *Miṣrawy*, March 7,
2017, www.masrawy.com/News/News_Reports/details/2017/3/7/1039372/
مصراوي-يرصد-انتفاضة-الخبز-في-المحافظات-وتكلفتها-الاقتصادي
ة-تغط-ةيخاص-.

118. 'Abdel Rahman Badr, "Tawabae' al-Tanazol 'Aan Tiran Wa Sanafir" ["The

Consequences of Conceding Tiran and Sanafir"], *al-Bedaya*, April 10, 2016, http://albedaiah.com/news/2016/04/10/110788.

119. Amr Hamzawy and Nathan J. Brown, "How Much will the Pandemic Change Egyptian Governance and for how Long?" Carnegie Endowment for International Peace, July 23, 2020, https://carnegieendowment.org/2020/07/23/how-much-will-pandemic-change-egyptian-governance-and-for-how-long-pub-82353.

120. Ibid.

INDEX

Note: Page numbers followed by "*n*" refer to notes, "*t*" refer to tables, "*f*" refer to figures.

Aktemur, Çağla (wife of İbrahim
   Özyavuz), 64
Al-Ahram (newspaper), 196
Al-Azhar University (Cairo), 197, 199
Al-Buhārna Mosque (Qatar), 97, 98–9,
   99*f*, 115, 115*f*
al-Darb al-Ahmar protests (Egypt), 206
Aleppo, 136
Alexandria Shipyard (firm), 204
Alexandria Spinning and Weaving
   Company, 204
Alexandria University, 197, 199
Alexandria, 127, 137
al-Gamaʿa al-Islamiyya (Islamist
   group), 131
Algeria, 11, 14, 139–61
   Article (40), 142, 145
   associational life in, 160
   civil society, 140, 141–2, 143–6,
      156, 159
   environmental Informality, 142–3,
      156–60
   farmer associations, 143
   Ghardaïa, 140, 147, 149–56, 157,
      158, 160
   local governance, 141–3
   military budget, 146
   National Forum for Dialogue, 146
   oasis political culture changes, 140–1
   social relations and power issues,
      150–6
   vacuum in politics, 144–5
   war of independence (1962), 145
   see also voluntary associations
      (Algeria)
Algerian civil war, 241*n*24
Algerian League of Human Rights, 145
Algerian protests (Apr 2019), 139, 146
Al-Ḥasa oasis, 94
al-Ḥudaydah (Yemen), 38
Ali Husayn, 40

Ali Muhsin, 36
Ali Yusuf, Sheikh Shaker, 97, 100, 101,
   102, 112–13
Ali, Salah Ba, 152
Alley, April Longley, 35, 36
al-Matanah (Banī Maṭar), 38
Alowaish, Ahmad, 87
Al-Sakhir Palace (Bahrain), 68
Al-Thunayyan *dīwāniyya* (Jahra), 90
Amazigh (ethnic group), 145, 159
Amazigh councils, 159
Ammerman, Nancy, 92
Amran (Yemen), 35
Amran conference (1963), 32
Amselle, Jean-Loup, 158
Anatolia, 48, 54, 55, 57
Anavatan Partisi (ANAP)
   [Motherland Party], 44, 60, 61
al-Anjari, Mishari, 80
Anjoman-e Zanan-i Sahel-i Minab
   (Association of Women of Minab
   Seashore), 182
Ankara (Turkey), 46, 59, 65
anti-labor-activism, 203
APEB (Association for the Protection
   of the Environment at Beni Isguen
   in Ghardaïa), 152
Arab Cumeyle tribe, 61
Arab nationalism, 74
Arab Shiʿa (Bahārna), 93–6
Arab socialism, 128
Arab uprisings (2011), 2, 17, 42, 69,
   111–13, 125, 134
Arabian Peninsula, 9, 67, 94
Arendt, Hannah, 70, 81
Arese, Nicholas Simcik, 135
Armbrust, Walter, 130
Arshad, Leila, 177–9, 185, 249*n*59
ʿarūsh/ʿarsh, 150
ʿasabiyya, 46
Aseeri, Ghadeer, 82–3, 84*f*